Blair's Just War

Blair's Just War

Iraq and the Illusion of Morality

Peter Lee
Lecturer in Air Power Studies, King's College London, UK

First published 2012 by
PALGRAVE MACMILLAN

Palgrave Macmillan in the UK is an imprint of Macmillan Publishers Limited, registered in England, company number 785998, of Houndmills, Basingstoke, Hampshire RG21 6XS.

Palgrave Macmillan in the US is a division of St Martin's Press LLC, 175 Fifth Avenue, New York, NY 10010.

Palgrave Macmillan is the global academic imprint of the above companies and has companies and representatives throughout the world.

Palgrave® and Macmillan® are registered trademarks in the United States, the United Kingdom, Europe and other countries.

ISBN 978–0–230–31927–1   hardback
ISBN 978–0–230–35570–5   paperback

This book is printed on paper suitable for recycling and made from fully managed and sustained forest sources. Logging, pulping and manufacturing processes are expected to conform to the environmental regulations of the country of origin.

A catalogue record for this book is available from the British Library.

A catalog record for this book is available from the Library of Congress.

10   9   8   7   6   5   4   3   2   1
21 20 19 18 17 16 15 14 13 12

Printed and bound in Great Britain by
CPI Antony Rowe, Chippenham and Eastbourne

For Lorna, Samantha and Fiona

His talk is as smooth as butter, yet war is in his heart; his words are more soothing than oil, yet they are drawn swords.

Psalm 55:21

But whoever lives by the truth comes into the light, so that it may be seen plainly that what they have done has been done in the sight of God.

John 3:21

Let your 'Yes' be yes, and your 'No', no, or you will be condemned.

James 5:12

Contents

Preface

I would prefer to live in a world where books like this were not written, where war was no more, military hardware gathered dust in museums and ancient enmities were long forgotten. However, with the whole of human history shaped by the spear, the gun, and, more recently, the precision guided missile, it looks as unlikely as ever that wars and talk of wars will cease anytime soon.

It was never my intention to write about war, let alone a war to which I had some personal connection. In 2001 I joined the Royal Air Force as a chaplain, hoping to make some positive contribution to the spiritual, moral and personal welfare of those who donned uniform and took up arms in service of their county. I hope, though there is no way of knowing, that along the way something I have said or done has been of comfort or encouragement to those I have had the privilege of meeting and serving alongside. What I can say with absolute certainty is that the men and women of the armed forces I have encountered have inspired me to laughter and to tears, to pride and to admiration. I have been moved to wonder and amazement in the cockpit of a Harrier as the pilot put the aircraft through its paces and the world passed by at 420 knots. Young men and women who have faced the enemy, lost friends and aged before their time have won my admiration for the professional and understated way they go about their business. Some have genuinely terrified me and I am truly grateful that they are on my side.

My interest in just war arose out of my involvement with wounded and injured British casualties who had been airlifted from battlefields in Iraq during the initial US-led invasion in 2003. I found it difficult to answer the kinds of questions asked of me both by the soldiers I encountered in the military hospital and those I met elsewhere. My research was therefore prompted not by an abstract philosophical interest in the morality of war but as a means of making sense, and trying to help others make sense, of political discourse, competing truth claims and shattered lives.

Having previously touched briefly on Blair's justification of the 2003 Iraq invasion I decided to conduct a more intensive study of the moral dimension of his case for war using just war as a framework for my analysis. I have also incorporated some ideas from the French philosopher Michel Foucault to consider the way issues of truth, power and morality were all intertwined in Blair's intervention discourse and contested by his critics. Among the assumptions I make, the most important is that arguing about war is not simply a matter of identifying and deploying absolute truth, with moral claims following naturally in its wake. Truth and morality are formed by, and in, the arguments we make, with those who wield the most power having the greatest advantage in ensuring that their claims to both are heard loudest and longest.

The book features close scrutiny of a significant number of Blair's speeches, interviews and press conferences, as well as evidence from the Iraq Inquiry. While some may feel that there is too much attention to detail, others may well take the opposite view. My own view is that understanding language and the way it is used is crucial if we are to fully appreciate Tony Blair's war discourse and the moral case therein. Language does not just describe the social world in which we live, it helps to create our world as well. No politician in recent times has been more attuned to the creative use of language than Blair, so we must look very closely at what he has said, how he said it and what he was trying to achieve in the process.

In exploring Blair's moral case for military action against Saddam Hussein and his regime I also question some of the ways that just war ideas are used and can be abused. Many just war advocates, though not all, attempt to take historical concepts from different parts of that long tradition and apply them unproblematically in the present. In the course of investigating the recent use of some ancient ideas about morality and war I have tried to do justice to their original philosophical and theological foundations. In places I show how some aspects of the original concepts have been brought into contemporary use while associated theological or philosophical principles have been resolutely left in the past.

War is as awful today as it has always been and the means of killing and maiming more efficient and destructive. This book does not argue for an end to war, even though like most people I long for that day to arrive. My view is that there are times when, in order to preserve the lives of thousands or millions of innocents, the judicious use of force is the only way to prevent even greater disaster. I echo the cautioning voices of those who throughout history have pointed out the horrors of war and its cost in lives and treasure. Consequently, it is the responsibility of every ruler or government to ensure that military power is only ever deployed for the most just of reasons and applied both proportionately and discriminately. They owe it to both combatants and noncombatants alike to avoid the needless loss of life. I did not believe at the time that Blair provided an adequate or persuasive moral case for involving the UK in the 2003 invasion of Iraq, with all its bloody consequences. After several years of study I am even more convinced that he did not.

This book has sought to avoid the extremes of the partisan polemicist and aloof musings of the distant and detached philosopher (if such a thing were possible). Some readers will want to place me closer to one extreme than the other, which will say as much about their viewpoints as mine. Regardless of whether or not you agree with my conclusions it has been my aim to provoke soul-searching in both supporters and opponents of the 2003 war alike, with a sufficient degree of academic rigour to do justice to such a serious subject. Most of all, I hope that in some small way this book honours those who die or are damaged in war; especially without good reason.

PETER LEE

Acknowledgements

I would like to thank the following organizations and individuals for their permission to use various copyright materials: Random House and its Hutchinson imprint for permission to use excerpts from Tony Blair's autobiography *A Journey*; Professor Lawrence Freedman for permission to quote suggestions he made to the Prime Minister's office in 1999 as Tony Blair was preparing to set out his Doctrine of the International Community; and the Information Policy Adviser at The National Archives for permission to quote from several documents submitted in evidence to the Iraq Inquiry. Scripture taken from the HOLY BIBLE: NEW INTERNATIONAL VERSION. Copyright © 1973, 1978, 1984 by International Bible Society. Anglicisation copyright © 1979, 1984, 1989. Used by permission of Hodder and Stoughton Limited.

I wish to express my profound gratitude to Professor Vivienne Jabri who, over several years, has provided academic guidance, incisive critique and exemplary intellectual rigour in a way that has been truly inspiring. The cadets and staff of the Royal Air Force College, and my colleagues at King's College London's Air Power Studies Division have consistently provided encouragement as this project has come to fruition.

My parents, Peter and Sheila, have shown me by example how to live life to the full and to make the most of every opportunity: for that I am truly grateful. My greatest thanks go to my wife, Lorna, and our daughters, Samantha and Fiona, whose love and support I try never to take for granted.

Introduction

'Do you think he should have sent us in?' It was April 2003, the 'he' in question was Prime Minister Tony Blair and the place to which the question referred was Iraq. The person who asked me the question was dressed, or at least partially dressed, as I was in standard, military issue camouflage uniform. I was a bit older and in the RAF while he was a soldier in the Army. Apart from that we had a lot in common: we were both married and spoke with similar Scottish accents; we were about the same height and build; we loved the same sports and couldn't stand the same football teams (Rangers and Celtic).

He fixed me with a piercing stare as he asked the question, fighting back tears as he lay in that hospital bed. I stared back equally intensely. Partly because I wanted him to know he had my full attention with all the distractions of medical activity going on around us; partly because the medication was affecting his speech. But mainly because I knew that if my concentration broke for a second my gaze would shift to the stained bandage that marked the spot where his arm used to be. Even then, my nostrils would not allow me to forget the extent of the loss the young soldier was trying to come to terms with.

I didn't know what to say to him. His good hand gripped mine with all the strength he could muster. If I said yes and offered a few platitudes I was sure he would detect the lack of conviction in my voice. And if I said no I would have belittled his life-changing personal sacrifice on the battlefields of Iraq. In a break with my normal habit I had the rare good sense to remain silent. After what seemed like ten minutes, but which in reality could only have been 20 or 30 seconds, he silently squeezed my hand twice to let me know that the conversation was over, turning away to hide the tears that could no longer be held back. As I walked away my own tears flowed: tears for his pain; tears for the life he would

1

no longer have; and tears for my inability to answer his question. Once I had composed myself I walked to the next ward, ready to go through the whole process again. And again. And again.

At the time I was a military chaplain and part of the medical and welfare network providing support to individuals who only hours earlier had been engaged in battle as the US/UK-led coalition stormed into Iraq. They had been deployed with the stated intention of removing the threat of Saddam Hussein's weapons of mass destruction to the region and the wider world.

Many other questions were asked of me by those whose lives were now scarred or maimed, mentally as well as physically: Should I have fought? How do I live with myself? Was it worth it? Have I let my country down? Will my partner still love me with my injury? These questions will be re-asked on a daily basis – possibly forever – by those whose limbs are missing, by those whose faces will cause others to turn away in the street and by those whose personal relationships have ended or are permanently altered. However, one question above all others dominated the reflections of those combatants whose lives were shattered in the line of duty, a question shared by millions of Britons and others round the world: did Blair do the right thing in sending us to war?

Since 2003 numerous books, scholarly articles and news articles have addressed different aspects of the 2003 invasion. The Butler *Review of Intelligence on Weapons of Mass Destruction* and Lord Hutton's *Investigation into the Circumstances Surrounding the Death of Dr David Kelly* – both undertaken in 2004 – were narrow in scope and resulted in more questions than answers. They also examined legal and procedural elements of the build-up to war while assiduously avoiding the moral aspects of Blair's justification of the intervention. As time has passed an increasing number of those who voted in support of, or provided tacit public support for, military action against Iraq express regret over their decision at that time. They frequently cite overblown intelligence information or castigate their previous failure to critique the evidence more thoroughly. As a consequence, the question asked in 2003 – Did Blair do the right thing in sending us? – has, for many observers, subtly changed. The more commonly asked question several years after the initial invasion is now: Why did I go along with it?

Such reasoning continues to attract interest to the Iraq Inquiry, launched on 30 July 2009. The Chair of the Inquiry, Sir John Chilcot, set out the terms of reference that would guide him and the other members of the committee: 'We will therefore be considering the UK's involvement in Iraq, including the way decisions were made and actions taken, to establish, as accurately as possible, what happened and to identify the lessons that can be learned'.[1] When the final report is delivered to Prime Minister David Cameron in 2011 it will no doubt identify lessons that can be learned. The remit of the Iraq Inquiry – like the Butler and Hutton Inquires before it – limits the extent to which it can throw light on Blair's justification of the invasion: because the aims of the inquiry exclude scrutiny of the pivotal *moral* aspects of Blair's arguments.

Much has been written about Blair, his political career in general and aspects of his involvement in Iraq in particular, with a tendency to dwell upon three areas. The first is a political emphasis on key events that assesses policy and procedures, speaks to witnesses and those involved in the decision-making process and seeks to reach logical and sustainable conclusions based on the evidence available. Examples of these are the numerous inquiries that have explored different aspects of the 2003 Iraq War.

The second approach disputes the legal basis for the invasion. Though contested extensively in the Iraq Inquiry, the legal basis of the invasion was hotly debated before a shot was even fired and continues to be disputed today. From parliamentary debates to newspaper stories, private arguments and the pseudo-judicial public inquiries set up by the very government they were supposed to investigate, the legal row goes on. It will continue to remain unresolved until a case is brought against Blair in either a domestic or international court and a verdict given one way or another: a wholly unlikely scenario. The third approach, more often found in scholarly works but occasionally demonstrated in more thoughtful newspaper pieces, touches upon the morality of Blair's interventionism through a straightforward, sometimes superficial application of just war criteria to the Iraq situation: just cause, right intention, last resort, legitimate authority, proportionality and so on.

These different approaches are based on the assumption that events are events and truth is truth so if we dig for long enough we will get there in the end. International law and historic just war arguments are treated as timeless and unproblematic codes to which Blair either conformed or not. Typically, on this basis, his actions are assessed by opponents to be illegal or immoral, while he and his supporters take the opposite view. However, the three approaches I have described overlook the complexity of Blair's moral argument, which has a number of interwoven parts and lies at the heart of his personal and political motivations surrounding Iraq.

Blair presented himself, and still presents himself, and his actions as ethical[2] in a number of ways. He drew upon traditional Western just war[3] discourses when he outlined his interventionist doctrine in

1999 – a key part of his internationalist approach that will be explored at length later. However, he went beyond any simplistic application of just war principles, aspects of which are now enshrined in international law in the form of the United Nations Charter. Over time, especially after 11 September 2001 and the attacks on the US, Blair creatively incorporated – consciously or otherwise – just war ideas that pre-date both the international system as we know it and the Enlightenment shift away from reliance on the concepts and influence of the divine in political affairs.

In addition, Blair regularly presented himself as ethical based on his willingness to stand by a friend in need at a time of crisis (President George W. Bush after 9/11) and his determination to oppose Saddam Hussein: the good man Blair confronting the evil Saddam. He thereby invited his listeners to become ethical like him by lending their support in tackling that evil. Further, Blair wove into his justification of military action against Saddam and Iraq a number of moral arguments that are not associated with contemporary just war or captured in international law. Examples of such arguments include: standing up for the weak; stepping in to help someone under attack; preventing a future threat; and civilizing a state that is not run properly for the benefit of its citizens. Many who have commented on Blair and Iraq emphasize hidden political or security agendas, flawed evidence and even deliberate lying, all the while overlooking the following crucial possibilities: that Blair was driven by a *moral* imperative that in his view transcended the constraints of international law; and that Blair said what he meant and meant what he said.

Prompted by the question I set out at the beginning of this Introduction – Do you think he should have sent us in? – I have reflected upon, researched, debated and analysed the questions surrounding Blair and Iraq for several years. Opinion seems to me to fall into three broad categories. Those who thought that the Iraq War was unjustified at the time, or even unjustified under any circumstances at any time, tend to see their judgement as vindicated by subsequent events. Meanwhile, Blair and ardent supporters such as Alastair Campbell, his former Director of Communications and Strategy, remain bullish about their actions many years later and seem unlikely to change their positions. In between these positions are the people who supported Blair's actions at the time and later came to regret or at least question the fact that they did so.

While I hope that this book will be of interest to anyone who wants to gain a greater understanding of events surrounding the Iraq War and its aftermath, and in particular the moral dimension, it is probably with those in the latter group that my arguments are most likely to resonate. My central thesis is that in trying to win public support for an unpopular war Blair very creatively interwove a questionable legal case with multiple strands of culturally recognized and accepted moral argument. This legal/moral tension is a thread that will run through the whole book. As his *legal* case eroded Blair placed increasing emphasis on *moral* arguments as a means of trying to win support from an increasingly sceptical public. By adopting this approach Blair managed to create, at least in the short-term, what I describe as the illusion of morality, an illusion that for many people has subsequently evaporated, leaving them asking: 'How then did I go along with it?'

The rest of this book is therefore devoted to a detailed analysis of how Blair managed to create the illusion of morality in his justification of the military action against Iraq and why for so many people the illusion dissipated very quickly afterwards. I will show that Blair succeeded in convincing many of the people for some of the time because his creative justification of the invasion called upon moral ideas that were culturally long-standing, familiar and influential. His moral sleight of hand occurred as he wove these ideas into his justification of war when he could meet neither the strict demands of current just war doctrine or international law. In addition I will explore some of the consequences of pursuing the course of action that Blair advocated so passionately.

There will be three elements in my analysis, none of which can be isolated from the others but which I will focus upon in turn as I seek to expose the illusion of morality in Blair's Iraq discourse. These elements can be broadly categorized as the moral, the political and the philosophical.

Moral arguments

There are two interconnected but individually identifiable ways of seeing someone, or seeing ourselves, as ethical. Both rely on individuals making decisions about how they are going to behave. These decisions and actions can be described as being either code-oriented or ethics-oriented. Code-oriented morality relies upon individuals conforming to the written and unwritten rules and conventions that shape social existence: for example, driving within the speed limit or being respectful towards elders. Ethics-oriented morality is focused on the creative choices that individuals make, their motivations for doing so and the ends that are being pursued.[4]

Codes that shape our going to war include just war, international and domestic law, and the conventions of parliament. For Blair or anyone else to emerge as ethical they must conform to the requirements of the codes. However, we can also act ethically in ways that are not so reliant on codes because some things cannot be codified. For example, every individual will have a unique basis for behaving ethically, a basis constructed out of a complex amalgam of influences such as ideological or religious beliefs, social conditioning, family influence, cultural heritage and so on. The basis of our ethical behaviour, in turn, impacts upon the way that we change our behaviour in order to act ethically. Therefore, even amongst those who supported the war against Saddam the individual motivations will have been very diverse. For some it may have been motivated to protect individual human rights in Iraq; for others it may have been to promote democracy; still others may have felt a divine imperative to, in some way, do God's will.

Regardless of what moved Blair to conduct himself ethically, and I will set out some possibilities in the course of the book, he faced the challenge of inciting or encouraging others to share his view – a key part of his speeches that will be analysed in some detail. In different eras and in different ways governments have always sought to influence not only their enemies but also their own populations. The Nazi regime in World War II was very explicit and Dr Joseph Goebbels was officially the Minister of Propaganda and National Enlightenment. The day after World War II was declared the British government formed the slightly less sinister sounding Ministry of Information whose threefold purpose was to control the press, shape home opinion and shape opinion overseas.[5] Note that propaganda was conducted both abroad *and* at home in the UK. By the time Blair was advocating war in Iraq it was the responsibility of his communications team, headed by Alastair Campbell, to manipulate press coverage of both the Prime Minister and the government and conduct publicity at home and abroad. The extent to which this could be done was of a more limited order than that conducted in World War II by both the UK and Germany but the principles were the same: shape what people know; shape how people think; shape how people behave.

The last element of ethical conduct to be examined concerns the intentions and ambitions of the individual concerned. What are they trying to achieve: social justice, eternity in heaven, to be a liberator of the oppressed? It is not possible to codify every aspect of peoples' intentions in relation to ethical conduct; everyone acts according to their own motivations and for their own ends, and we should leave open the possibility that people do not act for the reasons that they say they are acting. Take the example of a road with a 30 mph speed limit. The first choice that drivers face is whether to conform to the (Highway) code or not and keep their speed no higher than the prescribed 30 mph. If they do it can be for numerous reasons: a desire to obey the law; concern for children playing at the roadside; to reduce fuel consumption and hence reduce carbon footprint; because they have been drinking alcohol and the police are watching. In exploring Blair's moral arguments and his ethical conduct, bearing in mind the just war principles he advocated when defining his interventionist credentials and the constraints imposed upon him by international law, many of the foregoing subtle issues will be identified and discussed.

In the process, different aspects of the way Blair creatively presented himself as ethical will be examined in the course of this book with reference to four questions:[6] 1) What is the part of his character or personality on which Blair based his moral arguments? That is, what are the beliefs, qualities and characteristics upon which his ethical behaviour was constructed (religious faith, social conscience, patriotism)? 2) How did he try to persuade or encourage others to recognize what he considered to be their moral obligations? 3) What are the ways in which he encouraged his listeners to change themselves in order to act ethically in the context of military intervention? 4) To what did Blair aspire when behaving in an ethical way?

The most familiar of Blair's moral arguments to be considered will be those rooted in the just war tradition. The classical criteria to which leaders must conform if they are to take their countries into a just war state that the war must be fought for a just cause; in pursuit of right intentions; legitimately authorized; stand a reasonable possibility of success; undertaken as a last resort; and be considered a proportionate response: that is, the good that ultimately emerges should outweigh the bad that would otherwise occur and which takes place in the course of the fighting.

To highlight how much Blair conformed to, and in places departed from, widely acknowledged just war arguments I will compare his words and actions with the writings of the two most influential academics in the field today: Michael Walzer and Jean Bethke Elshtain. I will look at some of the major historical just war writers whose ideas were called upon in the present, knowingly or otherwise, by Blair, Elshtain and Walzer. I will also show how the three selectively included and excluded key ideas in constructing their different views of war and intervention. In the process it will be demonstrated that, contrary to much popular and academic thinking, the idea of just war as a settled historic tradition of thought is itself a mirage. Instead, it will be shown to be a collection of ideas that have been reformed and restated multiple times based on wildly differing theological and philosophical principles. By bringing both contemporary and historical just war concepts together I will illustrate one of the reasons why Blair's illusion of morality evaporated so quickly and irretrievably after the 2003 invasion: because some of the ideas he relied upon were taken out of their historical context and applied in a global political system where they no longer hold sway.

One final way that Blair's justification of war will be assessed is by exploring the way he took widely respected moral actions from everyday life and transplanted them into the international arena with reference to Iraq. For example, in the UK – and most other countries – if a passer-by observed a mugging and stepped in to protect a vulnerable person she would be lauded as heroic for her brave, ethical conduct. Blair viewed action against Saddam in a similar light, even though international law does not automatically allow action to be taken against rulers who mistreat their own people, no matter how noble, or ignoble, the intentions of the one who would intervene.

Political context

The events leading up to the 2003 invasion, as well as the subsequent political and military difficulties as Iraq moved from coalition occupation to an interim parliament and finally an elected government, have been picked over at great length in the press as well as the official inquiries carried out thus far. Unfortunately it is not possible to explore the morality of the war and Blair's role in justifying it without retreading on old familiar terrain. Despite the familiarity of many of the political events and arguments that are to be re-examined I am confident that a close look at the moral grounds for invasion will broaden our understanding of what took place, Blair's role in it, and the immediate and long-term consequences for the UK and Western interventionist policies.

At this juncture I want to make a bold claim that on one level seems obvious but which I hope the remainder of the book will justify: that politics, morality and discourse (that is, the way we describe and enact politics and morality) are inseparable and mutually creating and enforcing.[7] I will show that Blair and others did not just describe political events regarding Iraq but also in the process *created* the meaning of those events.

Take anthrax as an example. Anthrax is caused by a naturally occurring bacterium called *Bacillus anthracis*. In itself it is morally neutral and its spores can be deadly when they come into contact with humans, cattle and other animals. Many countries possess anthrax and do so for medical research purposes. However, it can also be weaponized and used against an enemy. It is most likely that there was no change in Iraq's possession or potential use of anthrax in the period from mid-2001 to mid-2002. What had changed was the global political context and US Defense Secretary Donald Rumsfeld would later make very clear the impact of 9/11 on the political stance of the US and its perception of the threat against it. He said to the United States Senate Armed Forces Committee on 9 July 2003:

> The coalition did not act in Iraq because we had discovered dramatic new evidence of Iraq's pursuit of weapons of mass destruction. We acted because we saw the evidence in a dramatic new light – through the prism of our experience on September 11th. ... that experience changed our appreciation of our vulnerability and the risks the U.S. faces from terrorist states and terrorist networks armed with powerful weapons.[8]

As a result of the changing political situation and the way the threat from Iraq was subsequently viewed and described on both sides of the Atlantic, the moral case – the need to defend against similar attacks in the future – put forward by the US and UK governments changed. Rumsfeld added: 'The objective in the global war on terror is to prevent another attack like September 11th, or a biological, nuclear or chemical attack that would be worse, before it happens'.[9] The discourse about anthrax changed in light of changing political events, in turn changing the moral argument for military intervention.

Blair said to Parliament on 24 September 2002, 'The biological agents we believe Iraq can produce include anthrax, botulinum, toxin, aflatoxin and ricin. All eventually result in excruciatingly painful death'.[10] Two distinct factors in Blair's words need to be weighed up: first, that he 'believed' Iraq could produce anthrax and, second, that it was not only lethal but provided an 'excruciatingly painful death'. On the first point, there is a huge difference between stating that there is incontrovertible evidence that Iraq could produce biological and chemical agents and merely *believing* that might be the case. The way that the discourse is constructed implies a threat where none could be demonstrated. Second, by referring to an excruciatingly painful death Blair implied a higher level of danger to be faced. What reasonable person would not want to avert such deaths? The way that Blair constructed his Iraq discourse did not simply describe moral dilemmas and the political situation; the discourse actively created the level of danger to be faced and shaped the urgency of the decision-making process. This shift leads us on to the final element that will be taken into account during my analysis of events: some of the philosophical underpinnings of my approach.

Philosophical issues

Any philosophical enquiry, and this exploration of the morality of the 2003 Iraq intervention and its aftermath is no exception, eventually turns to the issue of truth: what is truth; how do we recognize truth; and how is it used? In writing this book I reject the view that the truth is an entity of its own that somehow just *is*, instead seeing truth as something that is disputed, argued over and created as part of political and moral debate. I will call once more upon the ideas of Michel Foucault who argued that truth cannot be separated from power: the individual or group or political entity that wields power can shape what comes to be widely accepted as the truth. Take an extreme example of political and religious power being used to dictate what could be known as truth.

In 1616 Galileo Galilei proposed, against the Catholic Church's interpretation of scripture at that time, that the earth revolved round the sun and not *vice versa*. Even more significantly, he could prove it scientifically. In 1633 he stood trial for heresy on the basis of his scientific beliefs and the 'truth' about the earth's orbit around the sun, which contradicted the religious 'truth' expounded by Pope Urban and the Catholic Church. He was subsequently imprisoned and his book *Dialogue Concerning the Two Chief World Systems* was banned.[11] It was not superior, better researched knowledge that led to an improved version of the truth and saw Galileo denounced for his views on the orbit of the earth round the sun. It was the application of political and institutional power that determined what counted as valid, or in Galileo's case invalid, truth. What the Pope did was create a 'regime of truth'[12] about Galileo's idea using the institutions of the Church and the authority to declare doctrinal purity or heresy. The Inquisition was used as a tool to suppress one truth for another and the Church's ability to print, publicize and promote what it ordained to be orthodox ideas could not be successfully challenged because of the extent of its power.

I will therefore explore some of the sanctions, techniques and procedures by which a regime of truth about Saddam Hussein, Iraq and the need for military intervention was constructed. The agenda was set by powerful political figures who controlled crucial secret intelligence, selectively releasing information to the media – and even to the ministers in Blair's Cabinet – to shape or influence opinion in a national and even global audience. Truth lay at the heart of the political debate at both governmental and UN level and it was contested in social confrontation in street protests, in parliamentary debate and in threatened UNSC vetoes.

In the chapters to follow I will work on the assumption that the very concepts of truth and morality are disputed when we come to analyse how Blair, his supporters and his opponents sought to dominate the communications war. Truth and perception of truth blur together when it comes to analysing something as complex and emotive as war, where lives are lost in the clash of ideology and personality and the self-interest that defines international statecraft.

Chapters

Blair's enthusiasm for military intervention emerged early in his premiership and came to define and dominate his foreign policy agenda. After less than two years as Prime Minister and with the Kosovo Conflict in full swing, his position on military intervention – he preferred the term 'humanitarian intervention' – were clearly established. He gave a defining speech in April 1999 in Chicago where he set out his vision for a new internationalism. This speech provided not only the political framework for the various wars Blair subsequently advocated but the moral basis as well. Chapter 1 sets out the background to Blair's commitment to military action in Iraq by exploring the moral basis of his wars in Kosovo and Sierra Leone.[13] I will examine his use of just war concepts and his treatment of international law as he justified his earlier interventions, thereby paving the way for his most controversial campaign: Iraq 2003.

Chapter 2 identifies Blair's various justifications for invasion in the year leading up to his plea to Parliament to 'do the right thing' on the eve of the attack on Iraq on 19 March 2003. Fighting for a just cause lies at the heart of just war thinking, with the most ancient of just causes – self-defence – enshrined in international law as set out in the United Nations Charter. With reference to his statements and speeches I will show how, as the invasion approached, Blair placed less emphasis on the established codes of just war and international law. Instead, he preferred to increasingly reinforce a weak legal case with a creative amalgam of moral arguments, some of which are not normally associated with war or recognized in our current international political system. I demonstrate how Blair used linguistic sleight of hand to interweave carefully selected arguments in such a way as to gain at least temporary support for the war from both Members of Parliament and the general public. The chapter will conclude by identifying a number of themes that will be explored in later chapters.

Blair's moral justification of the Iraq intervention will be compared and contrasted with the wider academic just war debate that was taking place at the same time as he was making his arguments in the political arena. Chapter 3 thereby shows the areas where Blair's approach conformed to ongoing just war arguments and points where he digressed. This is done by juxtaposing Blair with the two most prominent Western just war theorists at the time of the invasion: Jean Bethke Elshtain and Michael Walzer, and their respective books *Just War Against Terror* and *Just and Unjust Wars*.

Chapters 4 to 7 explore three recurring themes in Blair's Iraq discourse: authority, legitimacy and war; regime change; confronting tyranny and protecting the weak. These chapters show how just war ideas from the past – whether used knowingly by Blair or not – made his arguments possible in the present. They also illustrate some of the ways in which just war has redefined itself over the past 1600 years. Instead of being a continuous tradition that has smoothly and continually evolved, using the themes in these chapters I show that there have been distinct breaks in the tradition with some of its ideas being carried forward in modified form and others being abandoned in the sands of time. As a result the meanings of some of its core concepts (such as divine authority vs UN legal authority) have been radically altered over time and cannot be applied unproblematically in the present.

Chapter 8 revisits the concerns of the combatants who inspired the writing of this book, particularly the tension that many felt in undertaking a war that was declared legal by the British Attorney-General but which, as one serving non-commissioned officer put it, 'did not feel right compared to the first time [the 1991 Gulf War]'. I examine the implications for some combatants of being ordered to fight in a war that they do not feel is wholly justified, looking particularly at the impact of this tension on both personal morale and motivation. This is followed by considering where moral responsibility ultimately lies on such occasions. The significance of fighting well, or failing to fight in a way that reflects the wider values of the country being represented by its soldiers in war, is explored in relation to a number of high profile incidents such as the Abu Ghraib prisoner beatings. The final section of the chapter explores the possibility of combatants emerging as ethical even in situations where the codes that normally govern a state's behaviour, such as international law, appear ambiguous.

The final chapter of the book reflects upon a number of the themes addressed in the previous chapters. I offer my views on whether Blair's contribution to just war debate has helped to nudge the just war tradition in a pro-interventionist direction or whether the result is likely to be a return to a more cautious reluctance to engage militarily across borders where there is a risk of encountering or engendering insurgency warfare. The difficulty of incorporating just war ideas from earlier eras in the current international system is highlighted as a weakness of Blair's approach. The conclusion summarizes key aspects of the preceding argument, demonstrating in the process why Blair's illusion of morality worked initially, at least to some extent, but ultimately failed.

1
Blair and just intervention

In April 1999 NATO was in the throes of a vast aerial bombardment of Serbia and its capital Belgrade as part of Operation Allied Force. The Serbian police and army stood accused of the oppression and ethnic cleansing of Kosovo Albanians and the NATO operation, launched on 24 March 1999, was intended to coerce President Slobodan Milosevic into withdrawing his personnel and ordering the brutality to stop. Milosevic wanted to ensure continuing political control of what was at that time the Serbian province of Kosovo. The desire to put an end to the horrific scenes that were being broadcast around the world on 24-hour news television prompted Prime Minister Tony Blair to undertake his first major military intervention and set the pattern that he would follow all the way to Baghdad in 2003.

Blair's position was simple: 'I saw it essentially as a moral issue. And that, in a sense, came to define my view on foreign and military intervention'.[1] The premise of this book is that Blair's involvement in Iraq, as it was for all his military interventions, was primarily motivated by moral concerns; the legal question – where it was considered – played a secondary role.

The chapter will proceed with an analysis of the pivotal moment at the height of the Kosovo campaign when Blair set out his internationalist credentials with a vision for the political, economic and security challenges facing the world, all underpinned by a distinct moral positioning. On 24 April 1999 Blair gave his defining Doctrine of the International Community speech to the Economic Club, Chicago. It was there that he first set out his case for intervening across state borders to prevent humanitarian disasters of the kind seen in Rwanda in 1994. He proposed a moral framework to serve as the basis on which future military interventions would be conducted. The just war foundations of his moral framework will be identified and then subsequently applied to two of the military interventions he conducted prior to his involvement in Iraq: Kosovo and Sierra Leone.

The principles that Blair expounded during these early years of his premiership would, for better and for worse, set the parameters of his subsequent involvement in Iraq, with the moral/legal tension playing an increasingly important role. As he reflected some years later: 'Posing and answering a moral question doesn't inexorably lead to a military solution, but it establishes a framework that can do so'.[2] If his words and actions in relation to Iraq are to be fully appreciated they must be examined in light of the moral arguments and military campaigns that went before.

A moral framework

Blair's approach to politics was to challenge anything and everything that he saw as anachronistic, established or traditional. He referred to this as 'taking away the givens'[3] within systems and organizations. He summarized his vision:

> So we began a reconsideration of the basic principles on which ... services were run, trying to measure them not against the 'givens' but against the contemporary reality, the potential and possibility opened up by change, the parameters we would want if we were relieved of all political constraint and just exercised freethinking.[4]

Blair took this basic premise for dealing with domestic political agendas and extended it to include challenges in the international arena. His 'freethinking' smacks of the romantic fledgling undergraduate who recognizes for the first time the limitations of his or her formative intellectual landscape and vows to explore new vistas, unencumbered by what is now seen as 'baggage' from the past. The more capable student soon realizes that true originality and freethinking is staggeringly rare and possibly nonexistent, leaving you, the reader, with the choice of situating Blair with the naive or the brilliant. The freethinking Blair conducted in relation to military intervention could be more accurately described as a bringing together of pre-existing ancient and modern moral arguments and applying them to new situations with boldness, flair and no little political opportunism. His strong desire to challenge the givens in international politics reached its peak in his speech to the Economic Club, where he set out his vision of how international institutions should operate, with an emphasis on distant conflicts and the willingness to intervene militarily:

> Many of our domestic problems are caused on the other side of the world ... These problems can only be addressed by international co-operation ... We cannot turn our backs on conflicts and the violation of human rights within other countries if we want still to be secure ... We need new rules for international co-operation and new ways of organising our international institutions.[5]

Blair's theme of international co-operation looms large and it emphasized human rights as sacrosanct and to be defended, even where those rights were violated behind the distant borders of sovereign states. Complicating the matter for Blair and other pro-interventionists is the UN Charter, which sets out alternate rights: the rights of states, irrespective of how they are governed, to non-interference from other states.[6] Blair tackled the issue head-on, identifying moral arguments that in his view outweighed the limitations of international law:

> But the principle of non-interference must be qualified in important respects. Acts of genocide can never be a purely internal matter. When oppression produces massive flows of refugees which unsettle neighbouring countries then they can properly be described as 'threats to international peace and security'. When regimes are based on minority rule they lose legitimacy – look at South Africa.[7]

Blair sets out here the conditions under which the principle of non-interference might be set aside, most notably in the cases of genocide, oppression leading to displacement and regional instability, and illegitimate regimes. Building on this foundation Blair went on to offer some suggestions for the codification of new rules to govern intervention across borders which under the UN Charter are ordinarily deemed inviolate:

> So how do we decide when and whether to intervene. I think we need to bear in mind five major considerations: First, are we sure of our case? ... Second, have we exhausted all diplomatic options? ... Third, on the basis of a practical assessment of the situation, are there military operations we can sensibly and prudently undertake? Fourth, are we prepared for the long term? ... And finally, do we have national interests involved?[8]

These five criteria for military intervention correspond remarkably closely to several key *jus ad bellum*[9] criteria of the just war tradition: just cause, last resort, reasonable chance of success, proportionality and right intention.[10] The reader may find it surprising, impressive even, that a British Prime Minister should be so familiar with ideas that have emerged over millennia to form an influential Western moral approach to war.[11] He may, of course, have covered this ground during his time at Oxford University but the most likely explanation is that he was assisted, for the purpose of writing his Chicago speech, by Lawrence Freedman, eminent historian and Professor of War Studies at King's College London. On 16 April 1999, in response to a request from Jonathan Powell, Blair's Chief of Staff, for ideas that might assist the Prime Minister in constructing his Chicago speech, Freedman submitted a five-page document.[12] Among many ideas contained within the document were Freedman's suggestions for dealing with the issue of non-interference and further ideas about when military intervention across state borders might be justified:

Yet this principle of non-interference must be qualified in important respects.

- Acts of genocide can never be a purely internal matter;
- when oppression produces massive flows of refugees which unsettle neighbouring countries then they can properly be described as 'threats to international peace and security';
- when regimes are based on minority rule they lose legitimacy. This was the foundation for the successful campaign against apartheid in South Africa.[13]

In addition, Freedman proposed five tests to help decide whether military intervention should be carried out:

1. Are we sure of our case? ... 2. Have we exhausted all diplomatic options? ... 3. On the basis of a practical assessment of the situation, are there military operations that we can sensibly and prudently undertake? ... 4. Are we prepared for the long-term? ... 5. Do we have national interests involved?[14]

The observant reader will notice the virtually identical excerpts from Freedman's suggestions and the transcript of the speech that Blair delivered. In itself the connection between Blair and Freedman is innocuous: it is the responsibility of Prime Ministers to avail themselves of informed and educated opinion. Blair was clearly enamoured of Freedman's ideas for great swathes of the latter's text were incorporated almost word-for-word in the speech that defined the Prime Minister's internationalism and set out the moral grounds for military intervention. Perhaps it is ironic or merely interesting in a coincidental sort of way that, only months before the Iraq invasion, Freedman received a knighthood.

In 2009 Gordon Brown, Blair's successor as both Prime Minister and leader of the Labour Party, instigated the Iraq Inquiry into the UK's involvement in Iraq between 2001 and 2009. The inquiry would be conducted by a committee comprising five members and chaired by Sir John Chilcot: 'non-partisan public figures acknowledged to be experts and leaders in their fields'.[15] In another of life's coincidences, one of the non-partisan figures appointed to sit on the panel that would try to glean lessons from the UK's involvement in Iraq – including the justification of military action – was none other than Professor Sir Lawrence Freedman: author of a significant portion of Blair interventionist doctrine in 1999. This chapter must now take another direction and apply Blair's moral framework for intervention to Kosovo and Sierra Leone. I leave you, the reader, to form your own opinion on whether or not it was appropriate for the man who provided the conceptual basis for Blair's interventionism to subsequently sit on a panel tasked with investigating Blair's Iraq intervention.

Kosovo

The moral framework for military intervention that Blair set out in April 1999 would continue to motivate him in the years to follow. But what was it that pushed him towards military intervention in the first place when so many other leaders seemed content to offer sympathy and platitudes and he was enjoying almost unmatched popularity with British voters? Blair recalls the outrage he felt at what he saw happening on the ground in Kosovo: 'Here were ordinary civilians being driven from their homes and turned into refugees, killed, raped, beaten up with savagery and often sadism, whole families humiliated or eliminated'.[16] His response was neither formal nor legalistic; he did not begin from the premise that Milosevic was breaking the law – either domestic or international. Blair's reaction was intrinsically personal and prompted by a concern for the suffering of others.

Outraged by what he saw on the TV screens and heard from displaced people and survivors of the action that was taking place Blair felt strongly motivated to act. It was only a few years since travesties of the war in Bosnia and Herzegovina had scarred the Balkan region and

Western Europe had once again witnessed mass rape, genocide and concentration camps. There is not the scope here to recount the complexities of that brutal campaign with its ethnically-driven violent excesses. However, one of the clear outcomes was a belief on the part of Slobodan Milosevic that the outside world would be most unlikely to devote political capital or military resources to stop him from advancing his ambitions for greater Serbia.

Milosevic calculated that Serbia's close historical, political and cultural links with Russia would ensure that the Russians would block any attempts by the UN Security Council to authorize military action in the region. He had also watched from afar during the 1990s as Saddam Hussein continued to defy world opinion and the UN by carrying out ethnic cleansing against the Iraqi Marsh Arabs and violent oppression against the southern Iraqi Shias. It hardly seems surprising therefore, though obviously we have the added bonus of 20/20 hindsight, that he felt secure in pursuing aggressive Serb nationalist policies.

Blair was educated as a boarder at Fettes College, Edinburgh, one of the most prestigious and expensive private schools in Scotland, followed by St John's College, Oxford. Blair, the celebrity Prime Minister who often gave the impression of supreme confidence mixed with a desperate desire for approval, did not seem at first glance to be the man who would step forward as the nemesis of Slobodan Milosevic. Yet it was Blair who became one of the driving forces of international opinion as he pleaded, persuaded and cajoled other NATO leaders into action against the Serb aggression in Kosovo.

In Europe Blair was confronted by other European leaders strongly averse to taking military action of any kind as a means of stopping the ethnic cleansing in Kosovo. The Germans were restricted not only by the sensitivities of internal politics but by a constitution that, for understandable historic reasons, would make foreign military intervention very difficult. Others, including the French, were only too happy to issue statements of condemnation and veiled threat but were not forthcoming on the matter of committing military personnel. The possibility of a ground invasion to force the Serb police and armed forces from Kosovo was out of the question from a European perspective.

In the United States President Clinton was more open to some form of intervention but was, like the Europeans, unwilling or unable to commit ground troops. Though Clinton would later describe the lack of action to stop the Rwanda genocide as his greatest regret as President, memories of a dead American soldier being publicly defiled and dragged through the streets of Mogadishu, Somalia in 1993 were equally raw. With the cut and thrust of American politics and Clinton's ongoing impeachment proceedings, the US President's ability to expend political capitol on a conflict a continent away was limited. He was, however, willing to devote the assets necessary for a coercive air campaign against Milosevic, an approach that would be supported by a number of European leaders.

One of Blair's great assets as a politician, at least prior to his involvement in Iraq, was his ability to relate to the concerns of people: regardless of class, gender or ethnicity. His emotional response to the death of Diana, Princess of Wales, only months after becoming Prime Minister, captured and perhaps even exaggerated the mood of the nation. The whole dynamic of celebrity culture at that time, even in death, changed the way many people viewed the world. The public reaction to Diana's death has had a long-lasting effect on the way public grieving is conducted by a traditionally reserved and private British people. Another example of Blair's ability to capture the prevailing Zeitgeist, which did not have an enduring impact, was his brief flirtation with 'Cool Britannia', a glamorous media-driven love-in in the late 1990s between the beautiful people of London, right-on rock stars, cutting edge artists and the new wave of British fashionistas. The celebrity Prime Minister was, briefly, if not quite the man of the people, the man of the moment. Blair did not quite scale the same heights of empathy as President Bill 'Ah feel your pain' Clinton but he enjoyed a degree of public optimism and trust that few Prime Ministers before him had been accorded.

In the process of making an argument Blair's flair for emotional delivery resonated with large swathes of any audience, for at least a few years until it became an object of satire and parody: fierce critics used much stronger descriptions. Making his presentational skills and ability to relate to people even more effective was his Director of Communications, Alastair Campbell. Campbell, oft ridiculed for his past work in the tabloid press, was fierce, incisive, loyal and seemingly willing to go to almost any lengths to both further, and protect, Blair's career. His ability to prepare the cherished 'sound-bite' for Blair's next appearance, and his even greater ability to ensure it appeared on multiple media outlets, made him political allies and enemies in equal measure.

A central tenet of the Blair/Campbell communication partnership was to keep the message clear, simple and to the point, a principle that can be seen in the way Blair set out his moral arguments for the various interventions he pursued. Take the language he used to describe Milosevic and the Serb actions in Kosovo:

> unspeakable things are happening in Europe. Awful crimes that we never thought we would see again have reappeared – ethnic cleansing,

systematic rape, mass murder ... the tear stained faces of the hundreds of thousands of refugees streaming across the border ... their heart-rending tales of cruelty.[17]

There can be no doubt that terrible crimes were being perpetrated against the Kosovo Albanians. However, in provoking an emotional response in his listeners as part of a process of persuading them to support his position, the complexity of the situation was over simplified using a good guy/bad guy approach. Blair failed to mention atrocities by the Kosovo Liberation Army (KLA) against Serbs resident in Kosovo. Though it should be acknowledged that these were not on the same scale as the Serb attacks a number of KLA officers were subsequently tried for war crimes. These may have been straightforward retaliatory actions or they may have been part of a violent insurgency campaign aimed at gaining Kosovo's independence from Serbia. Either way, if Blair had intimated that there were 'bad guys' on the other side as well (the side opposing Milosevic), his more subtle, and accurate, arguments may not have been so convincing and thereby not achieved the results they did. He was just as dramatic in his portrayal of Milosevic as he argued that the Kosovo intervention was morally justifiable:

This is a just war, based not on any territorial ambitions but on values. We cannot let the evil of ethnic cleansing stand. We must not rest until it is reversed. We have learned twice before in this century that appeasement does not work. If we let an evil dictator range unchallenged, we will have to spill infinitely more blood and treasure to stop him later.[18]

Blair provided a number of reasons why the Kosovo war should be counted as a just war. I have already set out his criteria for just intervention: 'are we sure of our case? ... have we exhausted all diplomatic options? ... are there military operations we can sensibly and prudently undertake? ... are we prepared for the long term? ... do we have national interests involved?'[19] By the time he made this particular speech the Kosovo war was already under way but Blair had clearly taken the view that these criteria had been satisfied. He also argued that they would provide a suitable template for future interventions aimed at preserving the lives of the victims, or potential victims, of ethnic cleansing unable to protect themselves.

The values that underpin Blair's just war were given in the same speech as 'liberty, the rule of law, human rights and an open society'.[20] These were not only values held by Blair but values he wanted to spread. However, two difficulties present themselves when his arguments are closely scrutinized. The first difficulty emerges in the relationship between morality and law at a most general level: does law precede morality or does morality precede law? Blair said that his just war – itself a *moral* claim – was based on a number of values; values that included the rule of *law*. When it came to military intervention therefore, Blair's moral basis rested on law: the law came first. While this segment of his interventionist doctrine may have provided the sound-bite so loved by the news channels, it was just plain wrong. Perhaps historians or philosophers more intellectually dextrous than I are able to argue the case that law precedes morality. However, my every observation of human history suggests the opposite. It is hard to envisage the development of human communities without an associated development of morally acceptable behaviours.

If early *Homo sapiens* robbed and killed one another at every turn we would not have survived as a species. Whether shaped by family bonds or wider social groupings there had to emerge some form of accepted social behaviour which we can describe as morality. Over time, accepted, and unaccepted, behaviours were written down and codified. An example of this in a religious context would be the Ten Commandments that define the Jewish and Christian traditions; commandments including: 'You shall not murder' and 'You shall not steal'.[21] Over much of the past two millennia, life in the West has been largely shaped by the Church's interpretation and application of the Ten Commandments and other moral imperatives set down in scripture. Over recent centuries in the UK, as elsewhere, many of society's – and indeed Christianity's – moral prohibitions have been formally set down in civil law and enforced by a judicial system.

To suggest that moral imperative follows on from the rule of law, instead of vice versa – is not realistic. The connection Blair made between the rule of law and morality in his speech may simply reflect the personal legacy of someone who had a brief legal career before entering into politics full time. It seems more likely, however, that Blair and his communications team put together a credible-sounding segment of his speech without thinking through the logic in too much detail. Perhaps not surprisingly, unlike the stronger moral reasoning Blair presented in Chicago in April 1999, this particular line of thought did not originate with Professor Freedman from King's College London. Blair may have stated that his moral case was based on the rule of law but in practice the opposite was true: he made a strong moral case for military intervention that could not or would not necessarily be supported or legitimized in international law.

The second difficulty with Blair's claim that his just war was based on values that included the rule of law stems from the legal status of the Kosovo campaign under international law. The two ways by which war can be waged legitimately under the terms of the UN Charter are quite straightforward in principle, if not in practice. First, every state has the right to self defence;[22] and second, the UN Security Council can choose to act to restore international peace and security.[23] In the case of Kosovo, the attacks were internal to Serbia and therefore within the same state. As a result, there was no issue of state self-defence to be addressed (except, strictly speaking, when Serbia came under attack from NATO). In addition, there was little or no danger of the violence moving beyond the borders of Kosovo.

Displaced Kosovo Albanians *were*, however, fleeing across the border and raising the possibility of instability in neighbouring Macedonia. The UN Security Council could have chosen to act to restore international peace and security on these grounds but was prevented from doing because Russia was prepared to use its veto to stop military action against Serbia. So despite what Blair said about Kosovo being a just war based on values that included the rule of law, the military campaign in Kosovo was justified on the *moral* grounds he set out and given a degree of legitimacy by the support of the European Union and NATO: it was not sanctioned by the UN. The only way Blair's comment about the rule of law makes sense is if he was referring to the Serbs breaking their own domestic law and ignoring his own disregard for international law, a disregard justified on what he saw as higher moral grounds.

It is that very tension between the moral case for saving the lives of Kosovo Albanians (or Bosnians or Rwandans earlier in the 1990s) and the legal restrictions imposed by the institutional rules and practices of the UN that Blair, drawing on Freedman, sought to address in Chicago. He proposed a number of changes to the way the international community operated, with an emphasis on the way the UN, and NATO, needed to adapt in order to respond effectively to future genocides or ethnic cleansing:

> A reconsideration of the role, workings and decision-making process of the UN, and in particular the UN Security Council. For NATO, once Kosovo is successfully concluded, a critical examination of the lessons to be learnt, and the changes we need to make in organisation and structure.[24]

Between the start of the Kosovo War on 24 March 1999 and the con-clusion of the air campaign on 10 June 1999 a number of significant developments took place. What was intended to be a two or three day, aggressive use of air power to coerce Milosevic into stopping his activities against the Kosovo Albanians did not have the desired effect. He concealed his military assets in the forests and appealed to the nationalist sensibilities of the Serbs to rally against what he described as the external aggressors. In the short term at least, Milosevic's position was strengthened as NATO's use of air power proved ineffective in the first weeks of the campaign. The initial rules of engagement given to the pilots meant that they had to fly above 15 000 feet to try to elimi-nate allied aircrew casualties. One consequence of the height restriction and the desire to protect NATO aircrew is that accuracy was reduced in non-precision guided weapons and civilian casualties became more likely. These rules were eventually relaxed to enable the aircraft to oper-ate more effectively at lower levels. As the NATO strikes proceeded Serb aggression escalated in Kosovo, as did reprisal attacks from the KLA.

Major environmental damage was caused by NATO air attacks on the Novi Sad and Panchevo oil refineries, the river Danube carrying carci-nogenic pollutants as far as Romania and Bulgaria. Both sides in the war claimed the moral high ground. Blair and other NATO leaders pointed to the brutal treatment of Kosovars, while Milosevic invited the world's media to observe the damage done by the attacks on the petro-chemical refineries: attacks that he referred to as ecocide.

As Blair pointed out there were lessons to be learned, particularly for the UN and the way it responds to the brutality of governments against their own people. His grand aspirations for the reform of the UN to make it easier to gain Security Council sanction for military intervention was to come to nothing. UN Security Council authorization for the deploy-ment of NATO forces in Kosovo was granted on 10 June 1999 as fighting ceased.[25] The UN Environmental Protection team provided post-war sup-port and advice to help reduce the long-term impact of the war on the environment. The UN's International Criminal Tribunal for the former Yugoslavia has brought a number of senior officials – mainly Serbs but also including KLA commanders and a small number from surrounding states – to trial for atrocities committed at that time.[26]

The key lesson that Blair appears to have taken from the Kosovo inter-vention was that he could wage war on the basis of a sound moral case, even if UN approval could not be obtained. Returning to Blair's proposed framework for military intervention, it is possible to assess the degree to which Kosovo satisfied his own moral code. A brief examination of the five criteria that he set out, and which correspond closely to longstanding just war doctrine, confirm the *moral* claims that Blair was making for the action in Kosovo, even though prior *legal* authorization for the military intervention was not granted by the UN Security Council.

Blair started by asking: 'are we sure of our case?' Blair's, and NATO's, case was that Slobodan Milosevic was using the Serb military and police to conduct ethnic cleansing against Kosovo Albanians. Thousands were being killed or threatened with death and tens of thousands of people were being displaced from their homes leading to suffering, hunger and further deaths. The case, or just cause, that Blair argued was the need to stop the oppression and the suffering of the weak and vulnerable. The idea of protecting the weak resonated across most of the world and the daily TV pictures of suffering and death enabled Blair to secure widespread support from the British people and others abroad.

As a moral argument the notion of helping the weak has a long history in the just war tradition, even though the principle of intervening across state borders on humanitarian grounds was not written into international law when the UN Charter was agreed at the end of World War II. However, such was Blair's reliance on this particular moral justification for military action in Kosovo, Sierra Leone and Iraq that it will be explored at length in Chapter 7. Recent use of this argument as a justification of military intervention on humanitarian grounds will be set alongside historical examples of its development and application in the just war tradition. The reasons for its falling out of favour as a just war argument will be analysed, as will its resurgence at the end of the twentieth century and the beginning of the twenty-first century.

The second issue Blair wanted to address before entering into a war was whether or not the diplomatic options had been exhausted. The main reason that just war emerged as a tradition of thought in the annals of history, and why it still remains relevant today, was to reduce unnecessary death and suffering by only fighting those wars that could not be avoided for the most just of causes. Consequently, every other option short of war should be explored as far as possible before military forces are committed. One of the variables in this particular equation is the imminence of the threat being faced.

The crisis in Kosovo accelerated rapidly towards the end of 1998 and into 1999. NATO leaders did not have the luxury of one or two years in which to enter protracted diplomatic negotiations or attempt to use economic sanctions as a means of halting Milosevic's troops. A decision had to be made and diplomatic pressure – reinforced by a military threat – applied quickly if the ethnic cleansing was to be stopped in its tracks. Representatives of both NATO and Milosevic's government met and negotiated in February 1999 at Chateau Rambouillet in northern France.[27] Terms were proposed by NATO's representatives that, if accepted by the Serbs, would have halted the ethnic cleansing in Kosovo, promote the autonomy of Kosovo and prevent the need for military action against Milosevic and his people.

Some diplomatic activity clearly took place but the question of whether *every* diplomatic option had been fully explored is still a matter of debate today. On the one hand, NATO did offer terms that would have avoided a war. On the other hand, the degree of sovereignty that Serbia would have had to surrender in agreeing to NATO's demands was considered too great and subsequently rejected. Henry Kissinger, former US Secretary of State, later criticized the proposals as provocative to a degree that could not have been accepted by any reasonable Serb and tantamount to an excuse for NATO to begin its air campaign.[28]

It can reasonably be said that *some* diplomatic negotiations took place, even though doubts remain about the depth of commitment to these on both sides. Blair and the other NATO leaders took the decision not to wait any longer since any delay, whether in pursuit of genuine negotiations or whether it was simply a ploy by Milosevic, would result in more deaths and displacement of Kosovo Albanians. The difficulty of upholding moral ideals in the face of political and military realities is highlighted in this example, but for Blair and other just war advocates it is still a better situation than no moral consideration at all.

A third just war criterion was proposed by Blair as part of his moral framework for military intervention when he asked: 'are there military operations we can sensibly and prudently undertake?' On the basis of the principle set out previously – that the purpose of only fighting just wars is to reduce unnecessary death and suffering – for a war to be considered just there should be a reasonable hope of military success. In this reasoning, any leader who knowingly committed military personnel to a campaign that was destined to fail would be guilty of the most immoral act. An army of 5000 soldiers sent to do battle – on equal terms as opposed to hit-and-run insurgency style tactics – with an army of 25 000 similarly prepared and equipped soldiers would stand little chance of success. The most likely outcome would be for more than 5000 soldiers to be wounded or killed in battle, unless a surrender ended the bloodshed before that stage.

As I write these words in mid-2011, UN sanctioned protection of Libyan civilians through the deployment of NATO and other air assets is encountering similar difficulties to those seen in the Kosovo campaign.

Colonel Gaddafi is hiding his tanks and other military hardware or locating it in primarily civilian neighbourhoods as a means of reducing the air threat against it. Furthermore, a number of his civilian supporters are occupying the compounds of military and political headquarters in the knowledge that their presence, when combined with media scrutiny, will make NATO airstrikes potentially very politically costly and therefore less likely to be launched. NATO's enemies seem to learn much faster than the Western states that make up the organization.

The *jus ad bellum* criterion of proportionality demands that the good that will ultimately result from going to war will outweigh the harm to be done in the process and the harm that would be caused by not going to war at all. More than any other aspect of just war, the issue of proportionality appears speculative and open to abuse by those who would add the descriptor 'just' to a war that is anything but. One of the ways of tipping the balance in favour of a positive outcome is, as Blair advocated in his fourth moral consideration, to commit political capital and resources for the long term. NATO's involvement in Kosovo continued for almost a decade, with the European Union taking over responsibility for policing in 2008 and the UK ending its formal military commitment at the end of that year. The UN continues to be involved in a number of guises as issues surrounding the Kosovo declaration of independence are addressed. Blair's, the UK's and NATO's long-term commitment to Kosovo has been realized, though, realistically, it will take decades before the world can say that stability has truly been achieved.

The final criterion Blair put forward to complete his framework for assessing the moral justification of intervention relates closely to just war's 'right intention'. One of the intentions that motivated Blair was the pursuit of national interests. The hard-headed *realpolitikers* of international relations would say that a leader's only responsibility is to achieve maximum advantage for his or her own people in every situation. Blair, however, was more idealistic and wanted to include a moral dimension in the political calculation. One way of measuring the degree of right intention in any proposed war is to attempt to place the action on a moral continuum somewhere between utter national selfishness on one extreme and perfect altruism on the other.

In the 1970s Hedley Bull, esteemed Professor of International Relations at the University of Oxford, entitled his famous study of global politics *The Anarchical Society*.[29] The word 'anarchical' here refers to the lack of hierarchy in the international system, such as a superior power or authority that somehow sits above all the states of the world and governs their conduct: it is every state for itself. However, the word 'society' suggests that global politics is not simply a war of all against all but rather shaped more like a society of equals with some broadly accepted rules to guide the conduct of its different members. If states were completely selfish there would be no end to war until one state either achieved domination over its rivals or destroyed them entirely. Contrarily, if altruism was pursued at all times then leaders would inevitably fail to act in the interests of their own people.

Blair considered a humanitarian disaster in the form of ethnic cleansing as a potentially destabilizing event in a region of Europe where the seeds of two world wars were sown. In this general sense he considered it to be in the interests of the British people to avoid another disaster. Given the potential costs involved in such an intervention, in terms of both finance and human lives, the benefits to the UK could be described as limited. Consequently, pursuing a war in Kosovo to save the lives of strangers can be considered, at least to some degree, an altruistic act.

To the foregoing moral criteria, which I have argued are closely based on traditional just war doctrine, can be added another form of moral argument – Blair's insistence on the need to confront evil. The advantage of this moral argument is that it would appear to need no further explanation or justification once Blair implied a link between Milosevic and Hitler. Let us look at another aspect of some of Blair's words that we have considered previously: 'We have learned twice before in this century that appeasement does not work. If we let an evil dictator range unchallenged, we will have to spill infinitely more blood and treasure to stop him later.'[30] The genius of Blair's argument is that he merely referred to two world wars, appeasement and a dictator and allowed his listeners to make the connection, a linguistic technique that he used extensively in the build-up to the Iraq invasion and which will be explored further in the next chapter.

Though distinctly religious language and motivations, such as the idea of confronting evil that Blair used extensively, are not part of international law today – and for many they do not even belong in just war debate – they played an important part in Blair's justification of war before, during and after the invasion of Iraq. The theme will be examined in Chapter 6, which looks at how religious – particularly Christian – ideas, words and imagery shaped and helped maintain the just war tradition from the fifth century until the Enlightenment before being replaced by ideas of justice based on law and human reason. In light of this history, the significance of Blair's use of religious words and imagery in recent just war debate will be explored. The strong emotions that such vocabulary invokes can be, and I will argue were, problematic in the war against Iraq. Ostensibly, Christian nations were pitted against a Muslim nation, providing ammunition for Islamist extremists and moderates alike to claim that their warnings of Western imperialism were coming to pass.

Returning to Blair's justification of the Kosovo War, for all the complexities of Serbia's internal politics, the difficulties he faced in securing the support of NATO leaders for military action, and the lack of UN sanction for the war in advance, there are few outside of Serbia who would now argue that action should not have been taken. The events of 1999 in Kosovo taught Blair a number of lessons. On the practicalities of coercing a determined enemy he came to the view that using air power alone was inherently limited; he considered the threat of assault by ground forces as essential in any future intervention. For Blair, the biggest legacy of the Kosovo intervention was not a concern for the tactical means of achieving strategic aims, it was a bringing to the fore of the importance of making moral judgements:

> Through Kosovo I came to the view – rightly or, some may think in light of Iraq, wrongly – that in such an uncertain landscape, the only way of finding direction was first to ask some moral questions: should this be allowed to happen or not? Should this regime remain in power? Should these people continue to suffer injustice? … Posing and answering a moral question doesn't inexorably lead to a military solution, but it establishes a framework that can do so.[31]

Blair's starting point is and was, unequivocally, a *moral* assessment, as opposed to assessing the possibilities available within what he considered to be a restrictive legal framework. Blair here asks some profound questions about what it is to be ethical and about the responsibility that people have towards one another's welfare. He also confronts the inbuilt paradox at the heart of the international system. On the one hand, the UN Charter sets out the rights of states to exist without external interference or even the threat of external interference.[32] On the other hand, *The Universal Declaration of Human Rights* concentrates on individuals and recognizes the 'inherent dignity and … the equal and inalienable rights of all members of the human family'.[33]

Two of the thirty articles of the Declaration state: 'Everyone has the right to life, liberty and security of person'; and, 'No one shall be subjected to torture or to cruel, inhuman or degrading treatment or punishment'.[34] Individual Kosovo Albanians and individual Iraqis all had and have human rights according to the Universal Declaration. However, even where these were being violated there is nothing written in the Declaration about enforcement of those rights where abuses take place. Furthermore, there is no mechanism in the UN Charter whereby violation of individual rights triggers military action against abusive regimes. Faced with this dilemma, Blair could not relieve the suffering of the oppressed by simply conforming to international law. His only other option, and the one he took, was to create the wider moral framework that has been examined at length above, which in his judgement outweighed the restrictions of the UN Charter.

When Blair asked whether the ethnic cleansing of the Kosovo Albanians should be allowed to continue and whether Milosevic's regime should be allowed to remain in place, his answer to both questions was a resounding 'no'. The only way, in his view, to ensure the safety of the Kosovo Albanians was to remove the regime that was oppressing them. The first of these actions – liberating the oppressed – would be counted as an ethical act in any moral framework I can think of. However, the only way Blair could achieve it would be by transgressing the letter of international law. He describes his 1999 policy on Kosovo in clear terms: 'intervention to bring down a despotic dictatorial regime could be justified on grounds of the *nature of that regime*, not merely its immediate threat to our self-interests'.[35] Blair was willing, enthusiastic even, to set aside conformity to the established and widely recognized codes of the UN in favour of his own self-created moral discourse which was focused heavily on individual conduct and frequently framed in terms of a contest between good and evil, aimed at regime change.

The success of NATO's coercive campaign to stop Milosevic's ethnic cleansing in Kosovo justified Blair's approach, certainly in his own view, despite the lack of UN authorization. He acknowledges this development in his thinking: 'Kosovo had not diminished my appetite for such intervention where I thought it essential to resolve a problem that needed resolution, and where a strong moral case could be made'.[36] Blair's actions had been based on a moral argument that he prioritized over international law and he was vindicated to a large extent by the UN's subsequent endorsement of the peace-keeping and enforcement activities of NATO and its constituent members. More importantly for Blair, Kosovo also provided a template which he would use for subsequent interventions.

Sierra Leone

The year after the Kosovo War, the next opportunity for Blair to commit the UK to military intervention arose in Sierra Leone. The government of President Ahmad Kejan Kabbah was on the brink of being toppled by the Revolutionary United Front (RUF): a rebel group led by Foday Sankoh whose main interests appeared to be diamond acquisition, murder, maiming, rape and torture. Complicating the political situation was a small contingent of UN military personnel in Sierra Leone that was ill-equipped to counter the actions of the RUF and did not have the necessary rules of engagement to take anything other than self-defensive action. This was a civil war with one group of Sierra Leoneans, with some support from Charles Taylor in Liberia, attempting to topple the government and impose a new regime.

In Sierra Leone, like other parts of the world where literacy levels are sporadic, many people participated in elections by means of fingerprinting: the ink residue providing evidence that a vote had been cast. Foday Sankoh's favourite intimidation tactic was to cut off the right hand, and sometime both hands, of government supporters. The RUF showed little or no intention of threatening the governance of the surrounding countries. Peace and security in the region beyond Sierra Leone was not threatened by events in and around Freetown, which – like Milosevic's ethnic cleansing in Kosovo – made it difficult to apply either the traditional state-oriented moral arguments of just war or the legal framework of the UN Charter to the situation. The UN was already failing to protect the Sierra Leoneans who were falling victim to the RUF's insurgency campaign.

Domestic stability was eroding daily as thousands of citizens were being killed or maimed, at the point in early 2000 when Blair was deciding whether to intervene militarily in Sierra Leone. Negotiations had been taking place over the previous two years with a number of agreements brokered then broken. In May the RUF accelerated their campaign of violence. With a British presence already established at Freetown's Lungi airport, an aircraft carrier and other naval assets only a few days' sail away and a rapid reaction force capable of almost immediate deployment, Blair took the decision to commit militarily. His aims included the safe evacuation of UK and other foreign citizens, the stabilization of Freetown and defeat of the RUF. The British presence of over a thousand ground troops, ships off the coast, Harrier strike aircraft and helicopter mobility quickly contributed to a degree of political stability and security.

The five criteria that Blair had set out the previous year as a means of providing a moral framework for such interventions stood up well. He felt sure of his case for intervening, based as it was on clear evidence of rapidly spreading atrocities committed by the RUF. These atrocities were taking place despite the numerous attempts to find a negotiated solution to the civil war over the previous years. Sankoh broke an existing cease-fire in order to pursue his latest campaign of violence. Blair was advised by his Chief of the Defence Staff, General Charles Guthrie, of the scale and availability of military assets to put a stop to the violence and start the process of stabilization.

Although the British operation was short lived it led on to further UN stabilization and justice programmes, a subsequent war crimes trial and eventually democratic elections in 2007. Sierra Leone faces many problems and its current degree of stability may still only be temporary but external support over several years has given the country the chance of a future brighter than its recent past. Finally, while there was a degree of UK national interest being pursued by Blair, the immediate reward was the safe evacuation of British nationals. In monetary terms there was, and is, little benefit for the UK. Illegal immigration had probably been reduced but Sierra Leone offered no great strategic advantage as reward for the efforts of Blair and the UK's armed forces.

When considered together, Blair's military interventions in Kosovo and Sierra Leone hardened his interventionist views and reinforced the way he saw himself as ethical. Both actions confirmed for him the relevance and success of the moral framework for intervention he set out in Chicago in April 1999. In addition to the moral framework Blair espoused was his burgeoning personal belief in the benefits of regime change. For Blair, Milosevic had been utterly immoral, confirmed by the latter's oppressive and brutal treatment of the Kosovo Albanians. Consequently, Blair saw himself, as did many others, as an ethical ruler simply on the basis of opposing the evil and immoral Milosevic. Some months after the Sierra Leone intervention he summed up his approach:

> On Sierra Leone there were those who said: what's it got to do with us? But I am sure Britain's and Europe's long-term interests in Africa are best served, if we intervene, not excessively, but to do what we can to save African nations from barbarism and dictatorship and be proud of it.[37]

Blair identified the evils to be confronted as barbarism and dictatorship. However, these characteristics that he identified with Milosevic's regime and Sankoh's RUF are not proscribed by international law: the UN Charter does not dictate the forms of governance that are to be considered acceptable amongst its members. Saving African or other nations from barbarism was and is, for Blair, an ethical act even where the barbarism offered no threat to third-party states: an ethical act that transcended international law. This view was reinforced in a subsequent speech in 2002 where he extolled the virtues and benefits of regime change through military intervention:

> I have been involved as British Prime Minister in three conflicts involving regime change. Milosevic. The Taliban. And Sierra Leone, where a country of six million people was saved from a murderous group of gangsters who had hijacked the democratically elected government ... I'll always remember driving through the villages near Freetown in Sierra Leone seeing the people rejoicing – many of them amputees through the brutality from which they had been liberated – and their joy at being free to debate, argue and vote as they wished.[38]

As well as confirming his moral judgement on the benefits of regime change, Blair presented himself as ethical in the act of saving the people of Sierra Leone from 'a murderous group of gangsters'. He further confirmed himself as ethical in two ways: first, through the act of opposing the murderous gangsters (the good guy/bad guy dichotomy that made him one of the good guys). Second, he presented himself as a liberator of the oppressed by setting free those who had previously been at the mercy of Foday Sankoh's killers. In his later recollections Blair was even more strident about the way he justified intervening in Sierra Leone, on moral and not legal grounds: 'We had acted without UN authority in Kosovo ... I never even thought about it for Sierra Leone. Yet it would be hard to argue that, morally, in each of those situations, we should not have intervened'.[39]

Though Blair referred on a number of occasions over the years to his role in liberating Kosovo and Sierra Leone, he did not apply a consistent moral standard. For example, one of the dilemmas that Blair said little about was how he distinguished between cases worthy of intervention and those that were not. He took the view that the UK had a special interest in Sierra Leone because it was a former British colony.[40] In contrast, when President Robert Mugabe spent years oppressing and brutalizing sections of the Zimbabwe population, Blair and his government were always reluctant to offer sharp verbal criticism, never mind devoting the military resources and political capital necessary to intervene. The moral case that Blair made for other interventions was not even attempted in the case of President Mugabe and Zimbabwe. Ever the pragmatist, Blair's flexible moral approach enabled him to set aside the concerns of Mugabe's victims, viewing the political challenge of intervening on their behalf as too great.[41]

In adopting such an attitude towards Zimbabwe and other states where oppression was clearly taking place on a large scale, Blair demonstrated a clear, hard-headed willingness to adjust his moral position when political expediency demanded it. When in his 1999 Chicago speech Blair spoke of being motivated by a mixture of 'mutual self interest and moral purpose'[42] he clearly meant it. Self-interest would be the yardstick by which it would be decided whether or not the moral argument would come into his political reckoning.

Summary

In the process of examining Blair's moral framework for war a number of distinct elements stand out. His five conditions for military intervention corresponded closely to, and draw upon, important just war criteria. In addition Blair creatively incorporated a number of moral arguments that are not normally associated with just war today, though they were several centuries ago: opposing evil and protecting the weak. Furthermore, he was convinced that regime change was both a necessary and moral response to actions as repressive and barbaric as those of Milosevic against the Kosovo Albanians. Most importantly for subsequent events in Iraq, Blair came to the view that his moral arguments transcended the constraints of international law to the extent that, by his own admission, he did not even consider going through the UN when deciding to intervene in Sierra Leone in 2000.

In the next chapter I begin to analyse the tension between Blair's moral conviction that he had to act in concert with President Bush against Saddam Hussein and Iraq and the pressure he was under to obtain UN Security Council sanction for war if he was to gain popular support for military action. Confronted by a weak and diminishing legal case for war in 2002 and early 2003, Blair's hopes of convincing sufficient numbers of the British people to support him rested on his ability to construct a convincing case. In Chapter 2 and beyond I examine the events surrounding the Iraq invasion in relation to the moral framework for military intervention Blair set out in 1999.

2
Are we sure of our case?[1]

Beads of perspiration glistened under the glare of the lights as Prime Minister Tony Blair gripped the despatch box and faced down his opponents in a crowded debating chamber. On 18 March 2003 the House of Commons seethed with anger and excitement as boos and cheers punctuated the statement that opened the Iraq debate. Neither before nor since has Blair look so convinced or convincing as he did in delivering the speech that defined his premiership, took the UK to war and shaped the British political landscape for the remainder of the first decade of the twenty-first century. His voice creaked with emotion as he outlined the litany of offences Saddam Hussein had committed, and continued to commit, against his own people. Past aggressions were revisited and Saddam's obfuscation before the United Nations was laid bare. Finally, exhausted of emotion and drained of colour, the Prime Minister set out his challenge to the Members of Parliament before him and the British public watching on their television screens: 'to have the courage to do the right thing'.[2]

The 'right thing', in this instance, was for the MPs present to vote in support of the motion to intervene militarily in Iraq and for those watching the debate on television to give Blair and his government their backing. His speech was a patchwork of moral and legal arguments woven together using the language of threat and defence, good and evil, strength and weakness. Following his successes in Kosovo and Sierra Leone, Blair was utterly confident that his justification of military intervention superseded all other arguments. What was not made clear by Blair, his ministers or his communications team was that the way in which he set out his arguments for action against Iraq played down the tenuousness of his legal case. The furthest he ever went towards acknowledging this was when he later wrote that there was both a case for and a case against war.[3] Furthermore, as this and subsequent chapters illustrate, his adherence to the just war-based moral framework for military intervention that he set out in 1999, and which had served him so well over Kosovo and Sierra Leone, was similarly nebulous.

As all talk of a second UN resolution faded away (that is, a follow up to UN Security Council Resolution 1441) Blair subtly shifted his emphasis from longstanding codes intended to govern and limit war between states towards a cocktail of disparate, almost desperate moral arguments. These enabled him, at the hour of decision, to gain the impetus necessary for the Commons majority vote that gave parliamentary approval to the invasion of Iraq. Although the various strands of Blair's justification of military action against Iraq were complex and interwoven, for the purpose of analysis I will separate them into two broad groupings: codes, written and unwritten to which behaviour should be conformed (international law or just war doctrine) and creative, individualized ethical arguments (I am good if I oppose evil). Of course, such a separation of moral arguments can never be absolute but it will serve as a way of understanding the means by which Blair's shifts in emphasis can be more readily understood. This chapter examines the pivotal aspect of Blair's justification of the Iraq invasion in light of the moral framework he established and applied previously: Are we sure of our case? Later chapters will explore his more contentious arguments and possible motivations: regime change; defending the weak; and opposing tyranny.

Before we explore these various themes there is a philosophical concern to be addressed, a concern that sits at the heart of everything that has been said and done in relation to Iraq: the quest for truth.

Power, truth and morality

If there was one area where Blair redefined the way that politics and politicians operate it was in the relationship between the government and the press. More specifically, it was in the way that the Prime Minister's communications department, headed by Alastair Campbell, sought to keep government ministers and Labour MPs 'on message' while seeking to shape the way that major stories were presented to, and in, the media.

Prior to his election as Prime Minister Blair had employed Alastair Campbell and Peter Mandelson to assist not only with the strategic planning of New Labour's policies but to control the way that policies were presented to the country. While initially this approach was very successful, after a few years of the New Labour government the public's view began to change. While Blair and his team have always described themselves as fundamentally honest in their concern to present the government – and particularly the Prime Minister – to best political advantage, the public were becoming increasingly hostile. 'Spin' started to be perceived by many as, at best, somehow less than fully honest, presenting only partial truths to suit the difficulty of the day, often through unattributed briefings. At worst, spin was perceived as deliberate deception for the sake of party political advantage.

By 2002 and the communication campaign to win over public support for military action against Iraq, the British public were already becoming inured to, and wary of, Number 10's formidable communications machine. Campbell himself acknowledged in 2002 that the media view of the New Labour brand had shifted from love to hate.[4] What Campbell was less forthright about – or accepting of – was the reason for the widespread cynicism about the government communications operation: the perception of truth. The most common perception, regardless of whether it was based in fact or not, was that government 'spin' equated to government 'lies'. This fault line over what counted, and still counts, as the truth over Iraq became hardened over the 12 months prior to the 2003 invasion and has remained in place ever since.

Michel Foucault, writing more than two decades earlier, provided a helpful means of investigating the complexities of 'truth' as presented by those who wield political power. He did not see truth as something that has a legitimacy and existence of its own and somehow just *is*. Rather, he viewed it as something created by those who wielded sufficient political power to dictate or shape, using the instruments of state and other mechanisms and procedures, what counted as the truth.[5] At first glance it might appear that only dictators in totalitarian regimes would have the authority to shape their populations' perspectives on what counts as truth and what does not. It is not only governments and leaders with access to secret police, torture squads and re-education programmes, of the kind for which the Soviet Gulags became infamous, that can dictate what counts as truth in public debate. A more subtle approach is needed in liberal democracies such as the UK but a British Prime Minister still has, and has always had, significant resources that can be used for the purpose of presenting a regime of truth, even if it does not represent what a court might refer to as the whole truth and nothing but the truth.

In the build-up to the Iraq War, Blair had greater influence than anyone over the mechanisms of government through which the truth or otherwise of particular statements could be distinguished. This occurred on three levels. First, his communications team tightly controlled information that was put into the public domain. Second, Blair's office used the machinery of government to control the flow of information directly relevant to war planning. For example, security classifications ensured that huge amounts of information that could have enabled members of the public to make a more informed view of the war were kept in the hands of a few government intelligence, security and military committees. Blair, and probably most other Prime Ministers, would argue, probably rightly, that policy cannot be set in the face of public speculation, anger or outrage, fuelled by a media maelstrom. This does not, however, refute the philosophical claim that only a particular version of the truth was being put into the public domain by him and those around him.

Third, Blair even limited the access of his own Cabinet ministers to sensitive material on Iraq. Lord Turnbull, Cabinet Secretary from September 2002, told the Iraq Inquiry that Cabinet ministers were not given access to the papers they would have needed in order to achieve an informed view of any impending military actions: 'None of those really key papers like the options paper in March '02, the military options of July, none of these were presented to Cabinet, which is why I don't accept [Blair's] claim that [the Cabinet ministers] knew the score.'[6] Blair's reluctance to discuss sensitive intelligence assessments and other papers with the Cabinet was explained by Sir Gus O'Donnell, Turnbull's successor as Cabinet Secretary, who said to the Iraq Inquiry, 'I think one of the reasons the Prime Minister was reluctant, at times, to take as many Cabinet discussions as possible was because he felt that they would become very public, very quickly.'[7] Preventing material from being made public, particularly material that might weaken the government's case for war or the public's potential support for war, was a key part of Blair's efforts to construct his regime of truth about Iraq and Saddam Hussein.

Viewed in this light, the concept of a regime of truth helps to explain the fault line that separates the pro- and anti-invasion lobbies and their respective claims to the truth over Iraq. A regime of truth is a subtly constructed edifice that is built on vast numbers of decisions taken by a number of individuals within the political machinery of state. Those who build and maintain a regime of truth, whether on Iraq or any other issue, will defend the edifice they have constructed on the basis that they have been presenting the truth. Opponents will reject a regime of truth if it is perceived to be selective or misleading, in the process also laying claim to the truth for themselves. Opinion is thus separated into distinct groups, each laying claim to the truth and rejecting the claims of those who adopt the opposing view. The crucial factor that enabled both supporters and opponents of the Iraq invasion to claim it was they who were telling the truth is that they each set their own parameters for what counted as truth: which is very different to saying that one or the other side deliberately lied.

Blair and the small group of close advisers who worked with him on the Iraq issue were able to select what material would be made public while restricting the availability of those assessments that weakened their case. One example of this was outlined by Sir Gus O'Donnell to the Iraq Inquiry regarding the Attorney General's legal advice to the Prime Minister. Inquiry member Sir Roderic Lyne was interested in learning whether Blair had conformed to convention when withholding the Attorney General's legal advice from Cabinet members in the months leading up to the eleventh-hour presentation of a revised view that authorized war.

> Sir Gus O'Donnell: I think to me it is fairly clear, absolutely clear. The Attorney General is the adviser for the Government and what that means is for Cabinet ... if it's a Cabinet issue then the Attorney General is giving advice to Cabinet, and it is laid out in the Ministerial Code and in the Cabinet Manual as well ...

> Sir Roderic Lyne: where the Prime Minister might be wanting to know what the legalities were on a particular issue would you not expect that the Attorney in providing that advice to the Prime Minister would provide it at least simultaneously to the departmental Minister handling the subject?

> Sir Gus O'Donnell: Yes.[8]

This small, but significant, technical point (on an issue I will return to later) illustrates how one apparently innocuous decision by Blair to with-hold information – which by convention should have been presented to at least one Cabinet minister – impacted upon his ministers' ability to fully appreciate the degree of difficulty presented by the legal case at that time. For Blair the issue seems to have been one of controlling or limit-ing information that might harden opposition within his own Cabinet and subsequently limit his options politically. Blair has made it clear that he did not see working closely with his Cabinet as an efficient way of dealing with an issue as contentious as war. He described his approach in July 2002: 'I reflected with *the closest team* on the different strands of the challenge.'[9]

Blair's critics have often accused him of lying and many public dem-onstrations against him have taken place between 2002 and 2011 with protestors carrying placards to that effect. Those who take the black-and-white view that Blair lied to drag the country into an illegal war have not yet produced the single, 'smoking gun' piece of evidence against Blair that vindicates their position. I take the view that no such evidence exists: Why would Blair lie when he was convinced that he was doing the right thing and he had the machinery of state at his disposal? No evidence of deception has emerged during the multiple investigations and inquiries that have taken place since the 2003 invasion, the only caveat being that government departments, and Blair himself, have been allowed to withhold evidence at every stage and Blair has refused to disclose personal letters he wrote to President Bush as war approached. He continues to defend himself vehemently: 'There was no intent to deceive. Indeed, such an intention would have been in any event absurd, since once Saddam was out, the truth would be out also.'[10] Note the prioritization in Blair's self-defence – the removal of Saddam comes first followed by a revelation of the truth. The difficulty facing Blair was that most people wanted the truth *first* before they would lend support to the removal of Saddam, a theme that is revisited in my analysis of the regime change argument in Chapter 5.

Still, the question of perception remains. What did Blair mean by 'intent to deceive'? Even accepting his self-defence at face value it cannot be said that Blair was *completely* open and transparent about his intentions, his aims and the advice he was being given at every stage in the build-up to war. His regime of truth could only be maintained by making – to both the public and Cabinet ministers alike – the arguments that advanced his case, limiting access to information and omitting some of the caveats and cautions that he had received, especially from intelligence sources.

Consider the observation of Baroness Elizabeth Manningham-Buller, Deputy Director General of MI5 in March 2002, who thought the threat from Iraq at that time to be 'very limited and containable'.[11] She wrote an assessment of Saddam Hussein and Iraq to the Home Office that stated: 'There is no credible evidence that demonstrates that Iraq was implicated in planning the 11 September attacks.'[12] Contrast this view from a leading member of the UK's intelligence community with the words of Blair in his speech at the George Bush Senior Presidential Library only two weeks later: 'But to allow WMD to be developed by a state like Iraq without let or hindrance would be grossly to ignore the lessons of September 11 and we will not do it.'[13] The thrust of Blair's speech was that Iraq was pursuing a WMD programme and therefore constituted a threat, the likes of which came to fruition on 11 September

2001. His speech would have had much less impact if he had included the cautionary observations of MI5.

In terms of the regime of truth he was constructing about Saddam and Iraq, Blair cannot be said to have lied in the statements he made during his speech in April 2002. However, neither can it be said that he gave a full and accurate presentation of British security assessments at that time (cautionary security assessments that were proven, in the fullness of time, to be accurate). Every government and Prime Minister, both in the UK and abroad, must make a judgement on every issue that comes their way as to how much information they put into the public domain. In making their calculations some form of political cost/benefit analysis will inevitably take place and the seriousness of the issue will be taken into account. They also construct a regime of truth that has an impact on the wider moral debate: in this case surrounding Iraq.

The case for war

The first difficulty in trying to assess the extent to which Blair had a case for war against Iraq is to identify what his case actually was. His speeches covered arguments as diverse as the need to protect Iraqi citizens to a desire to confront the evil of Saddam to the threat from WMD. Depending on the political situation at the time Blair placed a different emphasis on the various aspects of his case for war. However, in his 2010 autobiography Blair stated that WMD 'was, after all, the *casus belli*':[14] the case, or justification, for war. This observation corresponds with public statements he made both before and after the March 2003 invasion:

The purpose of our acting is disarmament.[15]

I have never put our justification for action as regime change. We have to act within the terms set out in Resolution 1441. That is our legal base.[16]

I accept entirely the legal basis for action was through weapons of mass destruction.[17]

The issue of Saddam and his weapons of mass destruction was an unresolved legacy from the 1991 Gulf War which took on renewed political significance following the Al-Qaeda attacks of 11 September 2001. During the Gulf War, when the US-led, UN-sanctioned coalition forcibly removed Iraqi occupiers from Kuwait, enormous damage was done to

Iraq's conventional and nonconventional military capability. A devastating 38-day air campaign was launched on 16 January 1991 against the political hierarchy, military command and communication structures, mobile missile threats against Israel and Saddam's conventional land and air forces. The great unknown variables in the calculations of the Allied political and military leadership was whether or not Saddam had effective chemical, biological or nuclear weapons and whether or not he would use them to repel an attack or to draw Israel into the political equation. The administration of President George Bush (Snr) made it clear in advance that the use of any such weapons would have the direst consequences for Iraq.

A short time after the campaign got under way, Iraqi aircraft stopped engaging the Allies because the losses were so severe. Attacks against Iraqi tanks were devastating and effective, destroying the will of many elements of the Iraqi forces to keep on fighting. When Allied ground forces finally conducted their part of the operation it took only four days to achieve the mandated aim of liberating Kuwait. By the time President Bush declared the suspension of combat operations on 27 February 1991 Iraq's armed forces, already heavily degraded in the 1980s by an eight-year war of attrition with Iran, were hugely weakened. Its ineffectiveness against coalition forces was probably Saddam's greatest humiliation. Over the next ten years no-fly zones were maintained over northern and southern Iraq and the remnant of the Iraqi war machine was effectively contained. In addition, economic sanctions and the UN oil-for-food programme severely restricted Saddam's capacity to re-arm.

UN Security Council Resolutions 686 and 687, passed in 1990 and 1991 respectively, required Iraq to relinquish any WMD in its possession, as well as related materials or development programmes. This placed Saddam in a political bind: if he fully and transparently co-operated with the demands of the UN Security Council he would make it clear to his neighbours, especially Iran, that he would be vulnerable to attack; and if he defied the UN there may be further consequences, or perhaps not, at some point in the future. He chose to maintain at least the impression of status in the region through the possible possession of WMD and embarked upon a decade-long game of brinkmanship with the UN. Brutal suppression by Saddam's military of the Iraqi Marsh Arabs and Iraqi Shias in the south of the country followed the 1991 war. However, in subsequent years containment appeared to work and even Saddam's internal repression of Iraqis was conducted on a much smaller scale than it had been in the late 1980s.

One of many frustrations endured by successive US and other governments was the difficulty of obtaining reliable intelligence on the extent to which Saddam was still pursuing, or not, the development and acquisition of WMD. UN inspections were disrupted and satellite imagery proved to be inconclusive at best, while the small number of human intelligence sources often turned out to be unreliable, opportunistic or politically motivated.[18] The biggest problem was proving, or disproving, a negative – that Saddam *did not* possess WMD. This had implications when, post 9/11, the political landscape changed and the US reassessed the situation through what Defense Secretary Donald Rumsfeld would later call 'the prism of our experience on 9/11'.[19] If it could be shown that Saddam threatened the US or UK both directly and imminently then military action would be both morally and legally justified on the grounds of self-defence under Article 51 of the UN Charter. If it could be shown that he posed a real and imminent threat to peace and security in the region then a separate legal and moral case could also be made under Article 39 of the Charter.

Blair later recalled that he and others, particularly his American allies, were sure that Saddam Hussein had a WMD programme.[20] However, Blair's certainty about Saddam's possession of WMD contrasts sharply with the uncertain intelligence picture that had been painted both before and after 9/11. The degree to which Western intelligence was 'certain' about Saddam's possession of WMD was crucial to the extent that he could then be seen as a threat, either regionally or globally. The other important part of the equation was the extent to which – even if he had a WMD capability – Saddam would be willing to use it against the West or his neighbours. The threat from Saddam would be calculated using these two variables: WMD capability and intent to use that capability.

The degree of threat posed by Saddam and his regime, and consequently the strength of the case against him, could be demonstrated in two possible ways: direct threat and indirect threat. Determined efforts were made by US, UK and other intelligence sources to demonstrate both. Direct threat was built on the suggestion that Saddam could, and would, attack his neighbours or others with WMD. Indirect threat depended upon showing a link between Saddam, WMD and terrorist organizations like Al-Qaeda who were ideologically motivated enough to use such weapons against the US and Western interests.

Direct threat would be by far the most difficult for Saddam to achieve because he would need chemical, biological or nuclear weapons, coupled with some form of long-range delivery system. Even at the height of Saddam's military capability prior to the 1991 Gulf War there had been no evidence that he had any kind of long-range missile capability, certainly not of a kind that would reach the UK or US. The possibility of him having such a delivery system after years of sanctions and the northern and southern no-fly zones was extremely small. This was tacitly acknowledged in the 2002 Joint Houses of Congress authorization of the use of American forces against Iraq. The Congressional resolution was presented in terms of the need to defend the United States from the threat posed by Saddam Hussein and the Iraqi regime: but it was framed in terms of an indirect threat. The suggestion of threat from Saddam was achieved by implying a link between alleged Iraqi chemical and biological weapon capability with a terrorist organization, Al-Qaeda, that had recently attacked the US.[21]

Essential to this authorization of the use of military force against Iraq are two distinct claims: that Iraq possessed chemical and biological weapons and was actively seeking nuclear weapons; and that Al-Qaeda or other terrorist elements were present in Iraq. Implicit in these claims is the suggestion that Al-Qaeda elements in Iraq were colluding with Saddam's regime, despite no evidence being offered in support of these assertions: on either side of the Atlantic. I have had a number of opportunities to discuss the pre-2003 security situation in Iraq with Iraqi exiles and members of the Iraqi military. The one issue I was most interested in was whether or not it was likely that Saddam would or could have been hosting Al-Qaeda or other terrorist organizations. The responses – admittedly few in number, though greater in number than those who corroborated the presence of an ongoing biological weapons programme – were identical, somewhere been scorn and ridicule. For them it was inconceivable that Saddam would have allowed a competing power base of any size inside the borders of Iraq. In addition, they thought it equally unlikely that religiously motivated organizations and leaders would have sought the cooperation of what I would term the 'secular' leadership of Saddam Hussein. To highlight the contrast, it is highly unlikely that Osama Bin Laden would ever have appointed a Christian into a senior position in his organization in the same way that Saddam Hussein appointed the Christian Tariq Aziz as his Foreign Minister and Deputy Prime Minister.

The reason for the lack of hard evidence offered at that time, and suggested in speeches by President Bush and others in the build-up to the invasion, was made clear in a 2008 Senate Intelligence Committee Report on Pre-war Iraq Intelligence: there was none. The Chairman of the Senate Select Committee, John D. Rockefeller IV said as the reports on the use of pre-war Iraq intelligence were released: 'In making the case for war, the Administration repeatedly presented intelligence as fact when in reality it was unsubstantiated, contradicted, or even non-existent. As a result, the American people were led to believe that the threat from Iraq was much greater than actually existed.'[22]

In 2002, as President Bush and the US administration were making forceful claims about the extent of the threat posed by Saddam Hussein and his regime, parallel claims based on British and other shared intelligence were being made by Tony Blair: 'He is developing weapons of mass destruction and we cannot leave him doing so unchecked. He is a threat to his own people and to the region, and if allowed to develop these weapons a threat to us also.'[23] Blair also repeatedly suggested or implied links – while not presenting evidence – between Saddam and Iraq, WMD, 9/11 and terrorist threats to the region and the world:

we must be prepared to act where terrorism or Weapons of Mass Destruction threaten us.[24]

But to allow WMD to be developed by a state like Iraq without let or hindrance would be grossly to ignore the lessons of September 11 and we will not do it.[25]

He is developing weapons of mass destruction and we cannot leave him doing so unchecked. He is a threat to his own people and to the region, and if allowed to develop these weapons a threat to us also.[26]

He has twice before started wars of aggression. Over one million people died in them. When the weapons inspectors were evicted from Iraq in 1998 there were still enough chemical and biological weapons remaining to devastate the entire Gulf region.[27]

Terrorism and weapons of mass destruction combine modern technology with political or religious fanaticism. If unchecked they will, as September 11 showed, explode into disorder and chaos.[28]

Terrorism and WMD are linked dangers. States which are failed, which repress their people brutally, in which notions of democracy and the rule of law are alien, share the same absence of rational boundaries to their actions as the terrorist. Iraq has used WMD.[29]

The common threat is chaos. That threat can come from terrorism, producing a train of events that pits nations against each other. It can come through irresponsible and repressive states gaining access to WMD.[30]

Blair's routine linking of Saddam and Iraq with WMD and terrorist threat can best be described as linguistic sleight of hand: implying a connection that may well have existed but without providing any proof whatsoever. He similarly cites 9/11 as an example of what happens when terrorism, WMD, modern technology and fanaticism coincide: they 'explode into disorder and chaos'.[31] Blair's dramatic rhetoric conjures up the destructive images of that fateful day in New York and the Pentagon, again without offering any evidence of a connection between Saddam and terrorist organizations. The Twin Towers *were* destroyed by terrorists motivated by a combination of religious fanaticism (though their supporters may claim religious devotion) and political ideology but there was not a weapon of mass destruction – that is, chemical, biological or nuclear weapon – in sight. The weapons of choice that day were standard airliners, their explosive power supplied by the fuel in their tanks and detonated by precise high speed collisions with their intended targets. Just as President George W. Bush and his administration were doing in the US, Blair's listeners were being invited to accept rhetoric as evidence and only a minority challenged him.

This view was confirmed and expanded upon by Baroness Manningham-Buller as she later recounted her views of Saddam in March 2002: 'we felt we had a pretty good intelligence picture of a threat from Iraq within the UK and to British interests, and you will see from that letter [submitted to the Iraq Inquiry] we thought it was very limited and containable.'[32] She went on to add: 'to my mind Iraq, Saddam Hussein, had nothing to do with 9/11 and I have never seen anything to make me change my mind.'[33] There is a clear disjuncture between Blair's pronouncements on the level of threat from Saddam as he sought to build support for action against the Iraqi leader and the assessment of the threat offered by the Deputy Director General – soon to be Director General – of MI5. The genius of Blair and his Communications Director Alastair Campbell was that in building a regime of truth about Saddam, the Prime Minister did not, and did not have to, lie. He just had to make sure that unhelpful comments and views within the departments of state stayed out of the public domain.

Aspects of Blair's statements are clearly factual, stand up well to scrutiny and appear substantive and authoritative. Saddam *had* possessed chemical weapons in the past, using them externally against Iran and internally against Iraqi Kurds in the 1980s. Al-Qaeda *had* launched a terrorist attack on the US that achieved a high level of destruction. It stands to reason that if Al-Qaeda managed to acquire WMD its threat to the West and to the US and UK would be much greater. However, to claim such a link was speculative at best and fanciful at worst. Blair could not demonstrate any connection between Saddam and Al-Qaeda or he most certainly would have. Blair simply and repeatedly threw together a concoction of possible threats, previous actions and hypothetical developments and invited his listeners to make connections that did not exist in fact: in other words, he invited people to draw their own conclusions and convince themselves.[34]

The lack of actual, as opposed to purported, threat to the UK is the reason the Attorney General ruled out self-defence against an imminent threat as a legal basis for action against Iraq and Saddam in the summer of 2002.[35] If the threat level changed during the period between July 2002 and March 2003 it was because the work of Hans Blix and the UN inspection teams pointed towards Saddam being less, and not more, of a threat than was previously thought. Take the now notorious 45-minute claim made in the dossier presented to Parliament on 24 September 2002. Blair said of the dossier:

> The dossier is based on the work of the British Joint Intelligence Committee. For over 60 years, beginning just prior to WWII, the JIC has provided intelligence assessments to British Prime Ministers ... The intelligence picture they paint is one accumulated over the past four years. It is extensive, detailed and authoritative. It concludes that Iraq has chemical and biological weapons, that Saddam has continued to produce them, that he has existing and active military plans for the use of chemical and biological weapons, which could be activated within 45 minutes, including against his own Shia population; and that he is actively trying to acquire nuclear weapons capability.[36]

Much has been said and written about the 45-minute claim made by Blair but it is important to address the issue here because the claim, no matter how briefly made, helped to present Saddam as a serious and imminent threat. There were suggestions at the time in the media that someone at Number 10 Downing Street or elsewhere in the intelligence chain had falsely inserted the 45-minute claim. Legal proceedings were undertaken and at the subsequent Hutton Report it was determined that no such falsification took place. What the Hutton Report did highlight was the precariousness of the foundation of the 45-minute claim in the September 2002 dossier.

Sir Richard Dearlove, Chief of the Secret Intelligence Service, had wanted a more qualified description of the 45-minute claim included in the dossier because it came from an uncorroborated single source.[37]

In the event, Blair's foreword to the dossier stated that Saddam's 'military planning allows for some of the WMD to be ready within 45 minutes of an order to use them'.[38] Similar wording was used elsewhere in the dossier itself.

However, there is another aspect to the story that bears further examination: not on the matter of what was wrongly alleged to have been *added* to the September 2002 dossier but concerning what was *omitted*. On 18 February 2008 Foreign Secretary David Miliband released previously confidential information relating to the drafting of the September 2002 dossier. The most intriguing and least mentioned of these documents is the unused Draft Conclusion. A confidential memo dated 20 September 2002 from John Scarlett, head of the Joint Intelligence Committee, to Alastair Campbell, Blair's head of communications who was involved in the presentation process, stated:

1. I attach the final draft version of the dossier, taking account of additional comments from you and others received over the last 24 hours. The Prime Minister's Foreword is now incorporated within the overall document. The conclusion has been dropped.

2. I am content that the text now reflects as fully and accurately as possible the intelligence picture on Saddam's mass destruction weapons.[39]

What was this unused Conclusion and why is its exclusion significant? The relevant section of the document provides a summary of available intelligence on Chemical and Biological weapons and includes the 45-minute assessment:[40]

Chemical and biological Weapons	In breach of UNSCR 687. Chemical and biological agents stocks retained Production has continued.
	Weapons available include bombs, airborne sprayer, artillery shells and rockets and ballistic missile warheads.
	Some weapons could be deployed within 45 minutes of an order.

Having mentioned that Saddam's weapons include bombs, airborne sprayer, artillery shells and rockets and ballistic missile warheads, the section finishes with the vague statement: 'Some weapons could be deployed within 45 minutes of an order'. This omission from the dossier is significant because its exclusion kept from MPs and the public some of the ambiguity that existed in the overall intelligence assessment and provided the reader with detail of different possible weapons that could be deployed. Specifically, it makes clear that some of the weapons that might be deployed were for battlefield use and would have provided a very limited threat. An airborne sprayer or artillery shells would not have posed a significant threat to Iraq's neighbours let alone the UK or US. Of the different ways that the 45-minute threat was presented in the dossier this one most clearly highlights it limitations. Because many people, especially journalists trying to produce a story against a deadline, turn to a conclusion for a brief summary of the contents of a document, its omission reduced the likelihood of opponents of any potential war from asking the crucial and obvious question: *Which* weapons could be deployed within 45 minutes of an order?

The Intelligence and Security Committee (ISC), via the Prime Minister, presented a report to Parliament in September 2003 that said:

> the most likely chemical and biological munitions to be used against Western forces were battlefield weapons (artillery and rockets), rather than strategic weapons. This should have been highlighted in the dossier.[41]

The document goes on to outline the (obvious) consequences of omitting the uncertainty level:

> As the 45 minutes claim was new to its readers, the context of the intelligence and any assessment needed to be explained. The fact that it was assessed to refer to battlefield chemical and biological munitions and their movement on the battlefield, not to any other form of chemical or biological attack, should have been highlighted in the dossier. The omission of the context and assessment allowed speculation as to its exact meaning.[42]

This issue of battlefield vs strategic weapons, which was not made clear by Blair or the September 2002 dossier, is at the heart of his case for war. WMD with a strategic capability could pose a threat to regional peace and security and therefore provide a basis for the UN Security Council to act. WMD which could only be used on the battlefield would have the range of only a few miles and only posed a danger to anyone in close proximity to it. Battlefield weapons would not provide a satisfactory basis for war. If Blair and his advisers did not know whether the weapons that could allegedly have been deployed had battlefield or strategic application they should have made it known. Given that a major war could potentially be based on the distinction, they should have – if they were being *fully* honest with the British people – made the public aware of their uncertainty.

In its response to the ISC report the government stated:

> The dossier was not intended to make the case for military action against Iraq; it was intended to share with the public the intelligence being presented to the Government which (along with much open source information) showed that Iraq was in serious breach of several UNSCRs.[43]

The government's position was that the dossier 'was not intended to make the case for military action against Iraq'. However, that statement has to be considered alongside Blair's insistence that WMD provided the *casus belli*.[44] If the September dossier was not setting out the case for military action, it *was* setting out a contribution to any case that would subsequently be made. This is a subtle distinction but when a regime of truth is being constructed it is small subtleties like these that keep the whole edifice intact. It is possible that there were some people who had been cut off from all media and public political discourse for several years and, in September 2002, were unaware that Saddam Hussein had been in breach of UNSCRs for several years and needed further information. It is much more likely that the dossier was part of Blair's stated desire to 're-order our story and message'.[45] One way to clarify the issue is to consider whether the dossier would have been published if Blair and his advisers had thought it would *lessen* any potential case for war. On balance, my view is that the dossier would not have been published if it was thought in advance that it could disadvantage Blair's political position in any way.

Let us return to the omitted conclusion of the September 2002 dossier. If Blair read the draft conclusion and failed to ask which weapons could be deployed within 45 minutes of an order, then he was derelict in his duty since it had a direct bearing on the level of threat offered by Saddam; ballistic missiles could pose a potentially significant threat while sprayers or shells would not. If Blair read and understood the implications of this draft Conclusion and deliberately dropped it then he, to some degree, misled the British people by omission by not making the doubts clearer.

A further, unlikely possibility is that someone else in an intelligence and presentational chain that included Alastair Campbell and John Scarlett took this crucial decision without consulting Blair. If so, that individual became culpable and Blair appears negligent in the way he ran his team. What should have been a cautious and qualified claim in Blair's statement to Parliament sent reverberations around the country. The following day the tabloid press – most notably the *Sun*[46] and the *Daily Star*[47] – led with the story of Saddam's ability to hit Britons with chemical weapons within 45 minutes of an order being given.

The headlines suggested, building on Blair's statement to Parliament in the way that tabloid headlines do, a level of threat that had not been shown to exist. More importantly, the intelligence assessment was, if anything, more cautious and qualified than Blair's reference to the 45-minute threat in his statement of 24 September 2002. Blair acknowledged to the Iraq Inquiry in January 2010, and recounted in his memoirs,[48] that 'it [the 45-minute threat] was never actually mentioned again by me ... in the light of what subsequently happened and the importance it subsequently took on, it would have most certainly been better to have corrected it'.[49] It is easy for Blair to concede this point almost eight years later when at the time his lack of clarity contributed to an unrealistic public assessment of the threat posed by Saddam and his regime. The reasons for his lack of subsequent clarification were not expanded upon to the Iraq Inquiry or in his book. Whether through commission or omission, Blair had left the *impression* with the British people that somehow they might be under imminent threat from Saddam and his WMD when such a conclusion was highly questionable.

It is utterly implausible that a government with such a shrewd media communications operation was not aware of the way Blair's words had been represented in the press, yet no attempt was made to subsequently play down the tabloid interpretation of events: probably because it suited Blair's and the government's aims. When Andrew Gilligan made the potentially damaging allegation that Blair's administration had somehow 'sexed up' the case for war, the Downing Street machine and Alastair Campbell in particular aggressively and successfully challenged the suggestion. Again, the question should be asked: would Blair or his team have clarified the misrepresentation of the threat level if it disadvantaged their case for action against Saddam? Once more, I take the view that the correction would have been made loudly, clearly and immediately. It can therefore be reasonably concluded that Number 10 allowed the sensational and inaccurate representations of the 45-minute claim to remain undisturbed and without clarification in the tabloid press because it was in some way deemed politically advantageous.

Blair's approach was to encourage the maximum perception of threat based on the information he had at his disposal, a tactic that continued right up until the eve of war. When we look at his statement to Parliament on 18 March 2003, the eve of the invasion, the law-oriented element of his argument required a measured presentation of the evidence for his case for war: in particular the threat that Saddam posed to the UK and his neighbours. However, what should have been a lesson in calm objectivity by a Prime Minister with a legal background was instead an example of the moral creativity that characterized his justification of the invasion by drawing attention away from the startling *lack* of evidence. His other moral arguments are explored in the chapters to follow.

In the earlier part of his speech Blair offered an extensive summary of Saddam's bluster and obstruction of the UN's weapons inspectors, all of which had been well known for years. This was followed by a frightening and impressive list of materials that could not be accounted for but which were suspected of being in Iraq's possession: thousands of litres of anthrax; a VX nerve agent programme; thousands of chemical munitions; a vast quantity of mustard gas; biological agents such as sarin and botulinum; and a covert Scud missile programme.[50] The list suggests a weapons programme of fearsome destructive capability, a threat to the region and the wider world as long as it remained under the control of Saddam Hussein. Even worse, at a time when the rubble from the destroyed World Trade Centre was still being sifted through for remains of the victims and evidence against the perpetrators, this was a threat whose destructiveness would reach new proportions if added to the arsenal of international terrorists.

Revisiting the transcript of this speech a number of years later, away from the sound and fury of the House of Commons and the immediacy and excitement of war, we see that a number of elements stand out in a way that many supporters of the invasion claim not to have noticed at the time. Blair listed poisonous materials that were 'unaccounted for', before going on to claim: 'Iraq continues to deny it has any WMD, though no serious intelligence service anywhere in the world believes them'.[51] Looking back, it is interesting to observe how a Prime Minister, a lawyer by training, was able to present a case for war based not primarily on evidence but on perceptions and beliefs. There is a profound difference between believing that a crime has been, or is about to be, committed and offering evidence for the same. The vocabulary used by Blair in describing the findings of the UN weapons inspectors reveals a great deal about the strength of his case:

> On 7 March, the inspectors published a remarkable document. It is 173 pages long, detailing all the *unanswered questions* about Iraq's WMD. It lists 29 different areas where they have been *unable to obtain information*:
>
> Documentation available to UNMOVIC *suggests that* Iraq at least had had far reaching *plans to weaponise* VX ...
>
> 550 mustard filled shells and up to 450 mustard filled aerial bombs *unaccounted for ... additional uncertainty ...*
>
> Based on *unaccounted for* growth media, Iraq's *potential* production of anthrax *could have been* in the range of about 15,000 to 25,000 litres ... Based on all the available evidence, the *strong presumption* is that about 10,000 litres of anthrax was not destroyed and *may still* exist.[52]

Blair's arguments were therefore based not on confirmed intelligence on the weapons of mass destruction that Saddam and his regime possessed but on what he, Hans Blix and the teams of UN weapons inspectors *did not know*. When the qualifications and uncertainties are extracted from Blair's speech and set out in sequence the degree to which he based his case on definite, acquired evidence becomes clear:

> unanswered questions ... unable to obtain information ... suggests that ... plans to weaponise ... unaccounted for ... additional uncertainty ... unaccounted for ... potential production ... could have been ... strong presumption ... may still.[53]

In October 2003 the Congressional Research Service compiled a report on Iraq and WMD for the US Congress that summarized the key developments in the UN weapons inspection process between November 2002 and March 2003. As well as setting out the various obfuscations, hindrances and cooperation of the Iraqi regime this report highlights the materials actually found by the weapons inspectors. The report makes clear that by February 2003 Hans Blix and his inspection teams had been provided with a list of the medium- and high-value sites where US Intelligence (which was working closely with UK and other intelligence agencies) expected to find evidence of Iraqi WMD.[54] The Congressional report summarizes what was *actually found*:

> the discoveries by UNMOVIC from November 2002 to March 2003 – [12] empty chemical weapons shells not previously declared; 2000 pages of undeclared documents on uranium enrichment in a private home; undeclared remotely piloted vehicles with wing spans of 7.5 meters; and cluster bombs that could be used with chemical or biological agents ...

These findings were subsequently qualified by the weapons inspectors, detail which the report to Congress also captured:

> With respect to the cluster bombs, the document reports that in February 2003 (February 2 and 5), inspection teams found a *component* of a 122mm CBW cluster *submunition* at Al Nouman.[55]

> According to UNMOVIC spokesperson Ewen Buchanan, Iraq claimed that it had declared the RPVs, saying that the information on wing spans was a typographical error – that the 4.4-meter span should have been 7.4-meter span.[56]

Recall that Blair, a trained lawyer, stood before Parliament and, on the matter of the evidence on which he proposed taking the country to war, listed a number of things that he did not know and whose existence he could not verify. Furthermore, the plaintiff (Saddam) was showing no intent or means to use these things that the best Western intelligence and the UN weapons inspectors could not prove he possessed. Yet because Blair was speaking from a position of power and influence with the whole machinery of state at his disposal his words were taken at face value by many people and accepted as authoritative. Imagine for a moment that Blair had omitted all speculation and highly qualified assessments when he appeared in the House of Commons on 18 March 2003 and asked MPs to vote for war. He could have told MPs instead that what had actually been found after a thorough search of the medium- and high-value sites amounted to 12 empty chemical shells, 2000 undeclared documents, a number of remotely piloted vehicles that may or may not have been declared and a component of a 122mm CBW cluster submunition. The outcome of the vote may have been somewhat different.

Summary

Blair's WMD-based *casus belli* was built on what he did not know about what had not been found, all laced with an equal share of optimism and sinister warnings. History will show that he achieved his aim of supporting Bush and the US in their war against Saddam Hussein and his regime. Despite the vote in Parliament supporting military action, many found Blair's case wanting. In just war terms he did not demonstrate a convincing just cause for intervening in Iraq that had the credibility, urgency or support of his arguments for acting in Kosovo or Sierra Leone. Given the paucity of the WMD evidence Blair presented to Parliament, a number of questions arise. How did he manage to achieve a vote in favour of war? Was the war therefore legitimately authorized? Was ridding Iraq of WMD Blair's sole intention when he set the course for war? In his most passionate hour at the dispatch box Blair came across as utterly committed, well intentioned and plausible as he augmented a weak legal case with a number of strong moral arguments in favour of military action against Saddam and his regime. From Chapters 4 to 7 I will explore these questions in relation to just war concepts that have provided the means to assess the morality of war for millennia.

Chapter 4 will consider the matter of where legitimate authorization for war comes from, and the degree to which Blair had legitimate authority – both legally and morally – to deploy British troops to war. Chapter 5 will assess Blair's intentions by assessing the degree to which, if at all, regime change motivated his actions: a charge widely made at the time. Chapters 6 and 7 will explore Blair's most altruistic reasons for intervening militarily in Iraq: a quest to protect those incapable of defending themselves and a desire to confront tyranny in the world. Before then, I turn in Chapter 3 to assess two contrasting just war perspectives on military intervention from the academy which will inform discussions in the subsequent chapters.

3
Views from the academy

As the twentieth century gave way to the twenty-first, Blair and his fellow political leaders were not alone in wrestling with the issue of military, or humanitarian, intervention and the circumstances in which it could or would be justified. Scholars were revisiting – and for many, discovering for the first time – just war as a means of disputing the legitimacy or otherwise of military intervention. Having looked at both Blair's moral framework for intervention and his case for taking military action against Iraq, this chapter will set out some of the ideas that permeated academic debate around that time. These ideas can then be used, in turn, to assess the relevance and effectiveness of the different aspects of Blair's moral justification of the Iraq War that are examined in the chapters to come.

The two most prominent just war theorists at the time of the invasion were Michael Walzer and Jean Bethke Elshtain, whose respective books *Just and Unjust Wars* and *Just War Against Terror* provided the basis of much of the academic debate. Walzer has been widely accredited with reinvigorating the just war tradition in the late 1970s, while in 2003 Elshtain provoked widespread debate with a pro-interventionist work that provided an intellectual foundation for America's war on terror. They have been chosen for analysis here because they offer helpful and contrasting perspectives not only on the matter of military intervention but on the use of historic just war concepts in present-day debate. By examining Walzer and Elshtain in this way we will also see how the different aspects of Blair's moral justification of war in Iraq used ideas, wittingly or not, that were far from original, having been present in Western thought for many centuries.

Walzer and Elshtain rely on distinct parts of the just war tradition. Elshtain looks extensively to the ideas of the great fifth century Christian theologian and ethicist Augustine and to a lesser extent the thirteenth century writings of Thomas Aquinas. Walzer, in contrast, avoids explicit reference to the early Christian element of the just war tradition and locates his just war theory in the legal frameworks that have shaped war in recent centuries. He uses concepts that emerged in the juristic works of Hugo Grotius and Emer de Vattel – *On the Rights of War and Peace* and *The Law of Nations* – in the seventeenth and eighteenth centuries respectively when the notions of sovereignty and an international system were emerging in Europe.

In the process of examining what Walzer and Elshtain have written about military intervention I will identify some of the assumptions, codes and values that they use to try to make sense of the complexities of morality and war. This will demonstrate the changing philosophical underpinnings of just war at different times in history, which in turn are related to the political and social contexts in which they emerge. These insights will identify only a fraction of the subtleties and nuances of such a broad tradition of thought but they will provide a theoretical basis from which to assess Blair's Iraq discourse and his moral case for action against Saddam Hussein. By putting Walzer's and Elshtain's ideas alongside Blair's they will provide an insight into the way that he incorporated moral arguments and concepts from classic Christian just war as a way of overcoming or augmenting weak, disputed legal arguments.

Walzer and just war

Walzer describes arriving at the use of just war arguments, almost by default, during the Vietnam War.[1] At that time international relations were dominated by political realism, where the pursuit of national interests overrides any need for moral considerations. This was particularly true of the Cold War stand-off between the US and the Soviet and Chinese communist blocs and the proxy wars fought in Asia. The dominance of political realism in both the theory and practice of politics, and in wider society, had resulted in a search by critics for a language of morality. Just war is what re-emerged from the theological faculties to be reclaimed by Walzer for International Relations, political theory and society at large.

Walzer's reputation in the academic world was already established by the time *Just and Unjust Wars* was published in 1977. Its timeliness may have struck a chord with a readership increasingly cynical about war in light of the events in Vietnam. His just war theory shifted the debate away from the use of religious texts and Church authority as moral sources at a time when American, and other, Catholic bishops were flexing their ecclesiastical muscle in the debate surrounding nuclear weapons and Mutually Assured Destruction with its apt three-letter acronym – MAD. By removing any explicitly religious dimension of just war, Walzer shifted the debate towards the secular mainstream and engaged a wider audience. In so doing, his approach paralleled the just war writings of Grotius and Vattel in the 1600s and 1700s respectively. As incipient notions of sovereignty and statehood emerged in tandem with secularizing Enlightenment thought, they based their arguments on human reason instead of the divine revelation and moral order that had previously been advocated by a powerful Church.

In setting out the moral basis of his just war theory, Walzer states: 'The morality I shall expound is in its philosophical form a doctrine of human rights.'[2] Human rights served as the cornerstone of his moral code, of which just war was a significant part. The right to life serves as the foundation of the UN's Universal Declaration of Human Rights, yet it was denied to countless civilian victims of the Vietnam War.

Just and Unjust Wars was not intended to be so much a philosophical enquiry as a practical reflection on war and morality. Hence, it is characterized by its reference to practical, historical examples of both just and unjust wars, as well as those wars that do not conveniently, or obviously, fall into one category or the other. In addition, Walzer explored the moral conduct of the combatants involved in the various wars he recounted. The outcome is a powerful application of general moral principles to specific examples of both the justification *of* war and conduct *in* war.

Walzer broadly summarizes the aspect of his moral code that enables the conduct of war to be described, disputed and justified, or otherwise, as the 'war convention', which for him is made up of 'the set of articulated norms, customs, professional codes, legal precepts, religious and philosophical principles, and reciprocal arrangements that shape our judgements of military conduct'.[3] As can be seen from this extensive list, he draws upon a wide variety of social and cultural norms in identifying his war convention. With regard to the relationship between law and morality, Walzer argued that the makers of the law were codifying and formalizing the morality that already existed within a particular shared existence.[4] So, inasmuch as laws emerge from previously existing moralities, laws, international conventions and protocols are all discourses that form part of the moral code that Walzer draws from in writing about morality and war.

Walzer's just war theory is strongly, but not entirely, shaped by the laws of war, which he draws from, amongst others, Grotius, 'who took over the tradition and began to work it into secular form',[5] and from

Vattel, who later continued the formalization of the laws of war that Grotius had embarked upon. Walzer turns to Vattel on a number of occasions, for example, on the matter of preventive war. Walzer uses Vattel's reading of the British and Austrian response to the growing power of the French in the seventeenth and eighteenth centuries as a means of forming his own view. At the turn of the eighteenth century it appeared that the Spanish Throne and Spanish Empire might be given to, or fall to, Louis XIV of France: already the major political power on the continent. Vattel later formulated a balance-of-power argument that would have justified military action against the French and Spanish, an approach that aimed to preserve the concept of sovereignty and the independence of weaker European states in the face of superior powers. Small states would be entitled to come together and make war on a major power to ensure that the latter did not become too powerful and subsume the small states around them.

Walzer rejected Vattel's historical legal argument for preventive war because it did not depend on a clear and immediate threat of attack and could be used to create illegitimate arguments in favour of unjust wars. The obvious link from this principle of just war to Saddam and Iraq is not difficult to see. There was concern on both sides of the Atlantic and elsewhere that the military action being advocated by the US and UK was more preventive – making sure a future threat could not arise – than pre-emptive: responding to an imminent threat.

Moving beyond the war convention, Walzer draws upon both human rights and state rights as sources for his moral code, of which his just war theory is a part. He argues that human rights provide the basis for states' rights:

> Individual rights (to life and liberty) underlie the most important judgements that we make about war. How these rights themselves are founded I cannot try to explain here. It is enough to say that they are somehow entailed by our sense of what it means to be a human being. If they are not natural, then we have invented them, but natural or invented, they are a palpable feature of our moral world. States' rights are simply their collective form.[6]

The relationship between the rights of individuals and the rights of states is deeply significant not only for Walzer's political theory and just war theory, the tension in the relationship is central to all debate about military intervention. Take an earlier example. Did Serbia's right to exist as a political entity without interference from another state outweigh the individual rights of the Kosovo Albanians who were being killed and dispossessed of their land and property? The UN Charter prioritizes the rights of states while the UN Universal Declaration of Human Rights is deemed to apply everywhere and sets out the rights of individuals. The main difference between the two is that states' rights to peace and security are enforceable at the behest of the UN Security Council while individual rights are not. In the case of Serbia, Blair's moral argument in support of the right to life and liberty of the Kosovo Albanians was deemed to outweigh the rights of Serbia to political non-interference: hence NATO's military action.

Although Walzer says that individual rights provide a basis for his just war theory, there is a caveat: the rights he is referring to are bound up with a particular political community – the state – and it is within these political communities that individual rights should be protected and guaranteed.[7] In response to four critics of *Just and Unjust Wars*, Walzer clarifies his position further on the relationship between the individual, rights and the state, though he remains more concerned with the political communities on which states are based:[8]

> Rights are only enforceable within political communities where they have been collectively recognized, and the process by which they come to be recognized is a political process which requires a political arena ... the only global community is pluralist in character, a community of nations, not of humanity.[9]

In other words, for Walzer the building-bloc of the global community, if we can call it that, is not the individual but the state, and it is the latter that also provides the basis of his just war theory. The state in this understanding is not, however, just some legal entity that needs to be protected or to protect itself. It is also the vehicle within which, for better or worse, the history of people groups has been shaped and lived. He refers to 'the commitment of individuals and groups to their own history, culture, and identity, and this commitment (though not any particular version of it) is a permanent feature of human social life.'[10] It is this commitment to a shared culture and heritage that motivates people to go to war to defend what has been built up over years, decades and centuries. The converse can also be a contributing factor to the failure of states: a lack of a sufficiently coherent shared social existence that binds individuals sufficiently that they would want to defend it.

For Walzer then, the ethical leader is the individual who acts justly to protect that common social existence identified most commonly as the state. Similarly, the ethical combatant is the one who fights justly on the field of battle to protect the common life he or she shares with others. Those who share a common life that has emerged historically in an independent state, have a right to share that social life without external interference. Crucially for Walzer, ethical leaders and soldiers protect their own common life but do not threaten or interfere in anyone else's.

Given Walzer's emphasis on political community it is hardly surprising that military intervention across borders is viewed by him with scepticism, and not addressed at great length. Walzer has granted three exceptions to the principle of non-intervention: secession, civil war or the kind of massacre of civilians that nowadays we would call genocide.[11] The common theme underpinning these three very limited permissions to intervene is that as a result of any one of them there would no longer exist what could reasonably be described as a shared common life of the people. However, while his main arguments remained unaltered in the second (1992), third (2000) and fourth (2006) editions of *Just and Unjust Wars*, he added a new preface to each to address different aspects of intervention in response to global events. The development in his thought is worth considering further.

Describing the issue as 'peripheral' in his original book, he recognizes that from the 1990s onwards intervention – or the more commonly used humanitarian intervention – has moved to the centre ground of just war debate.[12] Walzer would subsequently move further in his acceptance of intervention than he first indicated, though he never went so far as to be an enthusiastic advocate. In his 2004 book *Arguing About War* Walzer revisited his just war theory and some of the criticisms and arguments that have surrounded it since *Just and Unjust Wars* first appeared in 1977. He gathered together a number of essays spanning a quarter century in an attempt to clarify some previous ideas with a view to engaging politically with events at that time.[13] Acknowledging the limitations of any theory of justice in war he prioritized the need to avoid (humanitarian) disasters.[14] Walzer did not shift his position on intervention out of a perceived failure in his theoretical position as much as it is a response to disasters, the horrors of a number of world events, especially in the 1990s. He concedes:

Faced with the sheer number of recent horrors – with massacre and ethnic cleansing in Bosnia and Kosovo; in Rwanda, the Sudan, Sierra Leone, the Congo, and Liberia; in East Timor (and earlier, in Cambodia and Bangladesh) – I have slowly become more willing to call for military intervention. I haven't dropped the presumption against intervention that I defended in my book, but I have found it easier and easier to override the presumption.[15]

This shift is significant because of the implications it has for international relations and the question of violating someone else's sovereignty. Walzer subtly changed the conditions in which one state can override the sovereignty of another, moving, even if only partially, towards the view that intervention can occur as long as his general just war criteria are still met: particularly just cause, right intention and last resort. In so doing, Walzer's move shared at least some common ground, though he would not go nearly so far in advocating intervention, with the Blair doctrine as set out in 1999. He acknowledged that 'the chief dilemma of international politics is whether people in danger should be rescued by military forces from outside'.[16]

Going further, it was not until 2006 and the preface to the fourth edition of *Just and Unjust Wars* that Walzer specifically addressed the issue of regime change in the context of his earlier just war theory and the possibility of military intervention. He noted that in World War II: 'regime change was the consequence, not the cause, of the war fought by the allies'.[17] Acknowledging the nature of Saddam Hussein's regime, and its history of violence towards its neighbours and sections of its own population, Walzer could still not accede to what he felt was an attempt by the US government to extend *jus ad bellum* to include the toppling of regimes – even murderous ones like Saddam's. He concluded that regime change on its own could not provide the just cause necessary for a just war.[18] The furthest Walzer was prepared to go in the direction of preventive intervention is what he describes as 'force-short-of-war',[19] preferring to go, where possible, no further than 'politics-short-of-force'.[20] His solution to the problems posed by the Iraqi regime included robust containment policies, broad Security Council support and increased engagement with nongovernmental organizations (NGOs) and UN humanitarian agencies.

As well as providing us with material with which to increase our understanding of some of the *ad bellum* subtleties of Blair's moral justification of the Iraq intervention, Walzer also provides useful ideas that are used later in Chapter 8 to reflect upon the moral position of the combatants who undertook the war. He apportions different levels of moral responsibility to leaders and combatants with regard to war based on the ways in which they respectively represent the shared values of their society.[21] For Walzer, leaders and combatants emerge as ethical when their actions are faithful to the shared moral understandings of the state of which they are a part. In achieving these shared understandings Walzer recognizes common rules, codes and even religious doctrine as constitutive of the moral individual within a particular, shared society.[22] So his ethical leader or combatant not only emerges in relation to the moral codes that govern conduct in a particular, usually state setting, that same individual also helps to create and reinforce the values of the society she, or he, is defending. In other words, society shapes the values of the combatants who defend it while at the same time those combatants help create the values of the society they represent.

It is in relation to Walzer's *jus in bello* criteria that the combatant emerges as an ethical subject of war in a highly codified just war theory. Walzer's position dominates – though not unchallenged[23] – contemporary just war thinking in viewing enemy combatants, regardless of whether they fight as part of an aggressive army in an unjust war, or as part of an army acting justly in self-defence, as moral equals. This moral equality rests, for Walzer, on the ability to distinguish between categories of people – combatants and noncombatants. Noncombatants are part of a broader category he refers to as innocent and who, because they pose no direct threat to their enemies, cannot lose their rights (for example, their right to life).[24]

Walzer writes of an Italian soldier, Emilio Lussu, overlooking enemy Austrian trenches in World War I:

> Those strongly defended trenches, which we had attacked so many times without success had ended by seeming to us inanimate, like desolate buildings uninhabited by men, the refuge only of the mysterious and terrible beings of whom we knew nothing. Now they were showing themselves to us as they really were, men and soldiers like us, in uniform like us, moving about, talking, and drinking coffee, just as our own comrades were doing at that moment.[25]

The important dynamic in this incident is not a decision against killing the enemy – for that intention is still present – rather it is one soldier's recognition of himself in his enemy's behaviour. The uniforms may have been different in pattern but the important thing is that they were being worn, symbols of citizenry and a shared social life characterized in that moment by the moving, talking in a common language and eating of familiar food by fellow comrades. Further, the uniforms identified friend and foe, legitimizing the killing of one by the other in carrying out legal military orders.

This tiny snapshot from a war almost a century ago embodies two elements of the political theory on which Walzer's just war is based. The first is what he refers to as a 'thick' understanding of morality tied up in the citizenship shared by members of a single political community. Even though there may be variations in the language, culture, religion and history between the two countries at war and the distinct, thick moralities they have developed, there is enough familiarity between them for what Walzer calls a 'thin' shared morality that carries *between* the different groups. Recognition of Walzer's ethical soldier is not granted on the basis of being human and therefore endowed with *universal* rights; rather, the rights are socially created within states and mutually recognized even as war is waged between them.

Walzer refers to enemy soldiers as moral equals, on the grounds that, in the bearing of arms, they share a common status as representatives of their respective states and shared social life, within which they are formed and which they help to form, regardless of whether or not they are on the side of the aggressor or whether they are warring defensively.[26] Combatants on both sides of a conflict share reduced rights to life, and increased rights to take life, based on their specific role in defending the state, rights that are not shared similarly with noncombatants:

> the enemy soldier, though his war may well be criminal, is nevertheless as blameless as oneself ... the war isn't a relation between persons but between political entities and their human instruments ... They can try to kill me, and I can try to kill them. But it is wrong to cut the throats of their wounded or to shoot them down when they are trying to surrender.[27]

Remember that Walzer's just war is set against the backdrop of both Vietnam and the Cold War. The legitimacy of the insurgent or guerrilla fighter, for him, is determined by the level of support they have within a sovereign territory and the degree of common life that the insurgents represent. He describes how in Vietnam rules of engagement were put in place to respond proportionately against a village from whence an attack had come against American forces. Such rules were based around providing ample opportunity for the villagers to leave an area or to hand over Viet Cong or other relevant information.[28] Soldiers were seen as ethical if they followed the rules set out for them, while the consequences of the rules were, for Walzer, often immoral since they resulted in vast numbers of displaced people: innocents who were victims of both sides in the war. By his own criteria, the Viet Cong were granted legitimacy – or not – by the level of popular support they received for their campaign.

On balance, Walzer favours the rights of individuals within states to form their own political and moral framework, unhindered by external interference, thereby undermining the *ad bellum* justification of the Vietnam intervention while leaving open the possibility that American combatants could still emerge as ethical depending on their individual conduct in using force both discriminately and proportionately. The significance of these principles for allied combatants engaged in the 2003 Iraq War and the subsequent counter-insurgency campaign are explored further in Chapter 8.

Elshtain, just war and the War on Terror

Elshtain locates the just war on an ethical 'continuum' that is bounded by realism at one end and Christian pacifism at the other: the political realist viewing ethical considerations as an unnecessary optional extra and the pacifist rejecting all recourse to violence.[29] She proposes: 'For pacifists, the reigning word is *peace*. For realists the reigning word is *power*. For just war thinkers, the reigning word is *justice*.'[30] In one of her earlier books Elshtain described just war as

> an authoritative tradition dotted with its own sacred texts, offering a canonical alternative to realism as received truth. Rather than beginning with Machiavelli (or, reaching further back, Thucydides), just war as continuous narrative starts with Augustine; takes up a smattering of medieval canonists; plunges into the sixteenth century with Luther as the key figure; draws on a few natural/international-law thinkers ... then leapfrogs into the era of modern nation-states – and wars.[31]

The language used here is both revealing and significant: full of religious imagery and terminology, with references to 'sacred texts', 'canonical' and 'canonists' and specific mention of the renowned Christian theologians Augustine and Luther. For Elshtain, just war is a received truth, carried through the ages in sacred texts written by authoritative individuals. She then acknowledged the separation of religious and international-law discourses within just war as the tradition approaches the present. It is this, admittedly not absolute, separation of moral and legal approaches within the just war tradition that represents in microcosm much of the debate surrounding the Iraq intervention and which comes through clearly in Blair's justifications. Where Walzer located his just war reasoning firmly within what he calls his 'legalist paradigm' – 'the fundamental structure for the moral comprehension of war'[32] – Elshtain, like Blair, granted increasing importance in her just war arguments to ideas found originally in the works of Augustine and Aquinas.

Christian thought dominated the just war tradition from the fifth century until the Enlightenment and the emergence of states and international law. The authority of God and those who could discern divine will within the tradition was replaced by the authority and application of human reason within a legal framework. Elshtain argues that the sovereignty of the individual is in some way linked to, and dependent upon, the sovereign state. She writes:

> A streamlined version of my thesis would go like this: as sovereign state is to sovereign God, so sovereign selves are to sovereign states. Given that sovereignty in the political sense 'named' self-determination for a territorial, collective entity, it is altogether unsurprising that the logic of sovereignty came unbound and migrated, becoming attached more and more to notions of the self.[33]

Historically, therefore, Elshtain allocates the primacy of sovereignty to God, which is consistent with her Christian outlook and demonstrated in her reliance on Augustine in her just war theorizing. Over time, the sovereignty which in the West had been seen as the preserve of God and governed by the Church, gradually shifted and was associated instead with the emerging idea of statehood. In turn, for Elshtain the self-determining sovereign state has primacy over individual existence, with individual identity and ethics formed in relationship to the state, the family and wider community. Because of the priority she grants to the state, Elshtain rejects as problematic any notion that the UN provides legitimate authority for military action, observing that 'historically, approval by an international body has not been viewed by just war theorists as a just cause requirement'.[34] Elshtain is accurate in this statement if simply because it is only with the advent of the UN in 1945 that the US has belonged to an international body with the potential and the mandate to decide on *ad bellum* claims.[35] Whether or not she agrees with the legal standing of the UN and its authority to provide the mandate for war or military intervention, the US is a signatory to the Charter which it co-authored and signed in 1945. America's 65-year membership of the UN covers but a short period when compared to the 1600 years of the just war tradition since Augustine.

Throughout her writings Elshtain repeatedly returns to Augustine as a means of challenging modern political practice and assumptions, particularly those that are strongly state-centric like the UN Charter and the kind of just war arguments put forward by Walzer. She summarizes what she sees as Augustine's contribution to contemporary politics and the way we understand individuality and selfhood as follows: '[Augustine] gives us the great gift of an alternative way of thinking and being in the world, a way that is in many vital respects available to those who are not doctrinally Augustine's brothers and sisters.'[36] And why is this of such importance to Elshtain, and further, to any who seek to analyse or comment upon political violence? Because, she adds: 'In the twentieth century, justification and rationalization of violence as the *modus operandi* of social change introduces an element of remorseless moral absolutism into politics.'[37]

Augustine wrote during a period shaped by different forms of violence: military violence used both to attack and defend the Roman Empire; religious violence as Christianity struggled to sustain its religious authority in the face of resurgent, traditional Roman religious practice; and doctrinal violence against heretics who sought to undermine the Church from within. Augustine was no pacifist, but neither did he support the unconstrained use or abuse of imperial military might. Augustine limited his advocacy of violence to only the most important of reasons, such as self-defence. In addition, the pursuit of a just cause should only be undertaken with a good intention: for Augustine this meant the desire to be a good Christian in this life to earn eternity with God in the next. Different aspects of Augustine's writings continue to be used to oppose violence today, in particular his just war writings which, for many, are part of the taken-for-granted moral and cultural fabric of the West. With regard to the paradox that is caused when the particular rights of states clashes with the universal rights of individuals set out by the UN, Elshtain draws on Augustine to show that modern security concerns are just a reworking of ancient security concerns: people have always feared domination and subjugation by their enemies and must always be on their guard.[38]

One assumption at the heart of Elshtain's political theory is that states provide the social conditions in which individuality and selfhood emerge, while at the same time individuals within a state shape its character. Furthermore, states, like individuals, are formed in different ways at different times in history according to the political, cultural and religious situations at the time. She also regards state sovereignty as conditional, based on the state's ability to provide internal security and a functioning society, as well as security in the face of external threats. Once these have been achieved then a state can be viewed as taking a full part in the international community.[39]

Elshtain rejects a narrow legalist view that sees all states as inevitably equal, adding an ethical dimension to the recognition of sovereignty. A state must maintain its independence through external security and sustain within its borders a safe and just society in which its members can coexist and thrive. The decisions about what it means for a state to treat its citizens fairly, or what aspects of statehood constitute a vibrant society, are themselves ethical judgements: the implication being that good states will reflect – and project – liberal values.

Contrarily, to describe another state as immature or unworthy of recognition is also to make an ethical judgement, by implication, from a position of political maturity. By making statehood itself contingent upon the type of communal life it promotes, the strict terms of the UN Charter are loosened somewhat by Elshtain, at least in theory. By extension, since communal life had broken down in Serbia/Kosovo, Sierra Leone and Afghanistan, military interventions in these places did not violate a fully developed statehood in any one of them. Elshtain goes further: the state, any state, cannot passively enjoy its advantages in some imagined isolated existence. Her Augustinianism calls for active engagement between states, with the stronger helping the weaker.

When we look further at Elshtain's justification of the US and NATO intervention in Afghanistan, complications begin to emerge. Accepting, for example, her *prima facie* case that the US acted justly in attacking Afghanistan in 2001 and overthrowing the regime that allowed Al-Qaeda to operate within Afghan borders as an act of self-defence, questions arise as to where moral authority lies a decade after the initial invasion? Do ongoing US and NATO actions retain moral authority from the original wrong perpetrated by Afghanistan-based Al-Qaeda planners in 2001? Who has the right to fight?

Elshtain argues that in the American War of Independence legitimate authority for military action against the British Crown came from the rebelling colonies as valid political entities deserving of their independence acting against illegitimate authority.[40] However, applying the principle of legitimate authority in the analogy of the US war for independence to Afghanistan throws up a number of problems. Where the 2001 Afghan regime *may* have been legitimately overthrown because of its relationship with Al-Qaeda who, in turn, attacked the US, it is possible under Elshtain's arguments for Afghan fighters, who were not part of the previous regime, to emerge as ethical. The legitimacy of these fighters would come from their relationship to the cultural and historical illegitimacy of the current Kabul regime, as well as the aggression of what they see as an occupying power.

In early 2001 Elshtain applied classic just war arguments to the question of humanitarian intervention.[41] She stressed the plurality of human existence in independent political communities and the value, and validity, of such plurality, while also identifying a common thread in the importance placed across cultures in the protecting of human life. Her starting point is 'solidarity within the particular communities of which we are a part – for every human being is a member of a way of life that embodies itself institutionally as family, tribe, civil society, state. This plurality is a constant feature of human political and moral life.'[42] She went on to add: 'We may launch ourselves into wider or more universalistic possibilities from this particular site, seeking to affirm our common humanity through organizations [and] institutions.'[43] The trajectory of her argument for just intervention is clear: the basis of her moral code is a shared social life, with universalized notions of justice and rights being expressed as circumstances allow. Due recognition and respect were given to other cultures and peoples who formed their own moral codes. However, following the Al-Qaeda attacks later that year a different emphasis emerged in her moral arguments concerning military intervention.

In *Just War Against Terror* Elshtain emphasized the use of international agreements and treaties as moral sources that should guide the use of power in the current global system. She appealed to the UN Human Rights Declaration to underpin her arguments: 'The principle I call "equal regard" underlies the Universal Declaration of Human Rights ... [which] as we are coming to understand, must sometimes be backed up by coercive force.'[44] This equal regard refers to the individual rights that should be enjoyed by people everywhere to life, liberty, and freedom. Elshtain went on to ask: '[S]houldn't an international body be its guarantor and enforcer?'[45] This, for her, is a rhetorical question; the UN should enforce the human rights that are enshrined in international law and states and individuals should support such action.

At this point, Elshtain's moral argument in favour of military intervention is shaped by the codification of rights and the need to ensure that they are guaranteed. However, a difficulty emerges in her desire to enforce the UN Universal Declaration of Human Rights because the rules of the UN also allow permanent members of the Security Council to veto any proposed military action to enforce or protect such rights. As a result, Elshtain's argument moves beyond the need to conform to international law and instead gives priority to the moral dimension in her argument. She went on: 'We, the powerful, must respond to attacks against persons who cannot defend themselves because they, like us, are human beings, hence equal in regard to us.'[46] Such a move reflects Elshtain's Augustinianism, reinforced by her reading of Thomas Aquinas. Augustine is renowned for the way he incorporated self-reflection and self-analysis into not only the Christian life but also into the way that people engage with both themselves and the world more widely. Elshtain's Augustinianism prompts individuals to examine themselves and the way they engage with the world, as ancient ideas encounter the complexities of modern life.[47]

Individuals cannot opt out of engagement with political and social life. This may manifest itself in different ways but I am particularly concerned here with just war and the way that individuals act ethically in relation to military intervention. It is such a sense of responsibility that underpins Elshtain's *Just War Against Terror* and, in particular, the need for America to act beyond its own borders to exert what she sees as its moral responsibility. This – an America that acts beyond its own borders – provides the opportunity for leaders to emerge as ethical by acting to help others under oppression and for combatants to conduct themselves ethically as they engage an enemy on the field of battle on behalf of their own people and others.

In terms of the responsibility to act to protect a neighbour Elshtain draws upon Aquinas's position on protecting the innocent:

> During the run-up to the Iraq War ... I reminded those debating the war that St. Thomas Aquinas, among others, insisted that preventing the innocent from certain harm could well be a justified *casus belli* – the innocent being those without the means to defend themselves ... What is the point of bold commitments to universal human rights – the most fundamental of which is a right to life itself – if such rights can be violated systematically and the so-called international community, rather than enforcing those rights, wrings its hands and expresses regrets?[48]

In turning to Aquinas and his arguments about protecting the innocent, Elshtain added a dimension of historical support for her contemporary position on war and intervention: a position that includes a commitment to liberal values and human rights, and enthusiasm for the use of force to protect them (even though Aquinas would not recognize these values and rights in the terms she sets them out). Elshtain's reliance on the state in her *schema* would lead – as a result of proscriptions set out in the UN Charter – to the rejection of the protection of the innocent as a legitimate *casus belli*. However, Aquinas wrote centuries before the emergence of the state and conceptions of state sovereignty and the use of his ideas enabled Elshtain to modify her just war position by transcending or bypassing the limits of modern understandings of sovereignty in international law. Her shift away from non-intervention or, at least, reluctant interventionism, parallels – indeed encourages – America's move towards military engagement: not only in self-defence as she argued in the case of Afghanistan, but in forcefully *promoting* liberal, American values in the cases of both Afghanistan and Iraq.

By basing her just war case for intervention on ethical, individual rights-focused arguments, Elshtain was able to go beyond some of the difficulties that arise if morality and conformity to law are seen as synonymous. The US was an original signatory to the UN Charter and undertook to observe the following: 'All Members shall refrain in their international relations from the threat or use of force against the territorial integrity or political independence of any state, or in any other manner inconsistent with the Purposes of the United Nations.'[49] Counterpoint to Article 2 is Article 51, which states: 'Nothing in the present Charter shall impair the inherent right of individual or collective self-defence if an armed attack occurs against a Member of the United Nations.'[50] Note, however, that the Charter refers to one *state* defending itself against the attack of another: it does not provide a legal framework for incidents where a state has been attacked by a sub-state group such as Al-Qaeda. To get round this technical difficulty, the United States, having been attacked by Al-Qaeda, held the Taliban regime in Afghanistan collectively responsible with Al-Qaeda for the violence that had taken place. It thereby conflated the quite separate degrees of moral and legal responsibility of Al-Qaeda and the Taliban and produced a state target – albeit a failed or failing state – against whom action could be taken. Further, Afghanistan failed to satisfy the criteria Elshtain set out for recognition of sovereign statehood. It could not protect its borders and provide external security, while internally repression and oppression was rife – particularly of women and girls – and did not provide a social existence where individuals could thrive.

By shifting towards a more morally-oriented position Elshtain avoids some of the difficulties raised by the legalistic contortions that were needed in appealing to international law as the basis for American reprisal action. In so doing, Elshtain prioritized concern for individuals, and their freedoms, above the rights of states to remain immune to external interference. In her approach, the ethical standing of individual political leaders depended on their willingness to act against the wrong-doers. Similarly, fellow citizens were encouraged to act ethically by supporting such action by their leaders and soldiers. Further, Elshtain presented herself as ethical as she proposed the projection of the liberal democratic values of her community, her state, onto others whose moral codes were formed differently to her own. This is most notable with regard to the differences in the right to equality as a woman and the right to freedom of religion between the US and Afghanistan.

Just war may be part of Elshtain's moral code but it appears that Elshtain's moves towards the forceful *promotion* of Western liberal values comes at the expense of a dilution of the traditional state-oriented application of the just war principles she previously advocated. Elshtain stresses the important role of the state in protecting the vulnerable: the way to protect individual rights is to ensure that strong and competent statehood is promoted, even where that means the pursuit of military intervention.

Summary

The just war writings of Walzer and Elshtain are informed by a whole range of issues: differing philosophical foundations, notions of citizenship, security, peace, gender, religious faith, individual rights, communal existence and legitimate use of force. Having examined both Walzer's and Elshtain's just war ideas and their application to military intervention, it becomes easier to identify distinct elements in Blair's justification of military action against Saddam and his regime. Walzer's just war, located in his legalist paradigm, clearly strives to present a moral case for war within the context of existing laws, both domestic and international. As a result he opposed the Iraq intervention on the basis that a just case had not been established, rejecting regime change as a legitimate cause in the process. In addition, the attack on Iraq in March 2003 could not be described as a last resort since other options were available, such as containment or further inspections.

These limitations were exactly the kind of restraints Blair sought to overcome with his doctrine of the international community, striving to make it easier to gain support for, and execute, military interventions. Walzer is not unsympathetic to the difficulties and oppression faced by citizens of far-off countries and has indicated a willingness, in the right circumstances, to set aside his non-interventionist tendencies. However, the case of Iraq did not satisfy the threshold of human suffering that Walzer would need to see before setting aside his opposition.

After the events of 11 September 2001 Elshtain showed a greater willingness to use just war vocabulary in advocating the use of military force not only to protect America but to promote its, and her own, liberal democratic ideals by means of intervention across state borders. She set out a distinctly Augustinian approach to such interventions, incorporating his self-reflection and his caution about the use of military force. In addition, she appealed to Aquinas's stated need to protect the innocent as part of a shared common life. By drawing on ideas that long predate the emergence of the international system and international law that we see today, Elshtain was able to provide a moral framework for intervention that was more permissive than Walzer's and not constrained by international law as we find it in the UN Charter.

Their observations about one another are instructive. Walzer noted that 'standard just war theory, which Elshtain expounded and defended, and which fit[s] the Afghan case very neatly, does not always fit the larger "war against terror" as it has developed since 2002'.[51] Elshtain acknowledged Walzer's questioning of her position on combating terrorism through military intervention, asking whether the US should err 'on the side of caution or the side of what I shall call hyper-vigilance. For Walzer, a democratic people should err on the side of caution.'[52] Walzer views *Just War Against Terror* as taking a rather more robust pursuit of terrorism than his more cautionary position, a position informed by greater emphasis on the rights of states than the rights of individuals. Elshtain appears to accept the point but does not consider his position to be very far removed from her own.[53] Having considered both perspectives, I take the view that in the 1990s there was little to differentiate between the two; however, following the publication of *Just War Against Terror* subsequent divergence is greater than Elshtain confirmed in her response to Walzer.

Elshtain has specifically aligned herself with Blair's position on the justification of military action in Afghanistan and Iraq. In 2007 Elshtain reflected that 'JWAT [*Just War Against Terror*] was primarily written as a response to the domestic debate in America, although I think the clearest articulation of the position I endorse or come close to endorsing ... is Prime Minister Tony Blair's'.[54] Giving this comment some wider context, she considered Blair's position to be more cautious, more wary of the use of power – though she 'would put more Augustinian wariness into any final version of that position'[55] – than Bush's. However, what Elshtain saw as a wary or comprehensively argued justification of intervention on Blair's part can be viewed from the British perspective as either exactly that or as the necessarily tentative outworking of the complex political, and party-political, dynamics that Blair had to overcome – both domestically and in Europe – in taking the UK to war. In contrast, Bush enjoyed a huge well of domestic political capital and broad public support for whatever actions he deemed fit in response to the events of 11 September 2001. Contrary to Elshtain's perception of caution in Blair's approach to war and its justification, in the UK Blair has consistently been perceived (assisted by some sections of the media) as fundamentally committed to, and identified with, the Bush position.

In the following chapters several aspects of Blair's justification of military intervention in Iraq are explored, taking into account the just war frameworks set out by Walzer and Elshtain. One of the most contentious of these aspects is examined in Chapter 4: was military action legitimately authorized? The chapter asks where authority for war comes from and whether Blair achieved it in relation to Iraq.

4
Authority, legitimacy and war

The most succinct early summary of the criteria that need to be satisfied for a war to be considered just, and the pattern that would be adopted and adapted by subsequent theorists to the present day, was set out by Thomas Aquinas in the thirteenth century. Drawing together disparate historical arguments from Augustine and other predecessors he concluded that three things were needed for a just war: it had to be legitimately authorized; fought for a just cause and undertaken with a right intention.[1] It says something of the social and religious setting in which he wrote that Aquinas prioritized the need for a war to be legitimately authorized above the need for a just cause and a right intention. For Aquinas, the right of the sovereign to declare war was not an inherent right but an extension of God's sovereignty and will, expressed in the way that society was divinely ordered with rulers set above everyone else. Today, with just war disputed within the context of international law – Walzer's legalist paradigm – priority tends to be given to the issue of just cause.

Blair's case for war against Iraq – his just cause, Aquinas's second criterion – was disputed at the time and aspects of it have already been discussed in previous chapters, with further analysis to follow. However, the question of whether or not the 2003 invasion was legitimately authorized or not is – from a UK perspective at least – the most controversial and disputed of all. This chapter will draw on evidence heard by the Iraq Inquiry, and other evidence, in assessing whether or not the Iraq intervention was legitimately authorized. However, the legal aspects to be discussed should be seen in the context of Blair's broader legitimizing moral arguments.

The chapter will be set out chronologically, beginning with an overview of Iraq's recent military and political history. Saddam's actions in the 1980s and 1990s, wars against his neighbours and atrocities committed against his own people, were intricately bound up with his ability to pose a global or regional threat at the start of the twenty-first century. The second section of the chapter will examine Blair's position from the time of the September 2001 Al-Qaeda attacks on the US until November 2002 as he sought to legitimize military action against Iraq by gaining UN Security Council authorization. The final section of the chapter will explore the legal and moral contortions Blair went through from the granting of UNSCR 1441 on 8 November 2002 to his failed attempts to achieve a second UN resolution explicitly authorizing military action and eventually to the disputed legal permission given to Blair by his Attorney General, Lord Goldsmith, on the eve of war.

My enemy's enemy

It is difficult, uncomfortable even, looking back at the relationship between the US, the UK and Iraq in the 1980s. The complexities of Middle-East politics became, in some respects at least, remarkably simple for the US after the Islamic Revolution in Iran in 1979. The relationship between the US, the UK and the regime of the deposed Shah was sufficient for many in Iran to see America and Britain as its new enemies. The UK's declining influence in the face of the US superpower relegated it to a minor role while anti-Americanism reached a peak with the storming of the US Embassy by Islamic militants on 4 November 1979. Initially, 66 Americans were taken hostage, 52 of whom would eventually be held for over a year. A botched rescue attempt in April 1980 embarrassed President Jimmy Carter and escalated tension further. Carter's humiliation was complete when the remaining hostages were handed over only minutes after Ronald Reagan assumed the Presidency on 20 January 1981. A deep enmity was created that exists to the present day between the US and Iran.

In neighbouring Iraq, Saddam Hussein saw an opportunity to seize dominance of the region by taking advantage of Iran's chaotic internal politics and launched a surprise attack in September 1980. An eight-year war of attrition then followed with the US increasingly supporting Saddam Hussein's Iraq against their mutual enemy Iran. In a vignette that would prove to be a subsequent source of embarrassment, in December 1983 Donald Rumsfeld, then US Special Envoy and later the US Secretary of Defense, met Saddam Hussein to discuss ways of improving relations between the states. Varying degrees of official and unofficial US support for Saddam and his regime then followed, until Saddam's use of chemical weapons against Kurds at Halabja on 16 March 1988.

If the relationship between Iraq and the US had not been shattered completely at that point, the decisive fracture came with Iraq's invasion of Kuwait on 2 August 1990. In claiming Kuwait as Iraq's nineteenth province Saddam Hussein not only violated the internationally recognized sovereignty of Kuwait but destabilized both the region and the world's oil markets. The international response was immediate and widely supported. On the same day the UN Security Council passed a resolution condemning the invasion of Kuwait and demanding that Iraq withdraw its forces to the positions they occupied prior to the attack.[2] Intense negotiations were undertaken over the subsequent weeks involving permanent members of the Security Council and Iraq. When these talks broke down the Security Council passed Resolution 678 on 29 November 1990 authorizing the forceful removal of Iraqi forces from Kuwait by a US-led coalition using 'all necessary means' – a phrase whose significance is revisited later.[3]

The final act in this political and military drama came on 3 April 1991 after hostilities had ceased and the terms of the resumption of peace were set out by the Security Council in Resolution 687. As well as recognizing the independence, sovereignty and borders of Kuwait, Iraq was required to relinquish any WMD capability it had. This would include the destruction of all chemical, biological and nuclear weapons, agents, components and sub-systems, as well as the means of their manufacture or development. Iraq would also have to surrender any ballistic missiles with a range of over 150km and, in addition, member states and international organizations were called upon to ensure that Saddam complied with the demands laid upon him.[4]

The road to war

Over the following decade Saddam Hussein played a determined and wily game of brinkmanship with those states that were determined to ensure his compliance with UNSCR 687, the US and UK being his fiercest critics. UN weapons inspectors were variously allowed access and then denied access, their work constantly disrupted by a leader who only a decade earlier had been supported by the US during the Iran–Iraq war. Saddam was in a politically difficult situation. If he cooperated fully with UN demands his weakness and military vulnerability would be made plain to the neighbours he had previously attacked. He took the strategic decision to try to maintain a position of influence in the Gulf region by defying international opinion and demands, provoking succeeding US Presidents in the process. This *status quo* continued for several years, with the exception of occasional movement by Saddam in response to events such as the 1998 Operation Desert Fox air campaign, which coerced him into temporarily readmitting UN weapons inspectors.

In 2001 two events in the United States would set its political and security agenda for the remainder of the decade and signal the last days of Saddam's regime. First, the election of President George W. Bush and a neo-conservative administration intent on advancing US dominance of global politics in the new millennium. This had particular significance for Saddam. At a joint press conference at Camp David on 23 February 2001, only a month after he was inaugurated, Bush and Blair faced the world's media. The President made it clear that they were watching Iraq closely and were determined to ensure that Saddam would not provide a WMD threat to the region: even if that meant taking action against him.[5] This was not an impromptu comment on Saddam and his activities, it was a public declaration that Iraq was already on the political agenda of the new President. Bush headed up a much more internationally assertive administration than his predecessor and quickly developed a good rapport with the British Prime Minister who already had experience of military intervention and regime change.

The second key event in 2001 was the most high profile terrorist attack the world had ever seen, when Al-Qaeda ideologues used hijacked airliners to destroy New York's Twin Towers and a wing of the Pentagon on 11 September. The visible result was almost 3000 deaths, mainly civilians but including 55 US military personnel and the 19 hijackers. The invisible but no less significant outcome was a scar etched into the American psyche that will forever be known simply as 9/11.

The events of that day were watched with horrified fascination on TV screens around the world, punctuated by scenes of jubilation in the domains of those who hate all that the US and the West stands for. Blair immediately recognized on 11 September 2001 that a geo-political tectonic shift had occurred.[6] The pro-interventionist Blair grasped the enormity of the events unfolding on the news screens and immediately committed both himself and the UK to standing shoulder-to-shoulder with the US, its President and the American people.[7] Blair's gift for grasping the prevailing political mood shone through yet again. His thinking appeared, and still appears, entirely consistent with what was happening in the US at that time. On 20 September 2001 Bush addressed a Joint Session of Congress and responded to the Al-Qaeda attacks by declaring a war on terror. Despite the conceptual and physical difficulties of pursuing a war against an abstract noun, Bush pressed ahead with Blair as his most ardent supporter.

The US invoked the right to self-defence in light of the 9/11 attacks but, at least in the eyes of the wider world, faced a difficulty. The state of Afghanistan had not launched the attack; Al-Qaeda elements operating independently within Afghanistan had launched the attack. This was no state-on-state war. However, Bush's war on terror would allow him to confront any ideology or terrorist groups, or any other target that fell within his broad and malleable definition. American public support for their President was overwhelming and the United States enjoyed an initial tide of sympathy after the attacks it suffered. NATO Article 5 was invoked with regard to Afghanistan, where one member under attack can call on all members to enact collective self-defence. Similarly, despite being attacked by a sub-state group (Al-Qaeda) and not an actual state, Article 51 of the UN Charter and the right of self-defence was invoked. However, after the swift toppling of the Taliban regime and the routing of the Al-Qaeda elements that could be located, whatever international support Bush had for subsequent domino strikes against other states began to erode quickly.

Bush had already signalled a willingness to act against Saddam, having identified him and Iraq as part of his axis of evil. All he had to do was link the Iraqi regime to the war on terror. Unfortunately for Blair, many British people – including many Labour MPs and members of his own party – did not share his enthusiasm for the war on terror and potential military action in Iraq and were not prepared to grant him political *carte blanche* to act as he wanted in support of the US.

In a joint Press Conference on 6 April 2002 Bush and Blair both set out their positions on Iraq. They each spoke about Saddam and WMD, raising the question of the threat level posed by Saddam and Iraq in the post-9/11 era. Bush was particularly bullish, saying: 'I explained to the Prime Minister that the policy of my government is the removal of Saddam and that all options are on the table.'[8] Blair adopted a very similar tone, telling his audience and the assembled press corps: 'You know it has always been our policy that Iraq would be a better place without Saddam Hussein, I don't think anyone should be in any doubt about that.'[9] For all the talk of regime change – and the subject is covered at length in the next chapter – Blair was presented with a major obstacle. Despite his view that the removal of Saddam would be beneficial for the Iraqi people, Blair was put in a difficult situation in July 2002 when he was advised by the Attorney General 'that regime change was not a basis for legal – for lawful use of force'.[10]

For Blair to build a substantial justification based on international law, or in accordance with the principles of just war, he would have to demonstrate either the need for self-defence, an imminent humanitarian crisis to which the Security Council could respond, or United Nations authority for some other reason.[11] Even worse for Blair, the Attorney General's position in the summer of 2002 was that 'there wasn't the evidence of imminence of threat which would justify us in saying self-defence was a basis for force'.[12] Others have debated and will continue to debate the specifics of the purely legal case for war against Iraq. I will therefore allow the Attorney General's words to sum up the legal case as 2002 wore on:

> The self-defence [argument] didn't work, the humanitarian crisis [argument] didn't work. Put in those terms, there wasn't a basis for military action. If there was going to be a basis for military action, it had to be as a result of the new United Nations Security Council Resolution.[13]

The words of the Attorney General here are highly significant in terms of who or what could legitimately authorize war against Iraq. If it could have been shown that the UK faced an imminent and credible threat, Blair could have legitimately taken military action against Saddam and Iraq solely on Parliamentary authority under the provision of Article 51 of the UN Charter. However, as the UK's senior lawyer had pointed out, there was no basis for a self-defence argument.

Blair was in a very difficult situation. At that stage he had no legal basis on which to self-authorize war yet he was utterly convinced of the moral case for removing Saddam Hussein. He had also committed himself to standing shoulder-to-shoulder with a US President who, on 10 October 2002, would be granted authority by the House of Representatives to use military force to disarm Iraq: authority that was not linked to any UN Resolution. The US may have co-authored and signed up to the UN Charter but with regard to Iraq it had no intention of seeking any approval beyond that granted by its own House of Representatives.

The Deputy Prime Minister, John Prescott, played an important, though ultimately unsuccessful, role in trying to keep the Left-leaning elements of the Labour Party behind Blair. He was a regular trouble-shooter for the Prime Minister and clearly understood that without UN sanction Blair could not have attained political support for military action against Iraq.[14] Blair met Bush on 7 September 2002 and sought support for a further attempt to obtain UN authorization for military action. Although Bush agreed to the request, it was not because he or his administration felt it necessary. He recognized that Blair would find it very difficult, as Prescott pointed out, to get the British people to commit to military engagement without a Security Council resolution. It was a paradoxical situation: if Bush was viewed as deferring too much to the UN his credibility and domestic support would have diminished; and if Blair was not seen to operate within the rules of the UN then whatever domestic support he had would decrease. Bush's calculation was that if he supported Blair in obtaining UN authorization for military action he would then have the continued backing of a committed ally and increase the possibility of achieving a broad coalition of the kind that had removed Iraqi forces from Kuwait in 1991.

The UN route

At the start of 2011 Blair was invited to return to the Iraq Inquiry to provide further clarification on a number of points he had made during an earlier appearance, in particular the difference in the approaches of the British and American governments. In a written statement to the Inquiry he detailed how the US Congress, since 1998, had a policy of changing the Iraqi regime. He described how this legal sanction was sufficient for President Bush to act against Saddam Hussein and Iraq without recourse to the UN, a position significantly at odds with his own obligations. Blair described writing to Bush in July 2002 and setting out the political advantages (necessities for Blair) of going down the UN route. He acknowledged that his Attorney General had made clear the need for military action to be sanctioned under international law.[15]

The Iraq Inquiry sought to clarify Blair's attitude towards the UN during the period April to September 2002. As previously stated, the US already had a policy of regime change in place over the previous four years. This issue lay at the heart of Blair's dilemma. He was fully committed to the idea of removing Saddam Hussein and he has made numerous references over the years since to his satisfaction at having done so. He also raised the matter of regime change in a speech on 7 April 2002 at The George Bush Senior Presidential Library, where he spoke of his pride at being involved in three previous examples of regime change: in Kosovo, Sierra Leone and Afghanistan. Blair then went on to describe the situation in Iraq, drawing parallels with these earlier interventions. He may have been discursively inviting his listeners to make the connection between regime change and Iraq but Blair did not make the point explicitly. He could advocate regime change as a solution to intractable political problems such as that posed by Saddam Hussein and Iraq while not explicitly calling for it. His statement to the Iraq Inquiry in January 2011 is interesting because Blair makes it clear that the UN route was to be pursued out of political necessity, not because he personally felt it necessary.

Once Bush stated his intention to seek a UN mandate for action against Iraq a number of influential factors came into play. The main concern was with the case for war. Without a compelling case for military action the likelihood of the US and UK obtaining the crucial support of the other permanent members of the Security Council – China, Russia and France – was negligible. From early September 2002 until 8 November 2002 when the Security Council passed Resolution 1441 intense diplomatic negotiations took place between these five key powers.

The two broad positions on Iraq could be summarized as follows. The US and UK wanted a resolution that would automatically trigger military action if Saddam and Iraq continued to flout the work of UN weapons inspectors under the leadership of Hans Blix. Such action from Saddam would confirm him as being in continued material breach of the UNSCR 687 and the demands placed upon him following the 1991 Gulf War to liberate Kuwait. France, China and Russia, for different political reasons, were determined that no automatic trigger clause would be inserted into any resolution. An example of the type of wording being sought by the US and UK is UNSCR 678 from November 1990. In that resolution the Security Council demanded:

> That Iraq fully comply with ... [all] relevant resolutions, and decides, while maintaining all its decisions, to allow Iraq one final opportunity, as a pause of goodwill, to do so;
> [The Security Council] authorizes Member States co-operating with the Government of Kuwait, unless Iraq on or before 15 January 1991 fully implements ... the above-mentioned resolutions, to use all necessary means to ... restore international peace and security in the area.[16]

In 1990 one final opportunity for Saddam to pursue a peaceful route was written into the resolution, with a 'trigger clause' also included: the deadline to activate the trigger being 15 January 1991. When it came to the second war against Iraq, a clause that automatically led to military action was most unlikely to have been achieved because not even the British Attorney General was convinced that there was a legitimate case for war, on self-defence or humanitarian grounds, in September 2002.[17] UN authorization of military action would therefore have to be based on some other regional or terrorism-related threat from Saddam based on continuing possession of WMD in defiance of previous UN Security Council resolutions.

Over the following weeks a distinct pattern of behaviour began to emerge in Blair's attempts to secure the required Security Council resolution: a pattern of governance that seems inconsistent in a representative political system that values the rule of law. Blair opted to keep from his Cabinet members much of the detail of the options he was considering, while his senior legal experts – the Attorney General and the Foreign Office's top international law practitioners – were barely consulted. The Iraq Inquiry questioned Blair on the extent to which his Cabinet Ministers were kept abreast of his intentions towards Saddam and Iraq:

> Sir Roderic Lyne: But you think it was absolutely clear when we were talking about going to the United Nations the implication was this could lead us into military action against Iraq.

> The rt. Hon. Tony Blair: I don't think there was any doubt about that at all. If you went back, unless people were not listening to the news or reading the newspapers, which is not my experience of the Cabinet Ministers, it was the issue the entire time. What I was having to do was constantly say to people: 'We have not taken the decision on military action. We are not at this stage of having put the ultimatum down.'[18]

If the matter at hand were not so serious – war with all its costs and consequences – it would almost be comical to hear a British Prime Minister expecting members of his Cabinet to rely on TV news and newspapers to stay aware of their leader's intentions towards military action against Iraq. While the relationship between Blair and his Cabinet did not impact significantly on the legality of the UK's actions in international law, it does raise wider domestic questions about the legitimacy of Cabinet government and the principle of collective responsibility. This notion of collective responsibility was also addressed by the Inquiry in questions to Lord Wilson, Cabinet Secretary from 1998 until September 2002:

> Sir Martin Gilbert: Now Mr Blair told us on Friday last week that he saw no need for [the Iraq Options] paper to be circulated to the Cabinet, because the issues were generally being discussed publicly. They were in the public domain. They were widely in the newspapers. Wouldn't, again from your perspective as Cabinet Secretary, a Cabinet Office paper prepared by the Overseas and Defence Secretariat with all its detail – it's a very detailed and structured paper – would this not have helped Cabinet Ministers to have a formed view of the situation?

LORD WILSON: Through my prism of collective government the answer to your question has to be yes.[19]

In terms of maintaining the legitimacy of the British political system, with appropriate checks and balances on the various powers held by key figures such as the Prime Minister, few emerge with much credit at this point on the road to war with Iraq. Blair was asking his Cabinet, in effect, to take collective responsibility for decisions and events about which key planning information was being kept from them. Most Cabinet ministers, equally, seem to have accepted their supine role without obvious complaint, though Robin Cook and Clare Short, Leader of the House of Commons and International Development Secretary respectively, would play increasingly important roles as voices of opposition or restraint. Later, Short was unremitting in her criticism of the way decisions were made in relation to Iraq:

So we were getting – his view that he decided, him and his mates around him, the ones that he could trust to do whatever it was he decided, and then the closing down of normal communications and then this sort of drip feed of little chats to the Cabinet.[20]

If the practicalities of Blair's *modus operandi* were laid bare by Short, the reason he was able to achieve it was set out by the Cabinet Secretary. He referred to 'the degree of loyalty that Mr Blair commanded in his Cabinet ... They went along with him. This is a man who had won them, you know, a fantastic election victory in 1997 and in 2001, and he was a very powerful figure.'[21] In his desire to have military action against Iraq legitimately authorized, Blair kept tight control of the flow of information on which his regime of truth was based and trusted only a small band of confidants. Ironically, in the process he was undermining the legitimacy of Cabinet government and the principle of the collective responsibility of its members.

Possibly more significant than Blair's relationship with his Cabinet was his relationship with those providing legal advice on any potential military action. Negotiations over a UN Security Council resolution on Iraq would fall under the remit of the Foreign and Commonwealth Office and its minister Jack Straw. On 24 September 2002, Sir Michael Wood, Chief Legal Adviser at the Foreign and Commonwealth Office, sent the Attorney General a draft of the text that the US and UK governments were planning to submit to the other permanent members of the Security Council as the basis of a resolution on Iraq. At that stage, the text of the proposed draft took a form similar to the resolution that authorized the first Gulf War in 1991. Crucially the text would allow member states to use all means necessary – diplomatic language for military force and war – to force Saddam to conform to the UN's requirements.[22] However, this was before the US and UK began to negotiate with China, Russia and France. Within a few weeks the situation had changed.

On 18 October 2002 Sir Michael sent the Attorney General another draft of the proposed resolution. It is interesting to note the Attorney General's observation that the draft text of UNSCR 1441 at that stage did not authorize the use of force,[23] something that did not change in the final draft of the text. It is even more interesting, however, that the UK's most senior lawyer was not actively consulted during the final two weeks of negotiation over the wording of the resolution.[24]

The UK's most senior *International* lawyer, Sir Michael Wood of the Foreign Office, described his understanding of the legal position facing the UK prior to the passing of UNSCR 1441 in November 2002. He rejected both self-defence and the need to counteract an impending humanitarian catastrophe as possible justifications for military action. He recalled that a number of resolutions had been passed in relation to Saddam's regime, from 1990 through to 1998 when UNSCR 1205 authorized the air campaign – Operation Desert Fox – against Iraq. However, he was insistent that a fresh Security Council resolution would need to be granted if military action was to be legally sanctioned. He went as far as to say that 'we wouldn't have a leg to stand on' if the UK sought to rely on a resolution from several years before.[25] A new resolution authorizing military action would be needed. Like the Attorney General, in the negotiating period prior to the passing of UNSCR 1441 on 8 November 2002, Sir Michael saw a number of drafts and, as late as 6 November, consistently advised that the 'the draft that they were working towards did not authorize the use of force without a further decision of the Security Council'.[26] A second UN Security Council resolution would be needed (after UNSCR 1441). When 1441 was eventually passed it included the following key points:

[The Security Council]
12. *Decides* to convene immediately upon receipt of a report in accordance with paragraphs 4 or 11 above [where Iraq fails to meet its disarmament or inspection obligations], in order to consider the situation and the need for full compliance with all of the relevant Council resolutions in order to secure international peace and security;

13. *Recalls*, in that context, that the Council has repeatedly warned Iraq that it will face serious consequences as a result of its continued violations of its obligations;[27]

The most important points are that the document warned Saddam the Security Council would meet 'to consider the situation' in the event that Iraq failed to cooperate fully with the UN's weapons inspections teams and that Iraq would face 'serious consequences' if it violated its obligations. The document was a classic diplomatic fudge that allowed all sides to claim that they had got what they wanted while achieving no such thing. UNSCR 1441 is a compromise document containing text that allowed the UK and US to point to the serious consequences that would result from non-compliance by Iraq. Meanwhile China, Russia and France could take the view that war had not been authorized because the traditional diplomatic language of war, 'all means necessary', had not been included. Jack Straw described his understanding as Foreign Secretary at that time:

> This resolution contains, if you like, an ultimatum. I mean, it talks about the final opportunity. It then in OP13 talks about serious consequences, which as Stephen Pattison explains everyone knows means military action if there was non-compliance. So it contained its own ultimatum.[28]

Straw took, and maintained, the view that the warning of serious consequences was both an ultimatum and authority for military action. In his comments he quotes Stephen Pattison, Head of the UN Department in the Foreign and Commonwealth Office and British negotiator of Resolution 1441. Pattison made it clear to the Iraq Inquiry that in his view:

> the resolution itself authorized the use of force. What was necessary for that authorization to come into effect was failure by Iraq to cooperate and comply and subsequent consideration in the Council. When those two events had taken place, the authorization contained in this resolution could be invoked.[29]

Contrary to the views of Straw and Pattison (and by extension Blair) were the legal opinions of the UK's two most senior International lawyers at that time. Sir Michael Wood and Elizabeth Wilmshurst have both been highly critical of the government's approach to the legal justification of the 2003 intervention. The Inquiry received a Minute from

Sir Michael Wood to the Foreign Secretary's office dated 23 January 2003. He expressed the view that even with UNSCR 1441 in place it would still be necessary to return to the Security Council for further authorization if military force was to be used legally by the UK.[30] In that regard his views were consistent with those of the France, Russia and China.

Sir Michael's position was reinforced by his deputy Elizabeth Wilmshurst who was similarly dissatisfied with the legal basis for action against Iraq. They both maintained their views throughout the weeks leading up to the invasion and have not changed those views since. The evidence of history appears to fall on the side of Wood and Wilmshurst when we look back to the wording of other resolutions where the UN Security Council has authorized the use of military force. When authorizing the use of military force in Korea in 1950 the Security Council 'recommended that Members of the United Nations *furnish such assistance* to the Republic of Korea *as may be necessary* to repel the armed attack and restore international peace and security'.[31] Similarly, in 1992 the Security Council authorized the use of military force in Bosnia and Herzegovina, calling on states to take '*all measures necessary*' to ensure that humanitarian assistance reached Sarajevo and other places that needed it.[32] On 29 November 1990 Resolution 678 sanctioned 'all necessary means' to remove Iraqi forces and restore the sovereignty of Kuwait. Most damningly, on 17 March 2011 – almost eight years to the day after the Iraq invasion – following weeks of increasing violence by Colonel Gaddafi's Libyan regime against his own people, the Security Council passed Resolution 1973 and authorized Member States 'to take all necessary measures' to protect Libyan civilians against the onslaught.[33] All necessary use of force short of a foreign occupation was put in place in a remarkably short space of time, with China and Russia choosing to abstain from the vote rather than exercise a veto because of the commitment to the action of the League of Arab States. The contrast between the level of international support and clarity of legal authorization for military action against Colonel Gaddafi and that granted by the UN for action against Saddam Hussein is considerable and clear.

With the meaning of Resolution 1441 clearly disputed and subject to interpretation – even within the Foreign Office – a number of factors, when taken together, highlight the lack of consistency across government at that time. The UK's senior international lawyers felt that a second resolution was needed and the Attorney General felt that a second resolution was the sensible course of action. However, Straw and Blair had led the Cabinet to believe that a further resolution would not be required and that 1441 authorized the use of force. Lord Turnbull, who by November 2002 had taken over as Cabinet Secretary, recalled as much: 'Jack Straw was very proud of the fact in a sense that they had got the better of the French in securing that wording. So they knew that the resolution wasn't essential, that the second resolution wasn't essential'.[34] The picture was made even more confusing when Blair began to talk publicly about going back to the UN for a second resolution before taking any military action against Iraq – a curious course of action if he was convinced at that stage that he did not need one.

Final resolution

Between November 2002 and the end of January 2003 Blair stated on a number of occasions that the UK would seek further UN authorization prior to any attack on Iraq. On 20 December 2002 he said in an interview: 'we have always made it clear that we will go back to the Security Council, but we will be prepared to use force'.[35] Politically it seemed more important than ever to have Security Council authorization for war if he was to gain or maintain Parliamentary and public support for his proposed actions. When he appeared before the House of Commons Liaison Committee on 21 January 2003 Blair's answers were, in turn, bullish and hesitant. On the one hand he stated categorically: 'The fact is we are going to have a second UN Resolution'.[36] On the other hand he did not rule out the possibility that military action would occur regardless: 'Of course I accept it is going to be more difficult without a [second] UN Resolution.'[37] This ambivalence is best explained by his approach to the legal route, which Blair saw as only a narrow strand, and not the most important strand, of his broader moral case. One exchange with a member of the Liaison Committee reveals a theme which recurs again and again over his time in office and which Blair first set out in his Doctrine of the International Community in 1999. That is, Blair's prioritization of wider moral concern over the strictures of law.

> (Q.) When you make a decision, which I hope will not necessarily be to commit armed forces to combat operations, what are the principal factors that you will bear in mind before making what could be a fateful decision?
>
> (*Mr Blair*) The two most important are is it right and is it do-able?[38]

The *moral* question, 'is it right?' is the first calculation he makes, with the question, 'is it legal?' at best relegated to be part of the second question: 'is it do-able?' The moral judgement stands on its own while the legal judgement – if it is applied – is something that needs to be weighed up along with political calculations and military assessments to ensure support for an intervention.

At his monthly press conference on 18 February 2002 Blair again reiterated the need to follow the UN line: 'the basis of our action has got to be the UN mandate and we can't go beyond that'.[39] However, Blair also started to water down his commitment to obtaining a second UN resolution and began to use vague phrases such as, 'The authority given by 1441 is an authority on the basis of weapons of mass destruction'.[40] He suggested that UNSCR 1441 granted sufficient authority for military action without mentioning the dissenting view of key, specialist government legal experts. By 11 March 2003 Blair moved further away from his previous bold statement that a follow-up Security Council Resolution to 1441 would be forthcoming:

> if there was a veto applied by one of the countries with a veto or by countries that I thought were applying the veto unreasonably, in those circumstances we would [proceed without one] but we're fighting very hard to get a second resolution through and, as we speak now, I still believe we will get that second resolution.[41]

By talking in these terms about the second resolution Blair surrendered two positions he had previously set out: first, his initial view that Resolution 1441 itself provided sufficient authorization for military action; and second, his confidence that a follow-up resolution would be forthcoming. He also took upon himself the ability and responsibility to judge the actions of other states such as France, Russia and China. Just as he did in Parliament on 15 January 2003, Blair was creating a new argument: the 'unreasonable veto' approach. However, the Attorney General has made it clear that such an argument was not legally valid and contrary to the advice he gave the Prime Minister the day before.[42] When challenged on this discrepancy at the Iraq Inquiry, Blair conceded that there was an 'inconsistency' between what he was advised and what he said in the House of Commons.[43] He continued: 'but I was saying it not in a sense as a lawyer, but politically'.[44] The implication is that making a political statement somehow removed from Blair the responsibility to conform to the legal guidance provided by his Attorney General: any inconsistency was entirely of his own making.

In Blair's regime of truth, publicly contradicting the private advice of his Attorney General was entirely acceptable for what he saw as the higher political purpose of holding together the coalition against Saddam. There are probably few moments in the entire Iraq affair that more clearly illustrate the point that Blair saw the legitimacy of his actions in terms that transcended mere legality. He was probably right when he later pointed out that if he had publicly prevaricated at that point on the legal question it could have undermined the coalition's attempts to put pressure on Saddam while also keeping pressure on the French and Russians to support military action.[45] In other words, the higher end justified the means. More immediately, however, Blair was not accurately representing the legal case to his Cabinet and the House. If the detail of the Attorney General's concerns had been made public at that point it is hard to see how Blair could have held his Cabinet together, never mind the international Coalition of the Willing. Members of the coalition such as El Salvador, Eritrea, Estonia and Ethiopia may well have reconsidered their support for military action.

There was still one major development to come in the pursuit of UN authorization of military action against Iraq. Blair recalls his own attitude at that time: 'I knew in the final analysis that I would be with the US, because in my view it was right, morally and strategically'.[46] Note, again, he does not include the word 'legally' in his analysis. For Blair, legitimate authority for military action did not equate to legal authority. The moral argument outweighed the legal argument and always had done.

The most controversial aspect of the legal basis of the war appeared only days before the eventual invasion when it became clear that a second UN resolution was not going to be achieved. In his statement to Parliament on 18 March 2003 – the eve of war – Blair stated: 'on Monday night, France said it would veto a second Resolution whatever the circumstances.'[47] On the face of it Blair was correct and factual in what he said since President Chirac had spoken in those terms a few days previously on 10 March. Complicating matters, however, was the French position between Chirac's comments on 10 March and Blair's comments to Parliament on 18 March.

The French Foreign Minister, Dominique de Villepin, contacted Jack Straw, his British counterpart, on 13 March, telling him that France was still open to suggestion and would consider any new ideas brought forward.[48] This message was conveyed to Blair's office on the same day, also making clear that the stumbling block for the French was the issue of 'automaticity'. The message Straw received from the French – and forwarded to Blair – was that 'France could work on any mechanism which contained an ultimatum as long as it was the Security Council which took full responsibility at the end of any deadline'.[49] The French position was more consistent with the text of Resolution 1441 which referred any breach by Saddam back to the Security Council.

In light of the conversation between Straw and Villepin, with the latter stressing France's willingness to find common ground, Blair's statement to Parliament begins to appear less than fully representative of the complexities of the situation. Blair felt that the point of last resort had been reached; the French, and others, did not.

Two factors appear to have been driving events. The military deployment by the US and UK and other coalition partners had taken on a momentum of its own and it would be logistically difficult to support 250 000 personnel in the desert surrounding Iraq for any sustained period. Concurrently, the more access the weapons inspectors got to sites, information and Iraqi scientists, the clearer it was becoming that Iraq posed no threat to its neighbours, the US or the UK. Blair's legal basis for the war, which was already tenuous at best, would be lost if it could be demonstrated that Saddam and Iraq had no WMD capable of threatening or harming its neighbours or anyone else. So it was decided by the US and the UK, and supported by a number of other states, that authorization for military action would be achieved through what became known as the 'revival' argument: whereby the authority for the use of force granted in 1990 under UNSCR 678 was deemed to be still in force. Blair summarized this turn of events quite simply: 'Meanwhile, we had resolved our own legal issues.'[50] The decision ultimately rested with the British Attorney General who, reversing a position he had held for many months, decided at the last minute, and after a trip to Washington to discuss the legal case, that the 'revival' approach was valid and would provide legal sanction.

Despite his bullishness at the time Blair later acknowledged the delicacy of the situation: 'There was clearly a case in law; but there was also a case against.'[51] However, he does not appear entirely consistent on the subject when he adopted a position suggested by his long-time mentor Derry Irvine: 'the problem was that we tried so hard to get a second resolution that people assumed, wrongly, we needed one legally.'[52] Regardless, Blair's revivalist argument is open to challenge on two grounds.

The most serious grounds are on the technicalities of international law. Sir Michael Wood took the view that because the Security Council passed Resolution 678 in 1990 authorizing war against Iraq, only a further resolution or decision by the Security Council could revive it.[53] For him, individual states such as the UK or US did not possess sufficient authority to revive the earlier Resolution on their own authority. Elizabeth Wilmshurst was similarly critical in rejecting the revival argument. In all of these discussions a common absence was the lack of consideration of what it would mean to the soldiers and other combatants being asked – ordered – to go to war when the legality on which it was based seemed to be a matter of interpretation rather than bold confidence. Sir Michael addressed this when he questioned the threshold of certainty that should be attained before war is undertaken. He advocated a higher degree of legal certainty than was being used by Blair.[54] Additionally, as Elizabeth Wilmshurst pointed out, military personnel should be able to deploy without having to worry about the strength of the legal foundations of their actions: an aspect of the intervention that is covered in Chapter 8.[55]

The second challenge to Blair's position stems from his actions over the preceding six months. If the revival justification was valid in March 2003 when, if there had been any change in circumstance Saddam was providing greater co-operation than previously, why was that particular argument not set before the British public and Parliament in 2002? Why did Blair spend six months repeatedly emphasizing the need to pursue the UN route and after Resolution 1441 talk about going back for a further UN resolution? The short answers are: it would have looked politically opportunistic; the tenuous nature of the case for war would be laid bare; there would have been time to challenge his position in the UK Parliament; and because Blair's own Attorney General had pointed him in that direction from July 2002 onwards before deciding in March 2003 that the revival approach was valid (against the views of the UK's two most senior international lawyers). When Blair finally gave up on the possibility of a second UN resolution and adopted the revival argument in March 2003 it still looked politically opportunistic. However, such was the momentum towards invasion that there was not the time for this turn of events to be effectively opposed in the British political system. Sides had been taken by politicians and members of the public alike, pro-war or anti-war, and there was little scope for changing anyone's view: least of all Blair's.

Summary

I will use a straightforward analogy to highlight some of the concerns that observers of the political process had about the legal advice given to Blair by his Attorney General, who was not a specialist in international law. Imagine for a moment that during his time as Prime Minister Blair had started to behave erratically and his advisers and close confidants began to suspect some malfunction of the brain. Imagine, further, that they managed to convince him of their concerns and encouraged him to see a specialist. Being Prime Minister he would have had access to all the expert advice he wanted. Let us say, for the sake of argument, that the most senior surgeon in the land was an ear, nose and throat specialist. To whom would Blair have turned to for advice on his brain problem? The highest surgeon in the land who had some understanding of the how the brain operated based on lectures attended decades earlier in medical school, knowledge gleaned throughout his or her career and the fact that the throat, nose and ears are all in reasonably close proximity to the brain? Or, a brain surgeon who was less esteemed overall but who was, as a result of dedicated, focused experience over several decades, the highest ranked *brain* surgeon in the country? When put this way, with the political and procedural niceties set to one side, doubt is cast on Blair's judgement when he ignored the international law specialists and listened instead to an unconvincing Attorney General. By using what seemed like the uncertain advice of a non specialist lawyer who eventually came round to provide the authority that Blair wanted over the two most senior specialist law officers, whose opinions would not and could not be changed in the political, legal and diplomatic circumstances prevalent at the time, he cast – at the very least – a cloud over the legitimacy of Blair's legal approach.

There are four things that undermine the claims of Jack Straw and Stephen Pattison that the term 'serious consequences' in UNSCR 1441 meant military action if Saddam failed to cooperate. First, Blair subsequently spent months declaring to the British people and the world that he would seek a second UN resolution before taking military action against Saddam Hussein. Second, the original draft of 1441 put together by the US and UK referred to 'all means necessary' – which everyone in the diplomatic world except for the British negotiating team knows is needed to sanction military action. A combination of French, Chinese and Russian negotiators ensured that this long-recognized phrase was removed and replaced with the intentionally ambiguous 'serious consequences'. The Attorney General was content that the original proposal in September 2002 authorized war while later drafts and Resolution 1441 itself did not. Third, if 1441 self-authorized military action why did Blair, his government and the Attorney General go through the contortions of 'reviving' the original authority for the first Gulf War with its crucial wording, 'all means necessary'? The final critique of the claim that 1441, or a combination of 1441 and the 'revived' resolutions, authorized military action against Iraq is the consistent views of the Chief Legal Adviser Sir Michael Wood and his Deputy Elizabeth

Wilmshurst. At no time did they believe that UNSCR 1441 authorized war. Furthermore, the UK's two most senior international lawyers took the view that a further Security Council resolution was necessary for the earlier resolutions to be revived and applied in 2003 anyway. Despite his misgivings Sir Michael stayed in office to assist the government at a difficult time while on 18 March 2003 Elizabeth Wilmshurst tendered her resignation in a letter that expressed concern that the UK was about to commit the crime of aggression, undermining the rule of law in the process.

On the matter of whether or not the 2003 invasion of Iraq was legitimately authorized it is Blair, perhaps, who summed up the situation most effectively when he acknowledged that a case could be made both for and against the action.[56] Weighing up all of the foregoing arguments and the vast amount of testimony to several government inquiries it is my view that the case *against* is most convincing. It can be no coincidence that, in the last days before the invasion, and most notably in his statement to the House to open the Iraq debate that ultimately authorized military action, Blair reduced his emphasis on a legal basis for war and stressed the moral arguments of which he was utterly convinced. He would later write: 'I understood the importance of the second resolution in terms of political survival and so forth. I confess I always thought it a bit odd in terms of the *moral acceptability* of the course of action or not.'[57] Blair went on to state, 'We had acted without UN authority in Kosovo ... I never even thought about it for Sierra Leone. Yet it would be hard to argue that, morally, in each of those situations, we should not have intervened.'[58] It is the central thesis of this book that, for Blair, the moral arguments for military intervention superseded the legal case, an argument that he confirmed with his own words. It is to these moral arguments that the following chapters now turn.

5
Regime change

One of the great contributions made by Aquinas not only to the just war tradition but to Western legal thought in general is referred to as his doctrine of double effect. From the time it was written in the thirteenth century until the present day this concept has been used to assist in making moral and legal judgements, both on the field of battle and in civil courts, when acts of violence – often involving death – have been carried out. Crucially, in making such judgements the issue of intention is related to outcomes. Take the nightmare scenario of a family being attacked in their home by a knife-wielding assailant.

At the point where a teenage daughter is about to be stabbed by the attacker her mother picks up a heavy ornament and smashes it against the intruder's head. Instantly, the attacker drops dead from the blow. For Aquinas, and for us today, the morality and legality of the action is dictated by the intention of the one who struck the crucial blow. If the intention of the mother was to preserve the life of her child then the act should be considered both moral and lawful. If, however, the mother hit the attacker with the intention of killing him or her, then the action should be deemed immoral and illegal. If the latter could be proved in a court of law then the mother could expect to receive a serious punishment.

Aquinas wrote: 'Nothing prevents a single act from having two effects, only one of which is intended while the other is besides the intention. Now moral acts take their species from what is intended, not from what is beside the intention, since this is accidental.'[1] The 2003 Iraq War, and Blair's justification of it, provides a perfect example of one act that had two (or more) effects. One effect of the intervention was to remove any threat of WMD that Iraq posed to its neighbours and the wider world: either directly or indirectly via links to terrorist organizations. Another effect was the toppling of Saddam Hussein: regime change. This chapter will address the question: Was Blair's primary intention regime change or was it the removal of WMD and the enforcement of UN resolutions?

I am going to suggest at the outset that despite Blair's frequent claims to the contrary, the evidence points to the former. This chapter argues, with reference to his own words before, during and after the invasion, that Blair's *intention* was regime change and that the *policy* of pursuing a WMD case via the UN was simply a political means of achieving the primary aim of which he was already morally convinced. The chapter takes a chronological approach, starting with an examination of Blair's attitude towards regime change prior to 9/11. Blair has consistently spoken with pride about changing regimes in Serbia, Sierra Leone and Afghanistan and that conviction came to the forefront as he stood shoulder-to-shoulder with Bush and the US on the issue of Saddam and Iraq.

The relationship between Blair's *policy* on Iraq and his *intentions* towards Saddam are subsequently explored, taking into account his public statements at the time, declassified evidence that has been submitted to the Iraq Inquiry and his own reflections over subsequent years.

The liberator

Seven months after the 9/11 attacks on the United States, fighting was continuing in Afghanistan and the focus of President George W. Bush's administration was turning to Iraq and Saddam Hussein. On 7 April 2002 Blair spoke at the George Bush Senior Presidential Library and highlighted regime change as the morally appropriate response to brutal regimes guilty of oppressing their own people. He took the opportunity to relate possible action against Saddam and Iraq to the regime changing interventions he had led previously in Kosovo, Sierra Leone and Afghanistan. He told his listeners: 'we must be prepared to act where terrorism or Weapons of Mass Destruction threaten us. The fight against international terrorism is right ... If necessary the action should be military and again, if necessary and justified, it should involve regime change.'[2] Having linked the issues of terrorism and WMD he went on to make a further connection between these two threats and the benefits of regime change. In establishing his own credentials as a regime changer with a concern to liberate the victims of tyrants he said of Afghanistan:

> I have been involved as British Prime Minister in three conflicts involving regime change. Milosevic. The Taliban. And Sierra Leone ... We acted with care ... The Taliban are gone as a government. Al Qaida's

network has been destroyed in Afghanistan, though without doubt a residual capability remains and we should still be immensely vigilant. The Afghan people feel liberated not oppressed and have at least a chance of a better future.[3]

As we look back on Blair's words at that time, particularly his comments about Afghanistan, they come across as naive and optimistic. Perhaps it was just the spin machine in operation and trying to put a positive gloss on events. It is obvious that a decade after the post-9/11 invasion of Afghanistan the Afghan people have not been liberated either from the Taliban, Al-Qaeda or the Westerners many of them see as occupying their land. The chance of a better future continues to hang in the balance for the people of Afghanistan. Determined insurgents want to fight on while American and British politicians are keen to withdraw, pat themselves on the back and declare that the mission has been accomplished – whatever that mission happens to be at any point in time. Yet there can be little doubt that when Blair spoke these words in good faith he actually meant what he said. He saw himself as a liberator of the Afghans. He went on to describe his involvement in Sierra Leone in similar terms: 'I'll always remember driving through the villages near Freetown in Sierra Leone seeing the people rejoicing – many of them amputees through the brutality from which they had been liberated – and their joy at being free to debate, argue and vote as they wished.'[4]

Setting aside the discomfort of Blair presenting himself in almost Messianic terms and the inconvenient technicality that the Sierra Leone intervention was not aimed at regime change but in ending a catastrophic civil war, his personal conviction about the benefits of regime change shines through. Although passionately committed to the idea of changing regimes as a way to end ethnic cleansing, genocide or other crimes against humanity, Blair did not at that stage come out and say directly that he wanted regime change in Iraq. What he did instead was present a speech-making master class in suggesting something without saying it. Having highlighted his experiences and the benefits of regime change in Kosovo, Sierra Leone and Afghanistan, Blair moved on to the subject of Saddam, WMD and terrorism, saying:

> We cannot, of course, intervene in all cases but where countries are engaged in the terror or WMD business, we should not shirk from confronting them … But leaving Iraq to develop WMD, in flagrant breach of no less than nine separate UNSCRs, refusing still to allow weapons inspectors back to do their work properly, is not an option.

> The regime of Saddam is detestable. Brutal, repressive, political opponents routinely tortured and executed.[5]

The key to Blair's message at this point lies in the sequencing of themes in this section of his speech. The themes are: regime change leads to liberation; we should intervene where terror or WMD pose a threat; Iraq is developing WMD; Saddam's regime oppresses his own people and has attacked his neighbours. Blair left it to his listeners to make the connections that he either would not or could not explicitly make – regime change in Iraq would be a good thing because Saddam has WMD, maltreats his people and needs to be stopped. Blair had managed to suggest regime change in Iraq while not actually saying it explicitly, thereby leaving himself the option of plausible deniability later on. However, the regime of truth that Blair was carefully constructing with his public statements did not fully represent the strength of his private views at that time.

In a memo to Jonathan Powell, his chief of staff, on 17 March 2002 – more than two weeks prior to a meeting with President Bush at Crawford, Texas – Blair was more strident about his intentions towards Saddam and his regime. He wrote: 'a political philosophy that does care about other nations – eg Kosovo, Afghanistan, Sierra Leone – and is prepared to change regimes on the merits, should be gung-ho on Saddam.'[6] The tension between Blair's desire to be 'gung-ho' on Saddam and the need for him to tread warily through the political minefield that surrounded him would shape the next year of his premiership and beyond. The order in which Blair set out his approach to Powell is consistent with other public and private communications he made, with the issue of regime change being raised first, followed by reference to WMD and the security/UN arguments. Members of the Iraq Inquiry questioned Blair about other aspects of this memo.

Sir Martin Gilbert quoted some of Blair's words back to him – 'So we have to reorder our story and message. Increasingly I think it should be about the nature of the regime'[7] – and asked Blair to expand upon the story that needed to be reordered. Blair felt that if he was going to achieve political support from those on the Left then he would have to focus his discourse on the nature of Saddam's regime and the harm it did both at home and abroad. However, in taking this approach he was putting himself further into a political bind. By concentrating his justification increasingly upon Saddam's regime he ran into the contradiction set out by the Attorney General, 'that regime change was not a basis for legal – for lawful use of force'.[8] Even more restrictive for Blair, the UN Charter prohibits even the *threat* of force against the 'territorial integrity or political independence of any state'.[9]

Another consequence of Blair's determination to make the reordered story about the nature of Saddam's regime is that it shifted his arguments and political judgement from a dependence on international law and physical evidence towards a basis in moral judgement: from a legalist paradigm to a moralist paradigm. Chapter 4 highlighted the difficulty of demonstrating a watertight legal case against the Iraqi regime. Increased incorporation of moral pronouncements would at least give the impression of amplifying the meagre substance of the legal case against Saddam. Moreover, as Blair, Bush and their expert communications teams appreciated only too well, most people respond best to simple and direct choices: good/evil, right/wrong, action/inaction. Blair had to convince his listeners that good and right and action were on his side.

Blair even acknowledged to Powell that the threat from WMD did not seem any more serious than it had three years previously.[10] When this lack of increased threat is set alongside Blair's desire to focus on the nature of the Iraqi regime, his belief in the merits of regime changing and the view that they should be more 'gung-ho' on Saddam, it is difficult to see how Blair could claim that his priority was anything other than a desire to see regime change in Iraq. His way of dealing with the thorny, potentially illegal and politically problematic issue was, and still is, to argue that regime change and dealing with Iraq's WMD were inextricably linked. He rejected what he called the 'very binary distinction between regime change on the one hand and WMD on the other'.[11] At this point it helps to clarify the distinction between the strategic claims that Blair was making and the related moral arguments. On a strategic level Blair's claim is credible. If his aim was to use military force to achieve the desired end state of eliminating the (alleged) threat posed by WMD it is difficult to see how this could be achieved while still leaving Saddam's regime in power. Conversely, if his strategic intent was the removal of Saddam's regime by military means it could only be achieved by tackling the WMD threat on the field of battle. However, there are two limitations in Blair's attempts to tie together the issues of regime change and WMD.

The first is a moral challenge that originates in the ideas of Aquinas and just war introduced at the beginning of the chapter. The question of whether the 2003 invasion was just or not hinges, at least partly, on whether or not it was undertaken with a right or legitimate intention. If Blair's primary intention was to achieve regime change in Iraq then his actions would run contrary not only to the long-established principles of just war (which provided the basis for his interventionist doctrine in 1999) but also the constraints of international law set out in the UN Charter. If his primary intention was to remove any Iraqi WMD threat then his actions – if they were undertaken as a last resort in pursuit of a just and credible cause – could be viewed as consistent with just war requirements. However, in early 2002 he acknowledged that the WMD threat appeared not to have changed in three years while enthusiastically advocating the merits of regime change and highlighting his previous willingness to carry it out. On balance, it seems more likely that Blair's *intention* in March/April 2002 was to pursue regime change against Iraq and that he had to find a means of achieving that intent, with WMD emerging as the most likely means of gaining support for his intended actions.

He described his 1999 policy on Kosovo in clear terms that have implications for how we should read his intentions towards Saddam: 'intervention to bring down a despotic dictatorial regime could be justified on grounds of the nature of that regime, not merely its immediate threat to our self-interests.'[12] The significance of this particular observation by Blair is that it accords with his message to Jonathan Powell that the 'story' about Iraq should concentrate on the nature of the regime. He had achieved regime change before and he intended to do it again. Complicating the picture is an apparent self-contradiction in Blair's statements on regime change. Having reflected in his 2010 book that removing a regime could be justified on the nature of that regime he told the Iraq Inquiry only a few months later in January 2011: 'Well, again as I have said many, many times on this, the nature of the regime could not justify in itself the intervention.'[13] These are two diametrically opposed positions that raise a number of questions, including: How is the discerning observer to know which one of these contradictory statements Blair *really* meant? Was his regime of truth flexible enough to sustain two such contradictory moral approaches? And did the nature of a regime justify intervention or not? The Iraq Inquiry did not press him further on these contradictions.

One of the difficulties in ascertaining Blair's meaning when he made these divergent comments is the nature of political communication during the New Labour era and his time in office. A central pillar of Blair's 'Third-Way' politics, where he painted himself and New Labour as transcending the traditional Left/Right dichotomy, was in communicating with different elements of the electorate or political spectrum by identifying with their needs or concerns. This approach underpinned every regime of truth that Blair sought to construct, whether it related to social policy, financial policy or military intervention. The short-term advantage for Blair and New Labour was that it presented them as being somehow 'for' almost everyone. The long-term disadvantage is that it often relied on contradictory messages being given to the Left and the Right on the same issue. It would be putting it mildly to say that for some observers on both sides of the political spectrum this approach came across as inconsistent, opportunistic and without ideological basis.

In his first year as Prime Minister Blair described himself as 'a pretty straight sort of guy'[14] in response to a controversy over political funding and the public at that time gave him the benefit of the doubt. Blair has always seen himself as that 'straight sort of guy' and has always come across as sincere, or at least he has striven to come across as sincere, when presenting ideas that are patently contradictory when viewed side-by-side. It therefore seems reasonable to assume that within his own regime of truth Blair believed both of the comments on regime change and the nature of regimes when he made them: that intervention and regime change could be justified on the basis of the nature of a dictatorial regime, and his insistence that intervention and regime change could *not* be justified on the basis of the nature of [the Iraqi] dictatorial regime. The challenge in making a moral assessment of Blair's Iraq intervention is ascertaining which of his truths on regime change should be given greater weight: the one that underpinned several years of interventionist policy or the one that temporarily emerged after the Attorney General advised him that regime change would not provide a legal basis for military action against Saddam. My inclination is towards the former.

The second limitation on Blair's attempt to link regime change and WMD originates in the inherent difficulties of using military force as a means of achieving strategic aims. Despite claims to the contrary by air power advocates who extol the benefits of precision guided munitions, military power cannot be wielded like a surgeon's scalpel and the results cannot be so accurately predicted. Shortly before the invasion Robin Cook, Leader of the House of Commons, would point out an inconsistency between Blair's case for war and his preparations for war. In what was widely regarded as one of the most incisive and destructive resignation speeches in living memory he stated:

> For four years as Foreign Secretary I was partly responsible for the western strategy of containment. Over the past decade that strategy destroyed more weapons than in the Gulf War, dismantled Iraq's nuclear weapons programme and halted Saddam's medium and long-range missiles programmes. Iraq's military strength is now less than half its size than at the time of the last Gulf War.

Ironically, it is only because Iraq's military forces are so weak that we can even contemplate its invasion. Some advocates of conflict claim that Saddam's forces are so weak, so demoralized and so badly equipped that the war will be over in a few days. We cannot base our military strategy on the assumption that Saddam is weak and at the same time justify pre-emptive action on the claim that he is a threat.

Iraq probably has no weapons of mass destruction in the commonly understood sense of the term, namely a credible device capable of being delivered against a strategic city target.[15]

The most damaging of Cook's observations, bearing in mind his experience as a Cabinet minister, was that Blair's *planning* for war was based on a best-case scenario where Saddam was deemed to be militarily weak, while Blair's *case* for war was based on the extent of the threat Saddam posed to the region and the world. In essence, what Cook did was bring together two strands of Blair's triangulation approach, each of which had its own logic when viewed in isolation but which created a contradiction when brought together. According to Cook, military planners were being given one message about Saddam's threat and were resourced accordingly, while Blair's justification to the general public was based on the perception of a far graver threat. Consequently, Blair's approach makes most sense when viewed from the moral perspective – which was always his priority anyway – and the issues of intention (regime change) and means (acting to remove the WMD threat) viewed as *philosophically* distinct, even if they could not be easily *strategically* separated.

When in his memoirs Blair referred back to that period in March/April 2002, the removal of Saddam Hussein was still at the forefront of his justification, along with the tension between his moral and legal arguments he set out. Blair summarized his pre-invasion position as follows: 'From my standpoint, by this time I had resolved in my own mind that removing Saddam would do the world, and most particularly the Iraqi people, a service. Though I knew regime change could not be our policy, I viewed a change with enthusiasm, not dismay.'[16] Following the sequence of Blair's logic it is clear that by April 2002 he was convinced of the benefits of removing Saddam. If Blair's *policy* was to annul the threat offered by Saddam it was only as a means of achieving his primary *intention* of regime change. The UN argument, as Blair recounted it here, comes across very much as a means to an end: the 'end' that Blair was seeking to achieve was the removal of Saddam and his regime. This particular reading of Blair and his motivations was reinforced by

Alastair Campbell in an interview in 2011 when, in the context of a discussion about the Libyan intervention, he looked back on the 2003 Iraq invasion and stated: 'The aim was to topple the regime and it happened fairly quickly'.[17]

These words expose in microcosm the difficulty that Blair faced at the time and which has followed him ever since: a sense that his public policy statements were not fully in keeping with his private views and motivations. Bush took a similar view that regime change was to be desired but he was not constrained in saying it publicly in the same way that Blair was constrained by the Parliamentary system and the internal politics of the Labour Party. There was concern in the UK about an increasing Al-Qaeda threat at the time, as well as desire to support the US following the events of 9/11. However, there was not the same sense of outrage and anger that the Americans were experiencing and which prompted members of the Bush administration to view international law as a diplomatic nicety that would not be allowed to limit their response to the terror threat as they perceived it. When we look at what was said by the President and the Prime Minister in their joint press conference in Texas, Bush was bullish about the American approach while Blair's frustration seemed to simmer just below the surface:

PRESIDENT BUSH: The Prime Minister and I of course talked about Iraq. We both recognize the danger of a man who is willing to kill his own people and harbouring and developing weapons of mass destruction. This guy, Saddam Hussein, is a leader who gasses his own people, goes after people in his own neighbourhood with chemical weapons, he is a man who obviously has something to hide. He told the world that he would show us that he would not develop weapons of mass destruction and yet over the past decade he has refused to do so. And the Prime Minister and I both agree that he needs to prove that he isn't developing weapons of mass destruction. I explained to the Prime Minister that the policy of my government is the removal of Saddam and that all options are on the table.

PRIME MINISTER: I can say that any sensible person looking at the position of Saddam Hussein and asking the question, would the region, the world, and not least the ordinary Iraqi people, be better off without the regime of Saddam Hussein? The only answer anyone could give to that question would be yes. Now how we approach this, this is a matter for discussion, this is a matter for considering all the options ...

QUESTION: Prime Minister, we have heard the President say what his policy is directly about Saddam Hussein, which is to remove him, that is the policy of the American Administration. Could I ask you whether that is now the policy of the British government and could I ask you both if it is now your policy to target Saddam Hussein, what has happened to the doctrine of not targeting Heads of State and leaving countries to decide who their leaders should be, which is one of the principles which applied during the Gulf War?

PRIME MINISTER: You know it has always been our policy that Iraq would be a better place without Saddam Hussein, I don't think anyone should be in any doubt about that for all the reasons I gave earlier ...

PRESIDENT BUSH: Maybe I should be a little less direct and be a little more nuanced and say we support regime change.[18]

Blair gave a curious response to the question about his policy on Iraq, telling the journalists that 'it has always been our policy that Iraq would be a better place without Saddam'.[19] Again, there is an apparent contradiction between these words and Blair's recollections in his memoirs where he wrote: 'I knew regime change could not be our policy'.[20] This inconsistency is easily accounted for because Blair did not declare in his press conference that his policy was regime change. He *implied* regime change when he suggested that Iraq would be better off without Saddam, without actually calling for regime change. Blair's linguistic dexterity just about managed to allow him to say what he wanted to say about regime change without actually being able to be as direct as Bush. More problematically, his comment, 'it has always been our policy that Iraq would be a better place without Saddam',[21] does not stand up well to scrutiny. How can Iraq being a better place constitute government policy? It can be a personal belief or even a government view but it cannot be a policy. At most, a better-off Iraq could be described as the intended result or hoped-for outcome of government policy. In clear contrast to Blair, Bush was direct to the point of bluntness. So much so that he even chided himself for his lack of nuance in his comments. This tension would continue, with differing degrees of obviousness, until the invasion itself.

Having examined Blair's position in early 2002 it became clear over the remainder of the year that his intentions did not change much, if at all.

The longest year

By July 2002 the political pressure was increasing on everyone involved as talk about Saddam started to be translated into consideration of the ways in which he could be tackled. President Bush and his administration were increasingly strident in their determination to act against Saddam with their policy of regime change. Blair was as committed as ever to standing shoulder-to-shoulder with Bush even if he could not quite manage to stand policy-to-policy. Press speculation was rife, fuelled by a combination of incisive journalism and both official and unofficial briefings on both sides of the Atlantic. Blair was also starting to come under criticism for what was increasingly seen as his obsequious attitude towards Bush and the US, especially on the matter of a potential war against Iraq.[22]

On 19 July 2002 Blair's intentions towards Iraq were becoming hardened and a Cabinet paper was issued that set out conditions for possible military action. Blair was questioned about the content of that paper:

SIR MARTIN GILBERT: The Cabinet paper for conditions on military action which was issued on 19th July 2002, a version of which has appeared in the press, recorded that you had told the President at Crawford in April 2002: 'United Kingdom will support military action to bring about regime change provided certain conditions were met.' Was that a turning point?

THE RT. HON. TONY BLAIR: It wasn't a turning point. It was really that all the way through we were saying this issue now has to be dealt with. So Saddam either comes back into compliance with UN resolutions or action will follow.[23]

Yet again the idea emerges that Blair's intention in supporting the US was to bring about regime change in Iraq. Blair did not deny the words attributed to him about regime change but went on to repeat his view that Saddam had to be dealt with and UN resolutions had to be complied with or there would be action taken. The brief discussion highlighted here adds further consistency to my analysis that Blair's primary intention was to support the US in regime change, with the other factors such as UN compliance providing a means by which his primary aim could be achieved.

Also on 19 July, Blair's chief of staff wrote to him with ideas and suggestions that the Prime Minister could put to President Bush, who was aiming to create a military plan for Iraq. Powell suggested that a similar approach to that taken in Afghanistan should be adopted for Iraq and should include a number of specific elements. Suggestions that were put forward as part of a 'road map for getting rid of Saddam' included: assurance that the UK would be there when the US decided to act; the need for an ultimatum whereby a lack of cooperation by Saddam would lead to military action; a legal basis 'based on WMD rather than terrorism or regime change'; and the need to make the case for war by releasing documents 'on human rights abuses, WMD etc' using what he referred to as a 'Rolls Royce information campaign'.[24]

Powell went on to add a number of other points for Blair's consideration and, significantly, Blair had handwritten his approval at the top of the page: 'I agree with this entirely'. Yet again we see evidence that the mindset in the Prime Minister's office, and in Blair himself, was driven by regime change, or as Powell put it, 'getting rid of Saddam'. Everything from the legal case to the information campaign would provide the means of achieving Blair's primary intention: getting rid of Saddam.

Despite stating that the legal basis would have to be WMD – because of restrictions emanating from advice given elsewhere by the Attorney General – it is clear that Powell and Blair were planning to set out moral arguments, framed in terms of the abuse of human rights, as part of their 'Rolls Royce' information campaign. One of the disturbing aspects of this interchange between Blair and his chief of staff is the blithe indifference that is exhibited over the matter of proposing and creating what would be a propaganda campaign against the British people to shape their attitudes and actions in respect of Iraq. Jack Straw as Foreign Secretary preferred the euphemism, 'preparation of public opinion', one of Blair's conditions for UK involvement.[25]

The extent to which the propaganda campaign succeeded is open to debate. On the one hand Blair ultimately achieved his aim of regime change, while on the other he did it without ever having strong backing from the British people. While Blair's Iraq arguments linger in the minds of the British public, MPs and members of the public will demand a level of evidence and imminence of threat far greater than that offered by Blair. A more immediate judgement of the events at that time was given by Lord Wilson, Cabinet Secretary from 1998 to September 2002. He said of the Cabinet meeting on 23 July 2002: 'what struck me was that some of the language used implied that we were closer to military action than I had imagined that we were'.[26]

By September 2002 the issue of Saddam Hussein and possible war with Iraq came to dominate British and global politics. Blair's words to his chief of staff six months previously concerning the need to reorder the message about Saddam and focus more on the nature of his regime can be seen played out in many of Blair's public speeches. In his monthly press conference on 3 September Blair was asked whether regime change was now British foreign policy. He went on to talk about the threat from Saddam and the need to deal with the problem via the UN. He then went into great detail about the crimes that had been committed, or allegedly committed, by Saddam's regime, going on to issue a stark warning:

> We are dealing with a regime that routinely tortures and executes its political opponents, that probably was responsible for up to 100 000 Kurdish people dying in a brutal campaign in order to enforce Iraqi rule, we are talking about a regime that was responsible for a million people dying in the Iran–Iraq war, the annexation of Kuwait and that we know, because this is why the resolutions are there, was trying to develop these appalling weapons and indeed actually used these weapons against their own people. Now the issue is making sure it is not a threat and either the regime starts to function in an entirely different way, and there hasn't been much sign of that, or the regime has to change. That is the choice, very simply.[27]

Despite the warnings from the Attorney General that regime change could not be used as a *casus belli* and Blair's extolling of the UN as the way to deal with Saddam, he kept returning to the theme of removing Saddam. In this exchange Blair was speaking about the threat that Iraq posed. However, rather than setting out the ways in which the *threat* would be contained or removed Blair preferred to go down the route of 'the regime has to change'.[28] Now it may have been the case that removing the threat without also removing the regime would be difficult or impossible, but Blair went straight to regime change as a response to Saddam and his government failing to change their behaviour. With British public opinion hardening against an attack on Iraq Blair indicated that he would release a dossier on Saddam and Iraq's WMD in the near future. For all the talk of a Rolls Royce information campaign, Blair was not managing to shift public opinion in his favour.

When the dossier on Saddam's WMD was finally released on 24 September 2002, it resulted in more questions than answers, as the previous chapter highlighted. What it did not do was provide overwhelming evidence against Saddam that turned the tide of public opinion towards military action. Blair was giving out mixed messages in his determination to keep the issues of WMD threat and the nature of

Saddam's regime firmly linked in the eyes and ears of those who were following developments. By the time Blair had a meeting with the Attorney General on 22 October one of the subjects to be discussed was regime change. The Attorney General later conveyed the strong impression that Blair was not following the advice that had been given to the Prime Minister only three months earlier. The Attorney General recalled: 'One of [the issues] was regime change. I'm not sure whether I needed to repeat that again in October, but it was a constant theme.'[29] The mere fact that the Attorney General saw fit to raise the matter again with Blair points to the extent that Blair was continuing to speak of the matter – egged on by a press corps that consistently wanted to ask him about regime change.

Blair's quandary was kept alive and even made more difficult by his senior coalition partner Bush. Bush continued to be clear and unequivocal about his intentions regarding Saddam Hussein and on 21 October he reiterated his position: 'The stated policy of the United States is regime change.'[30] This statement was made at a time when the US and the UK were negotiating intensively with the other permanent members of the Security Council towards Resolution 1441. Bush's public utterances on his determination to achieve regime change undermined attempts to secure a UN resolution when regime change as a policy contradicted international law. Blair's close association with Bush, as well as all of the evidence that pointed to and still points to Blair sharing Bush's views on regime change, consistently undermined his own appeals to the UN and his stated desire to seek approval from the Security Council for military action.

Following his latest meeting with the Attorney General in October 2002 Blair seemed finally to get the message that he had to stop referring to regime change and present his case solely in terms of the UN and the need for the Security Council to enforce the resolutions that had been passed against Saddam and Iraq: hence Resolution 1441. Despite his more careful choice of words in the final weeks of 2002, the best efforts of his communications team and the information campaign that he was pursuing to convince the British people of the merits of supporting military action against Iraq, people were still not buying the message that Blair was selling. Even worse, Cabinet could not be described as supportive and neither could the Labour Party or its elected MPs. Blair later recalled his own position as 2002 drew to a close and paints it as very bleak:

> I was about as isolated as it was possible to be in politics. On the one
> hand, the US were chafing at the bit and essentially I agreed with

their basic thrust: Saddam was a threat, he would never cooperate fully with the international community, and the world, not to say Iraq, would be better off with him out of power.[31]

If Blair was isolated at that time he did not need to go far to find the cause. The Labour members who had elected him to lead their political party and the voting public who elected the New Labour government were largely opposed to going in the direction he wanted to lead them. However, he still had some political advantages that allowed him to proceed even without majority public support. After Blair won the 2001 General Election by a landslide, such was his overwhelming majority in the House of Commons that he was virtually unassailable: as close to an elected dictator as the British political system will allow. His powers of patronage combined with the ambitions of individual MPs ensured that many of those who were not enthusiastic about his direction of travel would continue to support or at least tolerate him.

Throughout December 2002 and January 2003 Blair remained 'on message' about WMD, the UN and the need to force Saddam into compliance with Security Council resolutions. In his speeches and press conferences he managed to steer away from the thorny issue that the US already had its self-granted authority and viewed the UN route with barely disguised indifference. If it proved to be politically advantageous then the US would continue with the UN approach but if it came to be problematic then the operation to change the Iraqi regime would proceed anyway. Blair spoke regularly of getting a second UN resolution and appeared confident that he would get one. By February 2003, however, Blair's confidence that he would obtain a second UN resolution started to wane rapidly. In addition, his Attorney General was still of the view that the second UN resolution would be highly preferable and probably essential. The senior lawyers at the Foreign Office still considered that any war with Iraq would be illegal without a subsequent UN resolution.

More problematic for Blair, Bush and other pro-interventionists was the speech given by Hans Blix, head of the UN weapons inspection teams on 14 February at the UN.[32] Instead of producing the anticipated 'smoking gun' evidence against Saddam, Blix reported that the Iraqis were, by and large, cooperating with his staff and that no WMD had been found. He also reported that amounts of chemical and biological agent had not yet been accounted for, though Iraq claimed that it had unilaterally destroyed stocks of anthrax and VX nerve agent. While not satisfying the demands of the US and UK in full, Saddam was providing greater cooperation to the UN inspectors than he had at any point previously. Far from being a source of satisfaction in London and Washington, Blix's report created the biggest problem yet faced: it was eroding the already flimsy foundations upon which military action was to be based. Robin Cook spoke to the heart of the matter when he described the obvious consequence of successful inspections which produced no evidence against Saddam – they reduced the case for military action.[33]

Then came one of the biggest protest marches in British history. On Sunday 16 February 2003 anti-war protestors descended on London from all over the UK and elsewhere. Attendance estimates varied, with police claiming a total of 750 000 marchers and the organizers claiming a figure of around two million. Whatever the actual number the visual impact was huge, as was the growing pressure on Blair and his government. His legal argument was disappearing as quickly as it took the UN weapons inspectors to get round the sites where WMD would allegedly be found. It also became increasingly clear that France, Russia and China would refuse to back another Security Council resolution explicitly authorizing the use of force against Saddam and Iraq. With all this in mind it should come as no surprise to discover that Blair openly and explicitly fell back on the moral case against Saddam and started to speak of that-which-would-not-be-mentioned in previous weeks: regime change. On 18 February he once again publicly compared the Iraq situation to the cases of Kosovo and Afghanistan:

> I think that whereas in relation to Kosovo or Afghanistan there was a very immediate casus belli if you like, an act that people could see was a provocation that we had to act against, it is more difficult to persuade people of the link between a state like Iraq with chemical, or biological, or nuclear weapons and the link with international terrorism. Now I believe it is our job to carry on trying to persuade people of that, and also to persuade people of the *moral case for removing Saddam*, who is a murderous and brutal dictator who has caused death and destruction to thousands, indeed millions of his fellow citizens.[34]

Blair made a serious miscalculation in trying to gain public support for his political ambitions for Iraq by presenting the moral case for military action against Saddam and his brutal, repressive regime at that stage. What he failed to appreciate was that most people with a modicum of intelligence and a vague awareness of world events, even if they were unable to actually pinpoint Iraq in an atlas of the world, *knew* or at least believed Saddam was a bad man by almost any moral calculation. They just did not feel strongly enough to launch a war against him since the hard evidence of him posing a major threat to either the UK or international peace and security was woefully inadequate.

The legal contortions undertaken by Blair and his Attorney General over the subsequent weeks as the invasion approached have been addressed already. With legal authority from the Attorney General granted, coalition forces attacked Iraq on 19 March 2003. On 20 March Blair addressed the nation and began his speech as follows:

> On Tuesday night I gave the order for British forces to take part in military action in Iraq.
>
> Tonight, British servicemen and women are engaged from air, land and sea. Their mission: to remove Saddam Hussein from power, and disarm Iraq of its weapons of mass destruction.[35]

In his choice of words Blair remained remarkably consistent with the argument I have put forward in this chapter: that regime change was his priority and his intention, with WMD providing the legal and policy means by which his intention could be achieved. According to Blair the mission of British servicemen and women was to 'remove Saddam Hussein from power, and disarm Iraq of its weapons of mass destruction'.[36] From November through to February Blair had kept away from the regime change argument, describing it as something that would occur in the process of removing Iraq's WMD threat. In his speech on 20 March he could have said, 'their mission is to disarm Iraq of its weapons of mass destruction', but he chose to speak of removing Saddam from power (regime change) first.

Some may feel that I place too much weight on the sequencing of these words or that I am too obsessed with the details. Maybe I am. Consider this though. Blair's premiership was built on the power of communication. From his description of 'the People's Princess' to his being a 'straight sort of guy' to the voice tremors as he spoke of the Queen Mother's death, every tiny detail was significant and well prepared. When Blair and Alastair Campbell were falsely accused of 'sexing up' the Iraq dossier all hell broke loose on a matter of detail. I attach no more or less significance to the details as Blair and his communications team did; we merely interpret them differently. Most importantly, and forgotten in much of what is said about Blair and Iraq, those who lost their lives in Iraq – of whatever nationality – and their grieving families deserve attention to detail. It matters to them why a son or a daughter or a partner or an arm or a face was lost: pursuing regime change as a primary intention or removing WMD as a primary intention.

Blair continued and continues to provide support for the argument that he prioritized the moral case over the legal case, regime change above WMD. In his book he wrote of the time when the second UN resolution looked unlikely to be achieved: 'I knew in the final analysis I would be with the US, because in my view it was right, morally and strategically.'[37] Blair refers to the moral position first, then the strategic position, with no mention of the legal case.

On 24 March 2003 Blair appeared in Parliament to tell the listening MPs and the British people: 'We are now just four days into this conflict. It is worth restating our central objectives. They are to remove Saddam Hussein from power and ensure Iraq is disarmed of all chemical, biological and nuclear weapons programmes.'[38] No matter how many times Blair insisted that removing WMD and forcing Iraq's compliance with UN resolutions was at the heart of his case for war – especially his legal case – time and time again he led with the desire to remove Saddam Hussein from power. His written account looked back on the events leading up to the invasion, especially the importance of working with other nations in a complex political environment: 'That is why building a coalition to topple Saddam Hussein mattered.'[39]

It is instructive that of all the reasons Blair listed by way of explanation for the course of action taken – purpose, moral and geopolitical rationale and objectives – notable for its absence is any mention of the legal basis for war. This may reflect Blair's wider attitude to intervention, and I believe it does, or it may just reflect the particular difficulties of the Iraq action, resulting in a decision, conscious or subconscious, not to mention international law. Blair's subsequent comment on the purpose of coalition building is equally revealing: 'to topple Saddam Hussein'.[40] Again, the desire for regime change writ large.

Summary

Regime change lay at the heart of Blair's interventionism, from his first use of military power against Slobodan Milosevic and Serbia to the thunder of the shock and awe air campaign against Iraq. To his intense frustration the moral arguments that appear to have been sufficient to prompt international military action and the removal of Milosevic and Sierra Leone's rebel leader Foday Sankoh, were not deemed sufficient to justify the removal of Saddam Hussein. It was clear for more than a year before the 2003 invasion of Iraq that Blair wanted to remove Saddam and his regime from power and his intention was matched and more by President George W. Bush and his administration.

Once Iraq was raised by Bush and Blair as a political problem to be dealt with it quickly became clear from a UK perspective that the constraints of international law encapsulated in the UN Charter would not be so easily set aside or ignored as they had been on previous occasions. The UN route and the legal dimension would therefore provide the means by which Blair could achieve the political outcome he desired, based on his moral certainty that ridding Iraq of Saddam Hussein was the right thing to do. Blair even made this prioritizing of regime change explicit:

> The objectives for both President Bush and myself in trying to secure a fresh resolution were clear: to give Saddam one final chance to comply; and make it clear if he didn't, then we would act, if necessary by force. In other words: change of heart or change of regime.[41]

Blair was not saying, change your approach or we will force you to comply. He was clearly and consistently advocating regime change. On one level, this is semantics. It would be very difficult to force Iraq's compliance with UN resolutions and still leave Saddam in place. However, the semantics are important because they lie at the heart of a key just war concept – the need to pursue war for a right intention – in relation to Blair and Iraq.

The difference is this. If regime change was always Blair's primary intention then he was adopting a legal position contrary to the letter of international law and a moral position contrary to the foundations on which international law was built. His Attorney General advised him in July 2002 that regime change was illegal under international law. If his intention was to uphold international law by forcing Saddam's compliance with UNSCRs then, as long as he could get the support of the UN Security Council, his moral intentions would be consistent with international law. Based on Blair's own speeches and writings it seems clear that his priority was regime change as a matter of personal moral conviction, with UN compliance being a second order political means of achieving his primary goal. In addition, however, even from a moral perspective regime change would be unacceptable as a political goal. The eminent just war theorist Michael Walzer rejected regime change as a just cause for going to war.[42]

Despite Blair's insistence on a number of occasions that ridding Iraq of WMD was his reason for invading Iraq, he kept falling back on the issue of regime change and ridding the world of a tyrant. Blair repeatedly provided ammunition for his critics who accuse him of being duplicitous about his motivations when he varied his answers according to the audience before him. My own view is that he was a convinced regime changer from the beginning, based on strongly held *moral* arguments. His pronouncements on ridding Saddam and Iraq of WMD were not based on the same degree of personal conviction but were motivated by the strategic need to provide the veneer of a legal basis for the invasion as a means of gaining or maintaining a measure of political and public support. He concluded his account of the 2003 Iraq intervention by, again, pointing to Saddam and not the WMD: 'All I know is that I did what I thought was right. I stood by America when it needed standing by. Together we rid the world of a tyrant.'[43]

Chapter 6 explores the first of two pillars of Blair's moral case: the need to confront tyranny. By considering both historical and contemporary argument the chapter shows why this aspect of Blair's moral case for military action against Saddam was ultimately unconvincing.

6
Confronting tyranny

Once Blair made it clear to his chief of staff that he wanted increasingly to make the Iraq 'story' about the nature of Saddam's regime, he was committed to a corresponding dependence on moral arguments. Looking back, it is easy to see why such an approach would appeal to him. Knowingly or otherwise, he had used ancient just war concepts when constructing his Doctrine of the International Community in 1999, particularly the part that dealt with intervention. From Kosovo to Sierra Leone to Iraq, one of the strongest elements of his interventionist discourse was the need to protect the weak and vulnerable from oppression and death at the hands of tyrants.

Amid the uncertainties of his legal case for military action against Saddam and against the backdrop of increasing political and public opposition to his desire for intervention, the moral case bolstered Blair's arguments and undermined the case of those who opposed him. The central theme of this moral approach to Iraq would follow the example of previous interventions and concentrate on the need to help those who were being harmed, and their human rights crushed, by a cruel dictator. Blair sustained this tactic throughout the year prior to the invasion and, on the eve of war, concluded his statement to Parliament with a call to arms based on his moral case:

> This is not the time to falter. This is the time for this House, not just this government or indeed this Prime Minister, but for this House to give a lead, to show that we will stand up for what we know to be right, to show that we will confront the tyrannies and dictatorships and terrorists who put our way of life at risk, to show at the moment of decision that we have the courage to do the right thing.[1]

Blair's final appeal was based not on compelling legal evidence but on 'what we know to be right'.[2] Being 'right' was a moral and not a legal claim. He invited his audience to share in his knowing what was right – that Saddam was a monstrous individual – and then to do what he suggested morally upright people should do: act against Saddam.

In the course of this chapter I assess different strands of Blair's moral argument as he sought to intervene and oppose the tyranny that he argued was at work in Iraq and would be extended if Saddam colluded with terrorists. In so doing I necessarily make a temporary and artificial distinction between opposing the tyrant and defending the victims of the tyrant, with the latter being addressed in the next chapter: opposing tyranny and defending the weak being, morally speaking, two sides of the same coin. The first strand looks at the classical just war principle of just punishment in relation to the actions of Saddam and his regime. Previous atrocities conducted under Saddam's authority include the use of chemical weapons against Iraqi Kurds in 1988 and the violent subjugation of Iraqi Shias during an uprising in 1991, including the displacement of vast numbers of Shia Marsh Arabs. The second strand examines the extent to which Blair's proposed intervention in Iraq could be seen as pre-emptive action against an imminent danger and how much of it could be deemed preventive: ensuring that a threat does not become viable at some point in the future. The final strand of this discussion explores Blair's use of religious imagery and language, most notably his casting of Saddam as an evil tyrant that any good person should want to oppose. Throughout, in making an assessment of this aspect of Blair's moral case, it is set against the backdrop of the just war tradition and examples of opposing tyranny that have emerged within it over the centuries.

Just punishment

Over several millennia, the idea of using military force as a means of achieving justice has emerged in philosophical debate, been incorporated into Christian theology and then relocated into the legal frameworks we see today. This has not been the smooth, conceptual transition that talk of a just war *tradition* is often taken to imply. The just war tradition has been influenced by violence, dispute, war and cultural upheaval every bit as much, and possibly more, than war has been shaped or limited by the ideas of the just war tradition. Some of the ideas of Augustine retain their power to inspire as effectively as when they were written 1600 years ago, although his references to God are now a source of shock, dismay and offence to many. From among the many commentaries on war and morality in his vast *oeuvre* came the following:

> The desire for harming, the cruelty of revenge, the restless and implacable mind, the savageness of revolting, the lust for dominating, and similar things – these are what are justly blamed in wars. Often, so that such things might also be justly punished, certain wars that must be waged against the violence of those resisting are commanded by God or some other legitimate ruler and are undertaken by the good.[3]

Here Augustine describes those who could legitimately be opposed by a just war – in this case perhaps more rightly referred to as just punishment. The characteristics that expose individuals to just punishment in war include cruelty, vengefulness and savagery. In addition, a specifically religious judgement of these vile individuals features in his writings. Good or legitimate rulers were instructed (somehow) by God to chastise those who ignored divine commands and who usurped the divine order that God instituted on earth.

This punitive aspect of Augustine's just war has recently been advocated as a *casus belli* by Elshtain in *Just War Against Terror*, both in the context of Afghanistan as a means of punishing the perpetrators of 9/11, and the need to punish Saddam Hussein and his regime for atrocities committed against the Kurds, Marsh Arabs and Shia Muslims in the 1980s and 1990s.[4] Elshtain takes a positive view of President Bush in relation to the punishment meted out in Afghanistan and Iraq. Elshtain also passes a judgement on the current international political system when she writes: 'It is a striking, and saddening, commentary that the emphasis had to be placed on the danger of WMD since Saddam's well-documented mass murder of his own people did not rise to the level of a *casus belli* in and of itself.'[5] It is easy to see why she identified herself with Blair and his moral case for confronting Iraq and Saddam.

Elshtain drew upon the Augustinian – or what she sometimes refers to as 'classical' – *jus ad bellum* precept of punitive war in support of a liberal view of military intervention because the UN Charter does not allow such action. What can be argued as just in her historically-oriented moral paradigm cannot necessarily be argued as lawful in today's legalist paradigm. However, Elshtain's resort to Augustine's arguments here is only partial. She excludes a key aspect of his discourse while applying his ideas in the present: the philosophical and theological underpinnings on which his just war theory was based. She fails to make clear the purpose of Augustine's punitive war against the cruel tyrant: to obey

God's commands and maintain God's order. Augustine's punitive war took place in support of his sovereign God, while Elshtain's punitive war argument today transgresses the rights of the sovereign state.[6]

The idea of opposing tyranny has appeared in different guises in the just war tradition. Several centuries after Augustine, Aquinas wrestled with whether or not Christians had a duty to obey tyrants. The dilemma at the core of Aquinas's deliberations brought together two opposing ideas. On the one hand there was Aquinas's theologically-driven desire to maintain divine order, even where that meant a tyrant would hold sway over the lives of the innocent. If authority was somehow rooted in God then to challenge a tyrant's authority would be to undermine God. Even where authority could be shown to have been acquired illegitimately there was not an automatic right to challenge the ruler, who may go on to govern effectively.[7] However, where the tyrant maintained rule through unjust violence against the innocent the divine order would be violated. Therefore, for Aquinas this would be 'an impediment to rightful authority, for he who seizes power by violence does not become a ruler or lord truly; and so anyone can reject such authority when the opportunity arises'.[8]

Aquinas was not entirely responsible for the idea that tyrants could be forcibly challenged. He drew upon the works of Marcus Tullius Cicero, Roman philosopher and political theorist, who wrote shortly before the Christian period. Cicero granted that a man of upright character could legitimately put a tyrant to the sword for the wider benefit of society.[9] Even taking into account the political context in which Cicero was writing (he was sympathetic towards those who had recently killed the tyrannical Caesar) the balance of justice fell on the side of the innocent who were being oppressed by the tyrant. Such an interpretation of justice lent itself to inclusion in the writings of Aquinas who adopted and adapted Cicero's ideas into his wider Christian writings.

In Cicero's enthusiasm for opposing the tyrant we can see a philosophical argument of the type later deployed by Blair with regard to Iraq. The appeal of Cicero's idea, even when translated into the minefield of twenty-first century politics, is that it does not rely on any specific understanding of statehood or sovereignty. Instead, tyrants were to be excluded from the whole community of humanity. If the whole of humanity would benefit from the removal of the tyrant then, in theory, any upstanding representative of that vast community could undertake the act of deposing the tyrant. In addition, Cicero's ideas were not encumbered with the complex theological underpinnings that characterized the works of the later Christian just war theorists.

In 1625 Hugo Grotius made a pivotal contribution not only to the just war tradition but the subsequent development of what would become the international political system and international law we find today. Where just war had previously been dominated by Christian, mainly Catholic, theologians, Grotius took the first steps towards a secular just war set in a legal framework. In his extensive works we find a complex and, at times, seemingly random relationship between moral arguments and legal arguments surrounding war. The reason for the complexity and ambiguity in his writings stems from the way he incorporated historical ideas into his own work. For example, Grotius would happily cite Greek philosophers, Romans legalists and Christian theologians in the framing of his arguments. The result was often confusing and anyone who has wrestled with his weighty texts will testify to the difficulties of identifying a single or even coherent philosophical basis for his work. Subsequent writers in the moralist tradition of war and theorists in the developing field of international law would take Grotius's ideas in different directions. The one thing that both of these schools of thought had in common was the way they continued Grotius's attempts to shift ideas surrounding war from a basis in divine revelation to a basis in the application of human reason.

According to Grotius there were three just causes for war: self-defence, recovery of something that had been taken, and just punishment.[10] In keeping with his general approach Grotius was not making an original proposal about the causes for war, rather he was summarizing the works of the ancients, including Plato, Seneca and Sallust. He was probably closest to Aquinas on the matter of just cause for war, who in turn remained Augustinian in his outlook. Aquinas quoted Augustine in naming the righting of wrongs, the punishment of a nation or the restoration of stolen property as just causes for war.[11] These causes for war were set out in terms of actions that had been committed in the past or currently being committed. He went further and added defence and revenge to his just causes for war.[12]

None of these historical just causes for war obviously lends itself to increasing our understanding of Blair and his Iraq discourse. Defence, or self-defence, was ruled out as a justification by the Attorney General since Saddam posed no direct threat to the UK. Recovery of property seized by Saddam could never have been a British argument since he had not taken anything that belonged to the UK. The final argument, just punishment, may well have had some resonance with Blair's case, which extensively referred to Saddam's tyrannical actions in the past, but it was never put forward as an explicit justification. The difficulty with just punishment as an argument against the Iraqi leader is that the concept would itself violate the legal norms encapsulated in the UN Charter. In addition, if Saddam's actions were punishable in the context of the international system, as opposed to Iraq's domestic laws, the appropriate place for dealing with him would probably have been the International Criminal Court (ICC). Ironically, two of the seven countries that voted against the Rome Statute of the International Criminal Court were Iraq and the US. The US was therefore extremely unlikely to pursue the prosecution of Saddam through the ICC when it rejects the court's jurisdiction over its own citizens.

Blair's repeated references to Saddam's gassing of the Kurds in 1988 and the killings of the Iraqi Shias potentially lend themselves to a just punishment reading. Both events occurred more than a decade earlier and there was no suggestion in 2002/3 that Saddam was about to repeat his actions against his fellow Iraqis. So the inclusion of these examples in Blair's moral arguments could not be viewed as part of an ongoing or imminent danger. So, Blair did not propose invasion as a punishment for past acts and there was no ongoing major chemical or genocide threat against Iraqi groups at that time. The only option left if Blair's arguments were to have any relevance in 2002/3 was that Saddam and his regime would pose some unspecified threat in the future. This approach had its own difficulties because it was moving into the realm of preventive war: ensuring that some potential or imagined future threat did not arise.

Preventative action

To the three just causes for war specified above – for previous or ongoing transgressions by an enemy – Grotius added another, which we might call either pre-emptive or preventive. A ruler could act against even the *threat* of an aggressor.[13] However, this just cause for war is constituted differently from those previously mentioned. The legal paradigm that provides the foundation for the first three of Grotius's stated just causes cannot support the fourth because a crime has not yet been committed for which self-defence, restitution or punishment is due. At this point Grotius's argument became individualized. The ethical ruler did not fight for a just cause in response to a crime that had already been committed; individuals became ethical in the act of opposing an aggressor who would inflict a *future* crime.

For Blair, the relevance of Saddam's attacks against his own people appears to be that such behaviour pointed towards a future capacity or intention to act in such a way again. From April 2002 to the invasion in March 2003 one of Blair's most consistent moral arguments against Saddam was that he had used WMD against his own people and had committed genocide against them. The constant suggestion was that without military action against Saddam he would repeat these atrocities in the future. The basis of Blair's reasoning would appear to be speculation, built on a hunch and reinforced by guesswork. If Blair had gone down the 'just punishment' route with his case against Saddam it would at least have had some basis in just war history and early ideas in international law. Instead, Blair's repeated reliance on factually accurate references to Saddam's past conduct, projected forward onto an imagined future, merely highlighted the weakness of the available evidence against the Iraqi leader in the present (that is, in 2002/3).

In his 1758 book, *Law of Nations*, Emer de Vattel went beyond the historical causes for war advocated by Grotius and his predecessors and added a further reason for resorting to military force. He wrote that a state fighting with a just cause had the right to weaken an enemy or potential enemy as a way of insuring against future violence.[14] This right can be described as preventive, ensuring that an enemy would remain weak for a considerable time and therefore pose no threat in the future. In advocating the prevention of a future threat Vattel provided a discourse that was present in intervention debate surrounding Iraq.

On 1 June 2002 President Bush addressed the graduating class at West Point Military Academy. He set out the way in which the war on terror would be fought: 'We must take the battle to the enemy, disrupt his plans, and confront the worst threats before they emerge.'[15] Bush sought to conflate preventive war against some future threat with pre-emptive war which usually takes place against a specific, imminent threat: or, to use another American expression, against a clear and present danger. Bush continued: 'our security will require all Americans to be forward-looking and resolute, to be ready for preemptive action when necessary to defend our liberty and to defend our lives.'[16]

Neither Bush nor Blair, in their advocacy of preventive military action, was presenting an original argument. More than two centuries earlier Vattel granted that, in certain circumstances, one sovereign power may intervene in the affairs of another. Where a tyrant was savagely brutalizing his own people, Vattel allowed that another sovereign power – if asked for help by those being oppressed – could intervene to remove, even kill, that tyrant.[17]

Two aspects of Vattel's position here are relevant to this analysis of Blair's justification of the 2003 intervention in Iraq. First, Vattel granted a limited right of intervention on the condition that abused subjects implored the assistance of a foreign power. In this regard, the foreign power would be allowed to intervene to help the side that appeared to have the more just case.[18] Elshtain, in justifying military action against Iraq, specifically invoked the 'attempted genocide against the Kurds; his destruction of the entire way of life of the Marsh Arabs; and his mass murders against the Shiite Muslims in the aftermath of the 1991 Gulf War'.[19] In each case these peoples of different areas of Iraq pleaded for external help at the height of the atrocities committed against them and in each case the lack of international response left Saddam Hussein in power. The failure to stop the 1991 atrocities reflects particularly badly on the UK, US and other members of the international coalition that still had significant military assets just across the Iraqi border at that time. The degree of suffering endured by the Kurdish Iraqis in the 1988 chemical weapon attacks may well have reached Vattel's threshold for an exemption to his normally strict observance of sovereignty and associated right to non-intervention. However, such an exemption does not exist today in a strict reading of the UN Charter.

The second aspect of Vattel's position on intervention that is relevant to this discussion is the role of the ethical individual. Vattel did not just frame his argument in terms of international law and his conception of sovereignty: the character of the tyrannical prince or sovereign played a significant role. He described tyrannical sovereigns as 'monsters ... scourges and horror of the human race, they are savage beasts'.[20] The ethical individual – 'the brave man' – was the sovereign who intervened in such situations to 'justly exterminate [the tyrant] from the face of the earth'.[21] When he said, 'Let us congratulate our age on the superior gentleness of it manners', it was not just because of any intrinsic value of political leaders, rather it was because they were 'productive of real and substantial effects'.[22] These substantial and real effects include the defeat and subjugation of the tyrant. Under Vattel's just war and emerging legal framework the arguments of both Blair and Bush would be considered both moral and legal. Furthermore, in Vattel's *schema*, as the rulers who acted to remove Saddam the tyrant the mere act of opposition in itself would constitute them as ethical.

Vattel's notions of preventing future threats and removing the threat posed by monsters whose presence is a scourge on the human race were captured by Elshtain in her justification of the 2003 Iraq invasion. Elshtain argued: 'There was massive and, to my mind, sufficient evidence of the threat [from WMD] before the war'.[23] She continued:

> Even more important – or at least as important – were the well-documented and continuing crimes against humanity perpetrated

on the bodies of the Iraqi people by the Saddam regime. I concluded before the Iraq war, and I continue to believe, that the first criterion [just cause] of a just war was met ... A world with one fewer brutal 'disturbers of the peace' would, by definition, be a more peaceful world over the long-haul.[24]

Elshtain's just cause argument comprised two elements. The first was that Saddam Hussein posed a threat to wider humanity – a globalized version of Grotius's Euro-centric notion of human society – rather than the United States necessarily, through his acquisition (*sic*) of WMD. In the second element she constituted Saddam Hussein as the Other – a brutal disturber of the peace – based on actions against his own populace which Elshtain described as crimes against humanity. These, she contended, were deserving of military action against him and his regime, even though no external attack against a neighbour was imminent. The latter argument corresponded closely to earlier ideas in the just war tradition. Grotius was keen to oppose the beastly leader who was preparing to mount an attack,[25] while Vattel granted that rulers who wielded sovereign power had the right to intervene on behalf of oppressed peoples.[26] Elshtain necessarily relied on the principle of opposition to Saddam Hussein as Other because he had – at the time of the invasion – committed no new crime for which he was liable to be punished under the codes of international law. When viewed together, Blair's approach was consistent with Elshtain's just war ideas in the present and the earlier just war arguments from the seventeenth and eighteenth centuries respectively.

While Walzer adopted a more sceptical position than Elshtain regarding the justification of the 2003 invasion of Iraq, and about intervention more generally, his just war employs an approach to humanitarian intervention that has a basis in Grotius's theorizing. He granted that in some circumstances, 'Humanitarian intervention is justified when it is a response ... to acts "that shock the moral conscience of mankind"'.[27] And these acts, for Walzer, involve 'enslavement or massacre' on a huge scale.[28] However, while ideas in Grotius's and Vattel's just war made it possible for Elshtain and Walzer to construct their own positions on intervention, the degree of tyranny required to justify intervention remains open to dispute. Walzer set a higher threshold of tyranny than Elshtain, while Elshtain buttressed her argument by adding external perceived threat to internal tyranny. Furthermore, Walzer maintained his reluctance to transgress sovereign borders and the codes that govern international relations.

When, after the 2003 Iraq War, Walzer reflected on the events that took place he concluded: 'Yes, the norm is not to intervene in other people's countries; the norm is self-determination. But not for *these* people, the victims of tyranny, ideological zeal, ethnic hatred, who are not determining anything for themselves, who urgently need help from outside.'[29] It is difficult to avoid the traces of Grotius's and Vattel's words in Walzer's justification of forceful intervention, even as the exception to his principle of non-intervention: 'Whenever the filthy work can be stopped, it should be stopped. And if not by us, the supposedly decent people of this world, then by whom?'[30]

Blair, speaking to the Iraq Inquiry, recalled what 'people' – though he did not specify who the 'people' were – were saying to him as he was making his decision to invade Iraq: 'Look, you can't sit around and wait for this [threat to come to fruition]. You know, you have got to take action and to take action clearly and definitively.'[31] The use of military power advocated here by Blair is presented as the exercise of virtue in the context of intervention. This preventive view of intervention was shared by Bush and presented at a shared press conference with Blair on 31 January 2003:

> See, the strategic view of America changed after 11 September. We must deal with threats before they hurt the American people again. And as I have said repeatedly, Saddam Hussein would like nothing more than to use a terrorist network to attack and to kill and leave no fingerprints behind.[32]

When Bush made this statement he was, at the very least, stretching the concept of pre-emptive strike towards a preventive doctrine. Understandably, he saw it as his responsibility to ensure that the American people were protected against future strikes but nothing in his words pointed to an impending attack against the US. Saddam Hussein may well have liked 'nothing more than to use a terrorist network' to hit out against the West, the US and UK in particular. However, Bush was only speculating. Nothing in Saddam's previous behaviour pointed to connections with international terrorism, especially not Islamist terrorism. His secular Ba'ath Party was ideologically opposed to the religiosity espoused by Al-Qaeda and there was no evidence to suggest any connection to the 9/11 attacks.

Several weeks earlier Blair had been even more specific about taking preventive action. Three days after Resolution 1441 was passed by the Security Council he stated:

> Tonight I want to take you through the dilemma that confronts us in meeting this threat and explain to you our strategy for it.

The purpose of terrorism is of course not just to kill and maim. As the name suggests, terrorism is about terror. It is to scare people, disrupt their normal lives, produce chaos and disorder, distort proper and sensible decision-making. The dilemma is reconciling warning people with alarming them; taking *preventive* measures without destroying normal life.[33]

Blair was speaking about taking preventive measures as a means of ensuring that lives were not threatened or taken in the future on the streets of the UK. Given the extent to which he associated Saddam, WMD and terrorism in his speeches it is unrealistic to expect that he was approaching Saddam and the Iraq question with any less commitment to preventive measures. Let us return to Blair's main approach to winning support for action against Saddam: making the argument about the nature of the regime and about the character of Saddam.

Deliver us from evil

When Blair spoke of confronting 'tyrannies and dictatorships'[34] in 2003 his arguments used language synonymous with that used in numerous historical and contemporary moral arguments from the just war tradition. Furthermore, in claiming that the nature of a despotic regime provided, in itself, sufficient basis for its removal, Blair's argument resonated with that made by Cicero two millennia earlier.[35] On the eve of the 2003 invasion Blair's Iraq discourse did not consist solely of a calm, measured assessment of his legal case for intervention based on an imminent military threat to UK or its interests. Nor was his argument simply presented in line with his own five criteria for just intervention proposed in April 1999. The following excerpts from Blair's statement to Parliament on the eve of the invasion highlight a number of aspects of Blair's moral argument, which elaborated on the nature of the Iraqi regime and called for action against the tyrant who was responsible for countless acts of brutality:

Saddam had used [WMD] against Iran, against his own people, causing thousands of deaths...

We can look back and say: there's the time; that was the moment; for example, when Czechoslovakia was swallowed up by the Nazis – that's when we should have acted ... Naturally should Hitler appear again in the same form, we would know what to do. But the point is that history doesn't declare the future to us so plainly. Each time is different and the present must be judged without the benefit of hindsight...[36]

Blair later acknowledged that he chose to finish his statement by setting out the moral case so effectively captured in the final paragraph quoted here.[37] This is fascinating because the key points he focused on are the moral arguments that formed no part of his UN-focused legal case. Blair set out a stark description of what Saddam's brutality meant in the experience of his victims, inciting his listeners to join him in opposing such a monster: the only ethical response that a reasonable person could make. The implication being that anyone who preferred to leave Saddam in place would be morally complicit in his tyranny. Yet this is only one aspect of Blair's creative use of moral argument identified here. Let us, in turn, consider examples of Saddam's tyranny set out by Blair and listed above: his use of WMD against his own people and the parallel with Hitler.

On 16 March 1988 chemical attacks ordered by Saddam against the Kurdish town of Halabja were orchestrated by his cousin General Ali Hassan al-Majid, subsequently known as Chemical Ali. As the Iran–Iraq war was nearing its conclusion, recognizing that the US was unlikely to strongly censure any actions taken against his Iranian enemy, Saddam had escalated his use of weaponized poison gas. The diplomatic events that followed Saddam's chemical attacks brought no credit to either the US or the UK. The strident criticism of Saddam and his regime over the gassing of the Kurds that would later become a feature of both Blair's and Bush's case for the 2003 war against Iraq, was strikingly absent from the UN's response to the event. So reluctant was the US to criticize Iraq, which was at that time a political bulwark against its bigger enemy Iran, it took eight weeks to produce a UN Security Council Resolution condemning the action. Under pressure from the US and UK, Resolution 612 did not even single out Iraq for criticism, stating instead that the Security Council '*Expects* both sides to refrain from the future use of chemical weapons in accordance with their obligations under the Geneva Protocol'.[38]

In contrast to Blair's speculative and optimistic use of evidence in supporting his legal case – based on what he did not know and what UN weapons inspectors had not found – the moral underpinning of his case was based largely on verifiable information. Saddam's regime indisputably gassed the Kurds and both he and his cousin, Chemical Ali, were later found guilty of that crime and sentenced to death by an Iraqi judge.[39]

This particular moral argument – Saddam's use of WMD against his own people – has two main weaknesses. The first is the lukewarm response of the British and American governments at the time it happened. Far from calling for military action against Saddam in response to the actions the British and Americans ensured that he was not even criticized very strongly. The second weakness in Blair's criticism of Saddam's gassing of the Iraqi Kurds is the timing of those events, 15 years before the 2003 invasion. By 2003 the Kurdish region of Iraq was already semi-autonomous and the most stable area of the country. Most importantly, there was no suggestion that any repeat of the chemical attack was imminent or even threatened.

One particularly emotive strand of Blair's eve-of-war speech was his talk of appeasing Saddam on the part of those who refused to support military action. He then went on to discuss what happened when Nazis were appeased in the 1930s and urged that such apathy should not be repeated with regard to rogue states that develop or use WMD. Blair later expressed regret over the inclusion of this section of his speech, noting somewhat disingenuously that he had not conflated Saddam Hussein and Adolf Hitler.[40] The fact that Blair did not explicitly state, 'Saddam is the Hitler of 2003', gives him only a small measure of deniability. In a speech whose sole purpose was to win Parliamentary support for military action against a tyrannical ruler who had committed atrocities against his own people and others, any mention of Nazism and Hitler was clearly inviting his listeners to draw the connections that Blair intended them to make: thereby provoking them to action by supporting his proposal. Speaking in the debating chamber where Winston Churchill inspired the British Parliament and people as they confronted Hitler and Nazism, what other interpretation of Blair's words is even remotely feasible? Yet again he reinforced his tenuous legal case with one of the most powerful and emotive moral arguments that can be presented to the British people: allowing a modern-day Hitler to operate unchecked.

Why did Blair think that by presenting Saddam as a tyrant and inviting his listeners to draw comparisons with the appeasement of Nazism in the 1930s he would gain public support? What moral discourse, deep-rooted within British (and other) history and culture, was Blair tapping into with his dramatic pleading for action against Saddam? I would suggest that he was attempting to portray himself as the hero, opposing the villain that was Saddam, and inviting his audience to do likewise. The ethical dimension of the hero–villain relationship, though not usually associated with just war tradition is at least as old. From classical Greek literature to the bible, from Shakespeare to Marvel comics, the ethical conduct of the hero is set before mere humans as both an inspiration and an aspiration from childhood through to adulthood.

The great British political 'heroes' have always been those who have led the country to triumph in war. It is no coincidence that the man regularly voted the greatest Briton ever is Winston Churchill, architect of the victory in World War II. Margaret Thatcher's triumph in reclaiming the Falkland Islands after they had been taken by force by Argentina in 1982 helped to transform her personal standing as Prime Minister. Though her economic policies were deeply divisive, Thatcher's legacy will always be illuminated by her determination and success as a wartime leader. There was an aspect of Blair's attitude to Saddam that went beyond mere heroic opposition to tyranny to a full-blown confrontation between good and evil.

Even though Blair's communications team sought to keep his deep religiosity away from the public gaze as much as possible during his time as Prime Minister, he has acknowledged the highly significant role personal faith has played in his life. From his introduction to the Christian faith during his university years to his conversion to Roman Catholicism and the setting up of a Faith Foundation following his departure from 10 Downing Street, religion has played a pivotal role in shaping Blair's moral framework and personal politics. Often overlooked by observers, supporters and critics alike, religious faith is a thread that ran, and still runs, through Blair's politics. In 2001 he made the explicit connection: 'So faith in politics isn't only about the relationship between faith and politics. It is also about having faith in the political process itself and its capacity to achieve a better society'.[41]

After he had left office Blair was asked in a television interview about his faith and whether it played a part in his decision-making when planning for war, particularly the war against Iraq. He replied:

> When it comes to a decision [to go to war], I think it is important that you take that decision, as it were, on the basis of what you think is right – because that is the only way to do it. And, I think people sometimes think that my religious faith played a direct part in some of these decisions – it really didn't. [Religious faith] gives you strength, if you've come to a decision, to hold to that decision. But that's, if you like, in terms of how it supports your character in a situation of difficulty.[42]

In keeping with the triangulation approach to communication that characterized his Third Way politics, Blair here leaves the impression of wanting to speak to two incongruent constituencies at the same time, delivering contradictory messages without alienating either group. First he said that his religious faith did not play a 'direct part' in his decision-making about war. However, in an interview in which he was extolling the benefits of religious beliefs he went on to describe how his own faith reinforced his decisions and help him to stand firm once a decision was reached. If his religious faith enabled Blair to maintain his political course in the face of considerable opposition to war then it clearly played a more direct part in events than he acknowledged. Going further, he regularly used the vocabulary of religion in the political arena as he sought to justify his various military interventions. As early as 1998 Blair was resorting to the language of good and evil as a means of identifying regimes and leaders that needed to be opposed or removed. Wars with Slobodan Milosevic and Saddam Hussein were not merely confrontations with tyranny but battles of good against evil. The following excerpts highlight the consistency in his approach over the years:

No one would be better pleased if his evil regime disappeared as a direct or indirect result of our action, but our military objectives are precisely those I have set out.[43]

This is a just war [over Kosovo], based not on any territorial ambitions but on values. We cannot let the evil of ethnic cleansing stand ... If we let an evil dictator range unchallenged, we will have to spill infinitely more blood and treasure to stop him later.[44]

Each step of human progress is a struggle between good and evil.[45]

This is not a battle between the United States of America and terrorism, but between the free and democratic world and terrorism. We, therefore, here in Britain stand shoulder to shoulder with our American friends in this hour of tragedy, and we, like them, will not rest until this evil is driven from our world.[46]

The struggle between good and evil was and is, for Blair, an essential part of the human existence. It is also an extremely helpful discursive tool because evil does not need to be explained, debated or rationalized: evil simply *is* and once it has been identified it needs to be opposed. Anyone who failed to join Blair (or Bush) on the side of good must have been, by default, either directly supporting evil or at least tacitly accepting it. The battle that rages between good and evil provides the only exception to Blair's all-encompassing Third Way politics. A side must be chosen. Blair's approach was echoed in an almost uncanny way by President Bush. Bush stated on 20 September 2001 in addressing a Joint Session of Congress: 'Either you are with us or you are with the terrorists.' His words were a transliteration of the biblical words of Jesus: 'He who is not with me is against me.'[47]

The relationship between Bush and Blair was cemented in the days following the 9/11 attacks. Bush was effusive in his admiration for the British Prime Minister when he said, 'I've got no better person I would like to talk to about our mutual concerns than Tony Blair. He brings a lot of wisdom and judgment, as we fight evil'.[48] Biblical imagery was also present in Blair's speeches, where he identified the need to engage in the battle between good and evil. Note the parallels between Blair's words and words of St Paul to the Ephesians in the New Testament:

> This is a battle that can't be fought or won only by armies. We are so much more powerful in all conventional ways than the terrorist. Yet even in all our might, we are taught humility. In the end, it is not our power alone that will defeat this evil. Our ultimate weapon is not our guns but our beliefs.[49]

> For our struggle is not against flesh and blood, but against the rulers, against the authorities, against the powers of this dark world and against the spiritual forces of evil in the heavenly realms. Therefore put on the full armour of God, so that when the day of evil comes you may be able to stand your ground ... take up the shield of faith, with which you can extinguish all the flaming arrows of the evil one.[50]

For Blair, once evil has been identified it has to be dealt with and because evil is not an entirely earthly entity, even if its consequences are. It takes more than earthly military hardware to combat evil: it takes beliefs. Blair's Christian beliefs, reinforced by his conversion from the Church of England to the Roman Catholic Church, are founded upon the bible and the guidance it provides to the adherent of the faith. In his wording Blair left open the possibility that others with beliefs, even if those beliefs did not coincide with his own, could also oppose the evil he had identified. He did not go as far as to explain how beliefs actually opposed evil, beyond implying that his listeners should commit themselves to supporting the political actions he proposed.

In the eighteenth century Vattel argued that nations had the right to self-preservation and could use force in defence of that right.[51]

The preservation of the nation was not merely a legal act, it was a moral act. However, this right to self-preservation is significant because it went beyond mere self-defence, allowing three further responses. Vattel granted, first, the right of rulers to use force to stop evil actions where possible, even preventively against another state.[52] Secondly, when acts of evil had been committed, that is, when a nation has been the victim of aggression or damage, the offended party has a right to full reparations – by means of force where necessary.[53] And thirdly, the offended party can punish an aggressor by rendering him unable to undertake further similar actions.[54] Although Vattel was keen to define the legitimacy of war in terms of law and move away from notions such as divine authority and the vocabulary of Christianity, he was not entirely successful. Perhaps it is not surprising that the son of a Swiss clergyman should resort to the language of good and evil when trying to describe the heinousness of a tyrannical aggressor. Blair, like Vattel, was educated in the law but could not resist the temptation – to use another biblical allegory – to resort to the language of the Church when the language of the courts proved inadequate.

Summary

In his determination to oppose tyranny and the evil that it spawns, Blair was willing to resort to the language and imagery of religion, and Christianity in particular. The use of 'evil' in his arguments seems out of place in twenty-first century just war, with its increasingly secular approach in a multi-faith world. It might even be more accurate to describe the use of 'evil' in Blair's war discourse as more of a spiritual than a moral argument. Strong traces of Christian just war doctrine that pre-date the emergence of the modern international system were present in Blair's speeches. The advantage of using such moral arguments is huge. The UN, with all its faults and failings, figures large in the current international system and many British voters wanted Blair to get unequivocal Security Council backing for the invasion of Iraq. His use of arguments and language that predate international law helped to create the perception of moral legitimacy, even when the substance on which the arguments were based was becoming less reliable and credible by the day as war approached.

Although the concepts are proscribed by international law there are traces of both just punishment and the preventive war in Blair's arguments for intervention in Iraq. There is an interesting dynamic in Blair's speeches as the war approached. His tenuous legal case was in danger of being eradicated all together as the UN weapons inspectors were increasingly confirming that Saddam presented no credible threat at that time. Blair's moral case consequently became more reliant on events that had definitely happened in the past – the gassing of Kurds and attacks on neighbours – and events which may or may not develop in the future: the perceived threat in the present (in early 2003) was increasingly eroding despite the best efforts of UK and US intelligence agencies. In this regard Blair's arguments had much in common with many centuries of early thinking in the pre-legalist just war tradition where enemies, especially tyrants, were viewed as the objects of just punishment for previous crimes. The just war theorists Cicero, Aquinas, Grotius and Vattel (among others) also allowed, to varying degrees, a righteous ruler to intervene against tyranny in neighbouring states. Blair's actions in Kosovo and Sierra Leone would qualify as morally just by this criterion because humanitarian disasters were clearly happening before the eyes of the world. For all Saddam's previous crimes against humanity in and around Iraq, in 2003 there was not the same ongoing humanitarian tragedy in Iraq that there had been in Kosovo and Sierra Leone. This dimension of Blair's moral case for action against Iraq was flawed and will be explored further in the next chapter as the focus shifts from opposing Saddam the tyrant to helping the people Saddam oppressed.

7
Protecting the weak

Row upon row, shelf upon shelf, the bleached skulls and bones of the victims provide a permanent memorial to the suffering of the innocent and the horrors of the Rwanda genocide in those fateful months in 1994. The world stood by as nearly a million Rwandans were murdered by other Rwandans, mainly Tutsis killed by Hutus. This crime against humanity was compounded by the rape and traumatizing of hundreds of thousands of Rwandan women, again, mainly Tutsis. The stories that emerged from Rwanda of man's inhumanity – and it was primarily men who were responsible – to both women and men were reinforced by graphic pictures of rotting, violated corpses and a vast movement of refugees fleeing for their lives.

Against this backdrop, in May 1994 Tony Blair began campaigning for leadership of the Labour Party following the premature death of the previous leader, John Smith. By 1995 he was leader of the Opposition when genocide returned to Europe for the first time since World War II with the killing of more than 8000 Bosniaks at Srebrenica. Both events significantly impacted upon the man who would go on to become British Prime Minister and a committed advocate of the use of military force as a means of preventing such atrocities.[1] If the world had been slow to learn lessons from the killing fields of Cambodia in the 1970s, Blair was determined to learn quickly from what happened, and did not happen, in Rwanda and Bosnia. By the time he took office Blair was already convinced that timely and appropriate intervention would save innocent lives, especially of those too weak to defend themselves.

From Kosovo to Iraq, crossing distant borders to preserve the lives of the innocent against the ravages of tyrants was the central pillar of Blair's justification of military intervention. In the tension between the rights of states to non-interference as set out in the UN Charter and the individual's right to life captured in the Universal Declaration of Human Rights adopted by the UN in 1948 Blair prioritized the latter. Each of Blair's interventions was a complex, multifaceted political endeavour and they resulted in varying degrees of success.

Consistent with the central ideas of the just war tradition going back many centuries, Blair sought to preserve lives and achieve a better state of peace for those places in the future. Consequently, his intervention discourse tended to concentrate on current and imminent loss of innocent lives: at least it did with Kosovo and Sierra Leone. His Iraq arguments were constructed differently and regularly highlighted Saddam's atrocities in the past as well as the potential risks he posed in the future.

The first part of the chapter will identify historic and contemporary just war arguments for using force to help the innocent. I show how the notion of defending those who cannot defend themselves has an ancient heritage in the just war tradition, a heritage that only began to erode as the idea of state sovereignty took root in Europe as the basis of the international system we know today. An analysis of Blair's oft-used moral case for military intervention contrasts the different approaches he took over his years in power. The second part of the chapter relates the actions Blair took to what we know of his political and religious motivations. The final part of the chapter discusses, with reference to Blair's own words, not only how he sought to save lives but also how he intended to shape the way that people lived in the future. Two interrelated principles featured frequently in Blair's war discourse: a desire to promote freedom and democracy, linked to the enforcement of human rights. In the case of Iraq, Blair also consistently associated action to help Saddam's victims with action to provide a political solution to the enmity between the Israelis and the Palestinians. As with other chapters, the problems that are raised when applying historical just war ideas in the present provide a philosophical backdrop to the discussion.

Defending the innocent

Just as opposing tyranny has a long history in the just war tradition, so has the notion of defending those who cannot defend themselves. However, before moving on to that moral justification for war or military intervention I want to consider what might prompt a leader into taking such action, beginning with a view from Augustine.

Augustine was primarily concerned with the eternal destination of human, especially Christian, souls. Augustine's masterpiece, *City of God*, set out at great length his understanding of the kinds of beliefs and activities that would earn the Christian eternity with God in the Heavenly City. Conversely it also set out how rejection of God and rejection of the behaviour that God demanded would consign individuals to the Earthly City in this life and eternal separation from God in the hereafter. Someone who achieved citizenship of the City of God was also considered by Augustine to be wise and he said of the relationship between the wise man and just wars:

> But the wise man, they say, will wage just wars. Surely, however, if he remembers that he is a human being, he will be much readier to deplore the fact that he is under the necessity of waging even just wars. For if they were not just, he would not have to wage them, and so there would be no wars at all for a wise man to engage in. For it is the iniquity of the opposing side that imposes upon the wise man the duty of waging wars; and every man certainly ought to deplore this iniquity since, even if no necessity for war should arise from it, it is still the iniquity of men.[2]

The wisdom of the wise man, in this example, did not emerge from the sum of knowledge he had accumulated but preceded his opposing of an unjust enemy. The war would be deemed just because the one who waged it was wise, obeyed the commands of God and sought to reinforce the divine moral order on earth. The wise man pursued the just war because he was already a citizen of the City of God and by virtue of that citizenship was unable to pursue any other kind of war. Contrary to modern readings of just war, the wise man did not simply emerge here as ethical because he undertook a just war; the war was just because it was a wise member of the City of God who waged it in opposing an unjust enemy. The wise man would act out of necessity, not through a need to fight but through the more important need to preserve his moral status by fighting for those who needed to be defended. To be clear, for Augustine the moral status of the leader preceded the morality of the war. Necessity therefore became part of Augustine's just war because the divine order prioritized the souls of human beings over the affairs of state, even in a war setting.

In another work, *On Free Choice of the Will*, Augustine introduced the idea that force could be used to defend the victims of an unjust aggressor: 'The death of an unjust aggressor is a lesser evil than that of a man who is only defending himself. It is much more horrible that a human being should be violated against his will than that a violent attacker should be killed by his intended victim.'[3] Augustine was not writing in the context of inter-state, cross-border intervention. He was referring to the broader principle of protecting the innocent from being violated, even if that protection resulted in the death of the violent aggressor. However, he still retained some reservations about granting the killing of even the most unjust attacker: 'I do not blame the law that permits such attackers to be killed, but I do not see how I might defend those who kill them.'[4] Augustine's reluctance to defend the killer of the unjust attacker is rooted in the bible, which – for those who accept its authority – reveals God's direct commands to humankind. Such commands include: 'You shall not murder'[5] and 'If someone slaps you on one cheek, turn to them the other also'.[6] Augustine struggled to reconcile the competing imperatives of divine justice: protecting others, turning the other cheek when under personal assault, and not killing others. Consequently, while Augustine's concern for the victims of violence provides some historical basis for just intervention today, it can only do so if the general principle is uncoupled from its theological and biblical foundations and his concern for the eternal destiny of the human soul.

By 1625 Grotius was busy working on that very process of separating divine authority from questions on the morality and legality of war. Instead, he related questions of war to emerging ideas of political, or state, sovereignty. Though the most clear-cut justification for war was the self-defence of a state under attack, he granted the option of pre-emptive self defence against imminent aggression. Going further, despite his tendency towards recognizing state borders as sacrosanct, Grotius granted one exception. He went beyond permitting pre-emptive attack in his just war to opening up the possibility that one ruler might intervene to protect the subjects of another ruler:

> But if the injustice [of a ruler against that ruler's subjects] be visible ... such tyrannies over subjects as no good man living can approve of, the right of human society shall not therefore be excluded ... And indeed tho' it were granted that subjects ought not, even in the most pressing necessity, to take up arms against their Prince ... we should not yet be able to conclude from thence, that others might not do it for them.[7]

Grotius did not develop this point at great length but the basis of the argument is that in some circumstances – when the offence or crime committed was serious enough – the rights of 'human society' (which for him meant European, civilized human society) and a desire to protect the innocent should outweigh the sovereign rights of the Prince in whose domain injury was being caused. The good – or ethical – Prince was the one who was prepared, at great cost, to intervene on behalf of others. The Prince who would intervene across borders on behalf of the innocent was prompted 'from the quality and circumstance of the person, which quality does not pass to others'.[8] In this regard Grotius captured aspects of Augustine's earlier argument that the just intervention is preceded by the just character of the one who would intervene on behalf of others. That is, the Prince who *already* had a character of high quality – the ethical ruler – would go to war to protect the innocent as an outward manifestation of that character.

As well as rooting the just war in the character of the wise man, Augustine also described characteristics and conduct of the individual who should be opposed in a just war. This person is able to experience evil without showing remorse and inflict horror and cruelty upon the innocent without acknowledging the misery of his actions.[9] The inhumane despot who must be opposed is characterized by a capacity for cruelty and evil, an appetite for destruction and an absence of grief. Blair could be quoting Augustine directly so similar are elements of his justification for military intervention to help the weak and vulnerable Iraqis who could not help themselves:

> The brutality of the repression – the death and torture camps, the barbaric prisons for political opponents, the routine beatings for anyone or their families suspected of disloyalty are well documented. Just last week, someone slandering Saddam was tied to a lamp post in a street in Baghdad, his tongue cut out, mutilated and left to bleed to death, as a warning to others.
>
> I recall a few weeks ago talking to an Iraqi exile and saying to her that I understood how grim it must be under the lash of Saddam. 'But you don't', she replied. 'You cannot. You do not know what it is like to live in perpetual fear.' And she is right. We take our freedom for granted. But imagine not to be able to speak or discuss or debate or even question the society you live in. To see friends and family taken away and never daring to complain. To suffer the humility of failing courage in face of pitiless terror. That is how the Iraqi people live. Leave Saddam in place and that is how they will continue to live.[10]

Every one of the actions by Saddam's regime listed by Blair as he added this layer of moral justification to his weak legal case for war was reprehensible in the extreme. The way he presented the abuse of innocent Iraqis was typical of his political discourse during his time as leader of

New Labour and as Prime Minister. When in opposition and campaigning to win his first term as Prime Minister he sought to personalize the
failings of the government by highlighting particularly tragic individual cases and presenting them as representative of the entire National
Health Service (NHS) and the failings of the Conservative Party. On the
eve of the 1997 General Election he told voters that they had 24 hours
to save the NHS. Although presentationally successful, this approach
was philosophically weak because it took isolated cases and generalized
them as representative of universal realities. The NHS was clearly not
going to die, disappear or self-destruct the day after the 1997 election and
not every Iraqi was experiencing the same degree of terror as those cited
by Blair: assuming of course that the people referred to by Blair were real
and not simply fabricated to make his argument stronger. Continuing
the assumption that the woman Blair mentioned actually existed, it is
fortunate that her command of the English language was good enough
to provide him with the rather rare, eloquent and persuasive phrase,
'perpetual fear'.[11] The implication of Blair's words was clear: fail to support me and you will be complicit in continuing atrocities against those,
like this woman, who cannot defend themselves.

Blair's desire to oppose the evil, barbaric and cruel actions of Slobodan
Milosevic, Foday Sankoh, Osama Bin Laden and Saddam Hussein against
the weak very precisely echoes the ideas Augustine set down many centuries earlier, as did Elshtain's concurrent support in the academic realm for
punitive action against Saddam Hussein and Al-Qaeda. However, in both
the political arena and the academic world these uses of Augustinian
ideas were only partial: both Blair and Elshtain failed to include in their
justification of intervention any mention of the divine order that such
actions were originally intended to reinforce. In addition, neither Blair
nor Elshtain captured in their rhetoric the reason for Augustine's reti-
cence over the use of force when humans would inevitably die: a reti-
cence based on his valuing of human life because it is had been created
by God, in the image of God.

On the contrary, an alternative reading of Blair and Elshtain suggests
that they called upon these ancient ideas of right and wrong as a means
of more effectively justifying wars that international law would restrain.
We can see a clear continuity between some of the ideas of Augustine and
Blair and Elshtain in advocating a punitive war against the immoral, cruel
and barbaric opponent. However, there is an important discontinuity in
the philosophical and theological basis of these arguments. Augustine's
ideas were based on a moral code defined by divine command and divine
order, while Blair's and Elshtain's occurred in an international system

in which references to divine justice would be unacceptable, in spite of the individuals' own beliefs.

The notion of reaching out to help the weak and vulnerable is commonplace in most societies and the British people tend to hold in high regard those who have done so. Numerous examples include: William Wilberforce, who campaigned for almost half a century to see the British involvement in the slave trade outlawed and then slavery itself abolished; Florence Nightingale, the 'Lady with the Lamp' who advanced patient care with the professionalization of nursing in the nineteenth century; William Booth, reaching out to the alcoholics, criminals and prostitutes of East London and beyond; Leonard Cheshire, who having seen and experienced the horrors of World War II as a bomber pilot, devoted the rest of his life to helping the disabled. An entire book could not list those worthy of mention. Despite any flaws in the characters of these individuals they are held up as the highest examples of moral and, in the case of some, religious, conduct. Blair was attempting to co-opt into his own interventionist ideals the support of a nation that reveres these and other moral exemplars from the past.

The notion of the 'good guy' protecting the oppressed from the tyrant, usually against the odds, is a deeply embedded moral discourse and every culture has its equivalent. Probably the most famous British example is Robin Hood, immortalized in numerous cinema and television films. Another example of this icon in modern culture is the lone cowboy, often of dubious or unknown origin. The altruistic goodie confronts and defeats the baddie holding some Western town to ransom: thus enabling the viewer to identify himself or herself with the ethical hero. In cinemas from Hollywood to Delhi to Beijing the character is easily identifiable. From the sword-wielding exploits of Zorro to the gun-slinging Man With No Name, audiences set aside any qualms about the legality of the methods of the hero on the basis that a higher moral purpose is being served in standing up for the innocent. By setting out his case for war in the way he did, Blair was relying on his audience(s) to embrace his moral dynamism in the same way that similar cultural stereotypes had been embraced for generations: thereby approving appropriate action against the barbaric Saddam. In a sense, therefore, Blair's view of himself as ethical helped propel him in the direction of intervention on behalf of the weak: how could he do otherwise?

Another icon of the British public, whose name changes from incident to incident, is the have-a-go-hero; the plucky individual who places himself or herself in harm's way to prevent robberies, rapes, muggings, assaults, and so on, happening to others. Society then rewards and reclaims that bravery in the award of medals such as the George Cross and holds up the recipients as exemplar, self-sacrificial citizens prepared to lay down their lives for others. Blair was inciting – deliberately or otherwise – his listeners to identify themselves with this kind of moral discourse and support his actions to stop the rapes, murders and torture conducted by Saddam Hussein's regime. Unfortunately for Blair, both at that time and afterwards, his critics only had to look at his and the UK's closest ally and the actions of the US government with regard to Guantanamo Bay to see a place where prisoners died and prisoners were tortured. His ability to be morally selective did little to bolster his case for action against Saddam.

The actions of the US against suspected Muslim terrorists or 'unlawful combatants' at Guantanamo Bay made it increasingly difficult for the coalition to gain the degree of international support for action against Iraq that had been achieved in 1991. Representatives of the Land of the Free removed these combatants, or suspected combatants, from in and around the battlefields of Afghanistan and bordering Pakistan and delivered them, hooded and manacled, to its naval base on Cuba: action that became known as extraordinary rendition. Having claimed a legal and moral right to self-defensive action against Al-Qaeda operatives based in Afghanistan, the US was not prepared to treat its captives according to international humanitarian law in the form of the Geneva Conventions. Worse, it was not prepared to honour the moral underpinnings of the Geneva Conventions, recognize the captives as *hors de combat* and treat them humanely. While Bush, Rumsfeld and others in the administration debated the degree of physical pain and discomfort that could be inflicted on captives without being classified as torture, millions of Muslims and others around the world had already made up their minds: none. Discomfort with the lack of due process for the rendered prisoners was not confined to Muslims and non-Americans. In 2009 one of Barak Obama's first acts as President was to sign an executive order ordering the closure of the detention centre at Guantanamo Bay within 12 months and suspending the military tribunals.

As pictures of manacled, hooded Muslim prisoners kneeling in their red prison uniforms were being beamed around the world, Blair and Bush were trying to amass a coalition against Saddam – both at home and abroad. Apart from undermining the moral case for action against the Iraqi leader there were practical implications as well. It became politically very difficult for the leaders of Iraq's neighbours to support the proposed US and UK military action. Not surprisingly many in the Gulf region were reluctant to support a coalition led by a country that was actively abusing Muslims, regardless of the atrocities of 9/11.

Blair's way of getting round the problem of a lack of support from Muslims was to dangle the prospect of progress towards a Palestinian state as a *quid pro quo* for supporting military action against Iraq. He even managed to convince President Bush of the political advantages and Bush pushed for the creation of the Road Map for Peace in 2002. At best the Road Map was a genuine attempt to resolve a conflict whose roots were lost in the sands of time and in which the protagonists on both sides claim that they are doings God's/Allah's will. At worst, the move was seen at the time as a piece of political opportunism where the Palestinians and Israelis would yet again be used as pawns in a bigger political game. An initial burst of diplomatic manoeuvring in 2002 led to some immediate progress but the drop in time, effort and diplomatic capital devoted to the effort in the years after the invasion seemed to reinforce the sceptical view from 2002.

Given Blair's commitment to peace in the Middle East since he left office as Prime Minister there should be little doubt that he has a genuine concern for those Palestinians who are homeless and stateless. However, his linking of the plight of the Palestinians and a desire for a Palestinian state to his case for war in Iraq was morally dubious. In more than a dozen speeches over the year prior to the invasion of Iraq Blair raised the Palestinian issue: usually outside of the context of whatever his theme was at the time. His concern for the Palestinians may have been, and still remains, genuine. It was, though, a secondary consideration when placed alongside his higher political end of building support for action against Saddam. Excerpts from speeches that address both the Iraq problem and Israel/Palestine and the Middle East Peace Process (MEPP) include:

> The Israelis must allow a state of Palestine, secure in its own borders. And in exchange the Palestinians and the whole Arab world must recognize and respect Israel's borders.[12]

> But Saddam is not the only issue. We must restart the Middle East Peace Process. We must work with all concerned, including the US, for a lasting peace which ends the suffering of both the Palestinians in the Occupied Territories and the Israelis at the hands of terrorists.[13]

> I have no doubt the Arab world knows it would be better off without Saddam. Equally, I know there is genuine resentment at the state of the Middle East Peace Process.[14]

> I do not believe there is any other issue with the same power to re-unite the world community than progress on the issues of Israel and

Palestine. Of course there is cynicism about recent announcements. But the US is now committed, and, I believe genuinely, to the Roadmap for peace, designed in consultation with the UN ... All of us are now signed up to its vision: a state of Israel, recognized and accepted by all the world, and a viable Palestinian state ... And that should be part of a larger global agenda. On poverty and sustainable development. On democracy and human rights. On the good governance of nations. That is why what happens after any conflict in Iraq is of such critical significance.[15]

Blair implied that a war with Iraq would be followed or accompanied by progress on the Israel/Palestine issue which, in turn, would serve as but part of a bigger agenda that would address sustainable development, democracy, human rights, and the good governance of nations. It is a very inviting moral calculation: all of these benefits as a return for war against Saddam and Iraq. On the simple calculus of the benefits to Israel/Palestine and wider humanity *versus* the costs involved in a war with Iraq it would seem immoral to refuse such a generous offer from Blair. That was the whole point of including such an emotive issue in his speeches. With the benefit of hindsight it seems clear that if the US and UK had expended as much time, resources and political capital in trying to resolve the ancient enmity between Israelis and Palestinians as they did in pursuit of war against Saddam they may well have been successful. One indicator of the political (in)effectiveness of Blair's and Bush's conflation of the MEPP and Iraq came on 1 March 2003 when the Turkish Grand National Assembly voted not to allow the deployment of American equipment and personnel on its land as part of the force that would take action against Saddam. Setting out to protect the weak and vulnerable in Iraq – if that was Blair's real intention – was a morally commendable act. Using the plight of another group of weak and vulnerable as a means of doing so is morally dubious at the very least. Before I consider the kind of future Blair had in mind for the Iraqi people let us look at some of his possible motivations and in particular the role of his Christian beliefs in shaping his approach to politics.

Blair's motivation

Occasionally in politics a throwaway word or phrase can almost take on a life of its own, becoming imbued with meaning that the original speaker or author did not intend. In recent British political history one such phrase was Alastair Campbell's line, in bringing to a close a journalist's interview with Tony Blair in 2003: 'we don't do God'. Campbell has acknowledged the comment on more than one occasion but has always insisted that it 'was not a major strategic statement'.[16] His intervention was promoted by a desire to avoid a repeat of an incident in 1996 when, in an interview with the Daily Telegraph, Blair revealed the extent of his commitment to his Christian beliefs, thereby opening himself up to myriad criticisms from opponents both outside and inside the Labour Party.

Blair came to his strong religious faith during his time at university, a time when many young men and women are challenging their own understanding of the world and their relationship with it. Young minds are highly receptive to new ideas as individuals set out to form themselves as specific kinds of people, often with a strong religious or political dimension. It is no coincidence that since the London bombings on 7 July 2005 there frequently emerges in both educational and mainstream media concern about the 'radicalization' of Muslim students. Such a view is limited and highly selective. Radicalization, at least for some, is part of the *raison d'être* for attending university. This can be described as a process of 'finding oneself' or, as I prefer, finding new discourses – political, religious or otherwise – with which to identify and conform. The phenomenon has been around since humans began reflecting on the nature of being and where they belong in the world. Historic high profile examples of radicalizing British students include the recruitment by the USSR of a group of highly intelligent and ideological young students and graduates from Cambridge University in the 1930s. Kim Philby, Guy Burgess and Donald Maclean among others worked for the Soviet Union against the UK's interests, won over to communism at around the same age as Blair was when Christianity became a major part of his life.

The religious aspect of Blair's 'radicalization' culminated in Confirmation in the Church of England, a service where the candidate is asked: 'Do you reject the devil and all rebellion against God?' and, 'Do you renounce the deceit and corruption of evil?'[17] The devil and the corruption of evil are subsequently rejected and renounced by the candidate. In Blair's case this rejection of evil was no symbolic gesture in a religious rite of passage. Opposing evil as he sought to protect the weak from violent oppression by means of military intervention became Blair's defining achievement as Prime Minister.

In his autobiography Blair writes movingly about the impact an Anglican priest, Peter Thomson, had on his life when he was at Oxford and how subsequently for Blair, religion and politics remained intertwined thereafter. In a remarkable revelation that has received little public comment Blair acknowledged that of the two, religion came first:

> Politically, Pete was on the left, but religion came first. Therefore, so, in a sense, it did for me. Not that the two were separated by him, or me, but the frame within which you see the world is different if religion comes first. Religion starts with values that are born of a view of humankind. Politics starts with an examination of society and the means of changing it ... This is vital in understanding my politics. I begin with an analysis of human beings as my compass; the politics is secondary.[18]

Throughout all the years Blair spent in frontline politics, including his decade as Prime Minister, with all the moral ambiguities that political decision-making involves, religion and his Christian faith shaped his actions and outlook on life. At the conclusion of his memoirs he was still able to write: 'I think life is a gift from God and should be lived to the full and with purpose.'[19] That purpose necessarily operates in two domains for the Christian, as it has since Jesus walked the earth 2000 years ago. Great theologians like Augustine and Aquinas, and countless others before and since, have wrestled with questions of how Christians should exercise their faith in relation to earthly politics in the present against the backdrop of an eternity with God in heaven – however that is conceived. It is this duality that set the parameters of Blair's political actions: making life better for others in the here and now, while looking forward to some form of heavenly judgement and reward.

In light of Blair's commitment to his faith over the years, Campbell's statement about not doing God left the erroneous impression that religious influence was somehow absent or banned from Blair's political decision-making process. Blair was determined as far as possible to express his Christian faith. John Burton was Blair's agent for 25 years and described how on one occasion Blair was determined to participate in an Easter procession in his constituency. Burton also captured, in what was a humorous anecdote, the effort to which they went in order for Blair not to be photographed in the vicinity of a Christian cross.[20] Public acknowledgement of any degree of Christian faith by British public figures is often met by ridicule, incredulity or faint embarrassment. So consistently is this principle applied in the UK that even bishops and archbishops can be criticized for bringing 'religion' into public political discourse: in effect, doing their jobs. Against this societal backdrop it is easy to understand why Blair said little about his Christian beliefs when he held public office and why his advisers would have preferred him to have said nothing at all: especially in the context of military interventions in a Muslim enclave of Serbia and two Muslim countries. However, those who have worked closely with Blair and who know him well will point to his Christian faith as central to understanding him and his political motivations.

The most contentious decision Blair made as Prime Minister was undoubtedly the ordering of British military personnel into action against Iraq in 2003. When his actions are considered in the religious terms I have set out there are likely to be strongly divided opinions on whether the judgement Blair faces as a Christian will result in eternal reward or eternal damnation. What makes such orders so significant is that they result in the deaths of allied and enemy combatants alike, as well as noncombatant bystanders. Blair was asked, as a Christian, about his morality and the possibility that he might be ordering the deaths of many people through war.

QUESTION: As the parent of four children and a Christian, how do you cope morally with the prospect of making decisions that could lead to the deaths of hundreds, if not thousands, of people, often perhaps in the most horrific ways?

PRIME MINISTER: Well you have to decide what the greatest risk is and what the morally right thing to do is, and as I say I have faced this twice before in Kosovo and Afghanistan. And I hate war, anybody of any sense hates war, hates military action, hates having to do it, but there are certain circumstances in which it is the right thing to do. Now I am not saying we have reached that point incidentally in relation to Iraq, I am simply saying that in relation to Kosovo and Afghanistan we took military action because I thought it was the right thing to do. Because you could not allow in the case of Kosovo ethnic cleansing and genocide to happen right on the doorstep of Europe and do nothing about it; because in the case of Afghanistan you couldn't allow a failed state to export terrorism around the world.[21]

Blair considered himself a man of action and that the most immoral of choices would be to do nothing when presented with evidence of evil being perpetrated against the vulnerable. Intervention in Kosovo and Afghanistan became 'the right thing' to do because innocent lives would be saved. In the case of Kosovo those lives would belong to the potential victims of ethnic cleansing and genocide, while Afghanistan was enabling terrorists to train and prepare for the murder of civilians in other countries on distant continents. In these examples, Blair made a 'lesser of two evils', or utilitarian, calculation. To reiterate an earlier argument, he managed to achieve support for these interventions because his supporters and opponents alike could witness for themselves on their television screens the death and destruction to which he referred. The same could not be said of Saddam and Iraq, no matter how completely Blair managed to convince himself of the threat. When, later, in a television interview with Michael Parkinson, he raised the prospect of divine judgement in relation to the wars he undertook Blair caused a storm of controversy:

> That decision has to be taken and has to be lived with, and in the end there is a judgement that, well, I think if you have faith about these things then you realise that judgement is made by other people, and … if you believe in God, it's made by God as well … but in the end you do what you think is the right thing.[22]

Blair's decision-making was shaped by his belief in God, his wider moral code, and in relation to the judgement of others: human judgement in this life and divine judgement in the next. As a Christian he was not wedded to one theological tradition. In his religious leanings, as with his politics, he appears most comfortable mixing with people across a spectrum of theological positions, perhaps most comfortable with those of a liberal disposition: agreeing with most people on something but rarely agreeing with anyone about everything.[23] His encounters with cardinals and the Pope must be very interesting affairs.

Given that Blair's religious faith and understanding appear no less complex than his political loyalties and affiliations, it is little wonder that when he spoke at the National Prayer Breakfast in Washington in 2009 Blair should have focused on the subject of God's grace. For those unfamiliar with the finer points of Christian theology grace can be described as the undeserved yet unconditional love of God. He said: 'It is through faith, by the Grace of God, that we have the courage to live as we should and die as we must.'[24] On that same occasion he set out his own vision for the place of religious faith in the modern world:

> I believe restoring religious faith to its rightful place, as the guide to our world and its future, is itself of the essence. The 21st Century will

be poorer in spirit, meaner in ambition, less disciplined in conscience, if it is not under the guardianship of faith in God. I do not mean by this to blur the correct distinction between the realms of religious and political authority.[25]

The opening comments in this quotation point to the centrality that Blair would afford religious faith in today's world. Whether people agree or not with the way in which he has conducted himself as Prime Minister he should not be accused of inconsistency. He continues to preach what he has practised for many years. The last sentence included here, however, is highly revealing both of Blair's own approach to politics and religion and his lack of understanding of people of other faiths. His commitment to the separation of religious and political authority bears all the hallmarks of a modern liberal democrat operating with a Western worldview that prioritizes individual rights and grants to Christian believers the capacity to redefine God in his or her own image.

Despite the work he has carried out through his own Faith Foundation Blair seems unwilling or unable to grasp that for many around the globe religious belief cannot be kept separate from political engagement in the world. Take Iran, for example. Ultimate political power in that country does not belong to President Mahmoud Ahmadinejad, it is wielded by the Grand Ayatollahs. Elsewhere, the fourteenth Dalai Lama is both the spiritual leader and the head of state of Tibet. While living in exile he continues to strive for Tibetan independence from China. In India, despite caste discrimination being outlawed in its constitution, the issues of caste, religion and politics appear as rigidly intertwined as ever. For billions of adherents of Islam, Hinduism, Buddhism, Sikhism and many other religions the notion of separating religious authority and spiritual authority, religious practice and political practice does not come as easily as it does to Blair. His appreciation of Muslim hostility towards his actions in Iraq might have been advanced more effectively if he, and other Westerners, stopped hoping for those who disagreed with him to start thinking and acting like Western liberals, with their separation of politics and religion, and instead spent more time trying to understand what causes people of other faiths to think and act as they do.

Returning to Christianity and the UK, there are two dominant caricatures of the British Christian. These can apply to both men and women and appear with great regularity in public discourse – from newspaper editorials to television sit-coms. The first is the bumbling individual who is uncertain about everything from their faith to their sexuality and almost wants to apologize for occupying public space. They are socially accepted, often fondly, because of their non-threatening views and demeanour and the most heinous crime they could commit would be to cause offence. The second caricature is the moralistic, judgemental and sanctimonious individual who knows that he or she is right, because they know God's will on any matter, and everyone else is wrong and most likely destined for hell.

While it would be unfair to deny Blair's inner wrangling over some of the decisions he made that resulted in the loss of life, he frequently, in public, exuded a certainty in his words and actions that I would place closer to the second of the two caricatures I have described. As I argue in Chapter 1, the tone was set by events in Kosovo in 1999, with Blair morally certain about the actions that had to be taken: Milosovic had to be opposed and replaced and the ethnic cleansing of the Kosovo Albanians stopped.[26] John Burton, who worked closely with Blair for 25 years, said of him: 'He believed that if it was possible to do something about injustice then you should do it – which is why it's very simple to explain the idea of Blair the Warrior. It was part of Tony living out his faith.'[27] Blair had a heightened sense of good and evil and the need to promote the former and oppose the latter in helping those who could not help themselves.

Liberation, human rights and democracy

Having considered some of Blair's possible motivations for opposing evil, countering oppression and defending those who could not help themselves, the final section of this chapter looks at the type of existence Blair wanted to usher in for those who had previously been downtrodden by brutal dictators, the key features of which were human rights and democracy. Blair identified the problems to be confronted as barbarism and dictatorship and he saw himself as the right person in the right place at the right time to stand up for those who had been, and were being, brutalized. To that end he regularly and consistently presented himself as a liberator in all his military interventions:

> [On Kosovo]
> Bismarck famously said the Balkans were not worth the bones of one Pomeranian Grenadier. Anyone who has seen the tear stained faces of the hundreds of thousands of refugees streaming across the border, heard their heart-rending tales of cruelty or contemplated the unknown fates of those left behind, knows that Bismarck was wrong.[28]

[On Sierra Leone]
I'll always remember driving through the villages near Freetown in Sierra Leone seeing the people rejoicing – many of them amputees through the brutality from which they had been liberated – and their joy at being free to debate, argue and vote as they wished.[29]

[On Afghanistan]
There has been a brilliant victory over the Taleban, who have ceased to be the Afghan Government. That is a welcome liberation.[30]

People in Afghanistan have been liberated from one of the most vile and oppressive regimes in the world, in fact most probably the most vile and oppressive regime, and one that was doing enormous damage to its country, to its citizens, in particular in its treatment of women inside Afghanistan.[31]

The Afghan people feel liberated not oppressed and have at least a chance of a better future.[32]

[On Iraq]
British troops are now patrolling the streets ... making it clear to people that we are there to help them, and we are there genuinely to liberate their country.[33]

there is no doubt in my mind, never has been and there is not any doubt now, that for people in Iraq this will in the end be a moment of liberation for them, however difficult it is now.[34]

though of course our aim is to rid Iraq of weapons of mass destruction and make our world more secure, the justice of our cause lies in the liberation of the Iraqi people, and to them we say we will liberate you, the day of your freedom draws near.[35]

I think anyone who has seen the joy on the faces of people in Basra, as they realise that the regime that they detest is finally collapsing, knows very well that this was indeed a war of liberation and not of conquest.[36]

The mere act of liberating the oppressed (even ignoring his premature comments on conditions in Afghanistan), by implication, should set Blair apart as an ethical person. However, this certainty about his own character and judgement contributed to the difficulties he encountered in justifying the Iraq invasion. In sanctioning the Kosovo campaign to prevent ethnic cleansing of Kosovo Albanians Blair's justification was based on his own moral certainty when presented with evidence of death and displacement. That moral certainty was at least partially rooted in a Christian faith that he sought to keep out of the public domain. When viewed in the light of Augustine's comments on the need for the wise man of faith to oppose injustice, Blair's actions can be interpreted as very much in keeping with the just war sentiments of the fifth century bishop. Furthermore, if Christians are commanded by God to follow the example of Jesus and live accordingly, then Blair's stated determination to liberate the oppressed resonates with aspects of the personal mission statement set out by Jesus in the bible: 'The Spirit of the Lord is on me, because he has anointed me to proclaim good news to the poor. He has sent me to proclaim freedom for the prisoners and recovery of sight for the blind, to set the oppressed free.'[37] While Blair may have felt that he was freeing Iraqis from oppression, no matter what role his Christian faith played in making or sustaining the decision, he was largely unsuccessful in convincing other British Christians of the worthiness of his cause, never mind those of other faiths and none.

The greatest difficulty for Blair when speaking of liberation from oppression in Iraq was that his arguments came a decade too late. In addition, the notion of liberation had no direct correlation with Saddam's alleged possession of WMD. The most plausible explanation for Blair's 'liberation' discourse was that it provided an additional means of procuring public support for military action against Saddam on moral grounds while distracting people from the weakness of his WMD case.

Blair was also consistent about what liberation would bring: freedom, democracy and human rights. Immediately prior to the invasion of Iraq in 2003 Blair spoke of 'uniting the nation's disparate groups, on a democratic basis, respecting human rights'.[38] This could only be achieved through a change of governance and contained a number of assumptions. First, Blair assumed that the fledgling democracy in Kurdish Northern Iraq could and would be spread, peacefully and gratefully, throughout the rest of the country. Quite aside from the question about whether or not Western-style democracy is historically and culturally appropriate in every setting, the idea of imposing it in an ancient civilization like Iraq is an oxymoron. The idea of imposing democracy is as logically consistent as having sex to preserve virginity.

This approach invited charges of a new imperialism against the US/UK-led coalition and its leaders. Echoes of old Western colonial policy in Africa and its *mission civilisatrice* abound. The idea of a civilizing mission to Iraq, a country whose first written laws predate the Old Testament, or the Jewish scriptures, would seem inappropriate to many Westerners and downright insulting to many in Iraq and the surrounding region. Once democracy was envisaged across the whole of Iraq the immediate problem would be the deep enmity of previously downtrodden groups towards those who had recently held power. It has been made clear by the Iraq and other inquiries – on both sides of the Atlantic – that inadequate post-conflict planning had taken place prior to the invasion and Blair was in no position to anticipate such an idealized transition.

The matter of human rights was, in itself, problematic. What human rights was Blair referring to? While the principle of universal human rights is strongly supported in the UK, the enactment of those rights and the interpretation of the European Convention on Human Rights is a source of dispute. David Cameron, the current British Prime Minister, has voiced concern about the UK's Human Rights Act in the context of UK's inability to deport individuals who may pose a threat to national security.[39] While almost every state has signed up to the Human Rights Convention, the philosophical basis under which they are understood varies across the globe. While there is no scope to do justice to the subject here, Western readings of human rights tend to be focused on the individual. If the concept is traced genealogically it leads back to the pre-Enlightenment idea of equality *before God*. In other parts of the world individual rights are set in the context of the more important rights of the community or collective.

If there is, and has been, no consensus within the UK over the application of human rights, what hope was there of imposing one of the British views (Blair's) on Iraq? At what point would the Iraqi people be allowed to decide for themselves what human rights are and how they should be interpreted, protected and implemented? It is deeply ironic that until the 2003 invasion Iraq's ancient Christian communities – Chaldean Catholics, Assyrians and Syriac Orthodox – lived in peaceful coexistence with the Muslim majority, while now they are targeted and persecuted for their beliefs. There is little evidence that a right to freedom of worship is currently being recognized or implemented in Iraq. Blair's moral argument for a Western model of democracy and human rights in Iraq was probably well intended as a means of protecting innocent Iraqis both in the present and the future. However, his ignorance of Iraqi society, religious divisions and culture – indicated by the lack of advance appropriate preparation for this major political undertaking – would suggest that it was not his strategic priority at the outset of military action.

Summary

A desire to defend the innocent from oppression, death and displacement consistently provided Blair's strongest moral argument for military intervention during his years as Prime Minister. His line of reasoning has a long heritage in the just war tradition. Having briefly examined Augustine's concern for fighting just wars to protect those who cannot help themselves it would appear that Blair's intervention discourse sat as comfortably alongside that ancient Christian perspective as it did with the ideas of Grotius. As the international system and something like modern international law was emerging – at a time when even the phrase 'international system' had not come into being – Grotius granted that the principle of non-interference across borders could be overlooked to protect the weak from a brutal and oppressive Prince. This is because for Grotius, as it would later be for Blair, the concerns and rights of humanity as a whole superseded the self-interest of a single sovereign ruler.

In light of Augustine's and Grotius's writings Blair's interventions, certainly the ones in Kosovo and Sierra Leone, can be viewed as just. Iraq was more problematic because the immediacy and scale of the humanitarian disasters that were unfolding on television screens before the eyes of the world in Kosovo and Sierra Leone were not present in Iraq. There had been widespread violent oppression by Saddam in Iraq but most of it had taken place more than a decade earlier, while Western powers like the US and UK watched and did nothing.

Blair's personal motivation for intervening militarily on behalf of the weak was strongly rooted in his personal moral framework, itself shaped to a large extent by his Christian faith and practice. As he set out his moral case he tried to tap into the special regard many British people have for those who have devoted their lives to the help and protection of others. He also set out a vision for a peaceful future in Iraq, characterized by democracy, freedom and human rights. In principle this moral intention should be praiseworthy but such was the paucity of planning for the aftermath of the military defeat of Saddam's forces that it undermined the credibility of this part of Blair's moral case for war. Blair wrote of his statement to Parliament opening the Iraq debate on 18 March 2003: 'So the moral case for action – never absent from my psyche – provided the final part of my speech and its peroration, echoing perhaps subconsciously the Chicago speech of 1999.'[40] The greatest rebuke of Blair's moral case for action against Iraq comes from his own case for action to stop a humanitarian disaster in Kosovo: a disaster that was imminent, serious, growing and demonstrable. No matter how hard he tried to create a moral case for military action against Saddam in 2003 there was no disguising the fact that, whatever threat Saddam had posed in the past or could potentially have posed in the future, he posed no imminent, serious, growing and demonstrable threat at that time: either to his own people or to others.

Having devoted several chapters to the legal and moral arguments for taking military action against Saddam, the next chapter moves from the *ad bellum* case for going to war to consider how it impacted, or otherwise, upon those charged with fighting in Iraq.

8
Fighting the fight

Military service has a number of characteristics that set it apart from other forms of service to the nation. Its two most obvious distinguishing features relate to the degree of commitment soldiers are required to make and the actions they are permitted to carry out under certain circumstances. Those who enlist or are commissioned as officers in the British armed forces, as elsewhere, are asked to be willing to give up their lives for their country. Associated with this potential self-sacrifice is the authority that is granted, within legal constraints, to kill others in defence of the country and its interests.

Given the potential cost to the individuals who bear arms there has always been some vague, moral understanding, described as the Military Covenant, between soldiers, sailors, marines, airmen, their families and the country that they will be appropriately looked after in times of war and peace. The covenant is assumed to apply to issues such as healthcare, education, housing and financial provision for serving personnel and dependants. If such a moral undertaking between the UK and those who defend it and its interests actually exists, then it is difficult to identify a time when it has been neglected or abused so flagrantly by a government as it was during the UK's involvement in the Iraq war and its aftermath. Recognizing the strength of feeling that had been welling up in the UK for several years – and perhaps seeing party political advantage at the same time – the Conservative Party brought the issue into the political mainstream. In the build-up to the 2010 election the Conservative Party pledged that a Military Covenant would be enshrined in law under a Conservative government. By April 2011 this pledge had still not been fulfilled. Consequently, in a breathtakingly hypocritical and opportunistic piece of political manoeuvring the Labour Party then pledged to enshrine a Military Covenant in law. Tony Blair (1997–2007) and his successor as prime minister, Gordon Brown (2007–2010), under whose Labour governments the armed forces had fought in Kosovo, Sierra Leone, Afghanistan and Iraq over a period of 12 years, had signally failed to set out any such Military Covenant in law.

The only written Military Covenant during that period was to be found in British Army publications, a version of which states:

> Soldiers are bound by service. The nature of service is inherently unequal: soldiers may have to give more than they receive. Ultimately, they may be called upon to make personal sacrifices – including death – in the service of the nation. In putting the needs of the Nation, The Army and others before their own, they forgo some of the rights enjoyed by those outside the Armed Forces. So, at the very least, British soldiers should always expect the Nation and their commanders to treat them fairly, to value and respect them as individuals, and to sustain and reward them and their families. This mutual obligation forms the Military Covenant and is binding in every circumstance. It has perhaps its greatest manifestation in the annual commemoration of Remembrance Day when the Nation keeps covenant with those who have given their lives in its service.[1]

This Military Covenant, as it is presented by the Army, has both weaknesses and strengths. The Army can speak authoritatively on matters pertaining to the conduct of officers and soldiers. It can even refer to the importance of Remembrance Day with confidence since the Army has participated in the annual commemoration since its post-World War I inception. However, the Army is unable to set out what the nation, through the government, will do to fulfil its side of the covenant. Further, if it cannot even define the nation's obligations towards Army personnel and their families it certainly cannot enforce them.

More positively, the Military Covenant as set out here alludes to a number of crucial relationships that have been damaged by events in Iraq, and to a lesser extent Afghanistan, in recent years. However, if we are to fully appreciate the impact of the Iraq War then, for the purpose of analysis, the 'Nation' as described by the Army in its Military Covenant will be divided into 'the government' and 'the people'. Although this is to some extent an artificial distinction it is accurately represented in the overall lack of support of the British people for the Iraq intervention: a support that dwindled further once it became clear that there were no WMD to be found and Iraq descended into bitter insurgency warfare.

The chapter considers where legitimacy on the battlefield comes from, starting with a historical view before going on to examine moral aspects of the relationship between Blair, the government and the armed forces in relation to Iraq. The subsequent section considers the relationship between morality and legal authority on the battlefield, with reference to the problems caused to some combatants when there is a disconnection between the two. For example, what happens when a soldier is given a legal order about which he or she is not morally convinced? What motivates him or her to persevere? The final section of the chapter examines the relationship between the public and the armed forces, and its importance in time of war. I explore the clear tension between the public's increasing opposition to the war alongside an increasing support to the personnel on the front line. This tension was characterized by the emergence of what I will call a cult of the military that valorized the sacrifice of soldiers' lives, almost as an act of protest at the same time. Remembrance was reclaimed by the public from the official, state-sanctioned commemoration held on 11 November each year, and focused instead on the parade of flag-draped coffins as they processed through the market town of Wootton Bassett.

Morality in war

The question of where moral legitimacy on the battlefield comes from has been discussed since soldiers first took up spears in combat. While just war theory has increasingly, over the past three centuries, tended to treat rulers' *ad bellum* justifications and soldiers' *in bello* conduct as distinct moral concerns, this has not always been the case. Even today, in the overall assessment of a war they remain interrelated and must both be present for a war to be considered just. When soldiers depart for the field of battle they do not leave behind the values of the society they defend; in the wielding of military power they both represent, and continue to contribute to, the ethical standards of their nation. The soldier's moral conduct on the battlefield impacts upon the political domain he or she represents, and *vice versa*. Not only that, the moral justifications of politicians and the ethical conduct of soldiers at war both impact upon wider society.

Since the time of Augustine and before there has existed a military/political hierarchy that shapes conduct in war, ethical or otherwise. Augustine located the soldier in this hierarchy as follows:

> when the soldier, obedient to the power under which he has been lawfully placed, slays a man, he is not guilty of murder according

to the laws of his city. On the contrary, if he does not do so, he is guilty of desertion and contempt of authority. If he had done this of his own will and authority, however, he would have fallen into the crime of shedding human blood. Thus, the deed which is punished if he does it when not commanded is the same as that for which he will be punished if he does not do it when commanded. And if this is true when the command is given by a general, how much more true is it when the command is given by the Creator.[2]

The hierarchy of authority created by Augustine with regard to war took the following form: the Creator [God], legitimate [political] authority, the general, the soldier. Freedom of thought and action declines as we move down Augustine's hierarchy of being from God to political leader and ultimately to the soldier. The prime minister or president of a Western liberal democracy would not – could not – refer to the authority of God dictating their actions as Augustine did, though it was common to read of references by Iraqi insurgents fighting against US or UK Forces to speak of doing Allah's will. In terms of the relevance of Augustine's words today we should recognize that even then the soldier operated *within* the constraints set out by his own authorities and not independently of them.

One of the questions that Augustine had to address was whether or not Christians could or should serve in the Roman Army. Although Christianity had been the official religion of the Roman Empire for almost a century many Christians either would not, or felt that they could not, serve in the Roman Army. Some were influenced by the teachings of the early Church Fathers who advocated pacifism, therefore refusing to take up arms for any cause. Other Christians were reluctant to join the very army that had been used several times in previous centuries to persecute their forebears for their beliefs. With the Roman Empire under attack and Rome itself being sacked in 410 by Alaric and his Visigoths from the north, Augustine was under some pressure to find a solution that would satisfy the political intentions of the Emperor while not undermining the Catholic Church and the doctrines of the Christian faith. The result was a rudimentary Christianized just war framework that would encourage greater participation by Christians as soldiers in the Roman Army. More than a millennium later, just war became increasingly rooted in the authority of the law, which replaced divine authority as the ultimate arbiter of war.

Augustine also had to address a moral conundrum that still resonates today with those who, as in the case of Iraq, were unconvinced by both the legal and moral arguments but were still sent to war anyway. He wrote of the consequences when a good soldier served a sacrilegious king. The key question was: Would obeying orders from a ruler who contravened Augustine's moral order and conception of just war automatically ensure that the soldier's actions in war were unethical?

Augustine left open the possibility that the soldier could still emerge as ethical in pursuing honour on the battlefield, even while obeying a sacrilegious ruler in executing an unjust war. In so doing, Augustine provided the basis for later just war writers to treat *jus ad bellum* and *jus in bello* as separate categories:

> Therefore, a just man, if he should happen to serve as a soldier under a human king who is sacrilegious, could rightly wage war at the king's command, maintaining the order of civic peace, for what he is commanded to do is not contrary to the sure precepts of God ... perhaps the iniquity of giving the orders will make the king guilty while the rank of servant in the civil order will show the soldier to be innocent.[3]

The king is described as guilty, not necessarily a result of his actions in relation to war but because he is sacrilegious and contravenes God's guidance. The soldier who waged the king's unjust war, on the other hand, could still be seen as ethical despite involvement in actions that opposed God's command. This is because the soldier, through his obedience, is helping to maintain civic peace, which is part of God's intended *order* for people to live by. The separation of the moral responsibilities of the king and the soldier reflects Augustine's Christian views about salvation as individualized rather than a shared communal responsibility. One person's actions could not get another person into heaven, just as one individual's behaviour could not stop someone else from gaining divine approval. So the one who ordered war and the one who executed war could only be held accountable for actions in their own sphere of influence.

When it came to deploying personnel and equipment for the purpose of invading Iraq, Blair's government, through Parliament, provided the authority. It had one very specific legal obligation that was fulfilled on the eve of war, as well as a number of moral obligations towards its armed forces. The legal obligation was straightforward. Admiral, now Lord, Boyce, then Chief of the Defence Staff, requested written legal authority for the invasion as early as January 2003 and received that authority – what he referred to as 'a one-liner'[4] – immediately prior to the invasion. He has described how it was essential for those about to be deployed, and their families, that legal cover was provided for the actions that they were about to embark upon. The legal proviso provided the opening statement of his Operational Directive of 20 March 2003.[5]

The first of the government's moral obligations was to demonstrate a legitimate and compelling *ad bellum* justification for the military intervention. I have already argued at length that Blair failed to make a legitimate or compelling case and consequently did not achieve the level of public support for his endeavours that he desired. This *ad bellum* case is linked to a second obligation held by those who have the authority to send men and women to their deaths on foreign shores or in defence of their own lands: the need to preserve life right up to the point where it becomes absolutely necessary to risk life. Soldiers should reasonably expect that they will be exposed to danger for only the best of reasons and once every other possibility has been exhausted. This moral obligation of the leader or legitimate authority to the combatant has one further dimension that became a source of controversy in Iraq. As part of valuing their lives and protecting them from unnecessary risk, soldiers should be properly equipped to carry out the task set before them.

Three equipment controversies dogged the Iraq imbroglio from the beginning, undermining the credibility and moral authority of politicians and senior military planners. The first problem was a shortage of body armour among front-line personnel during the initial cross-border incursion, which resulted directly in at least one death. The controversy was rooted in the way that Blair tried to justify the invasion, with senior military planners impeded in their preparations by the Prime Minister's desperation to avoid giving the impression that the decision for war had already been made. In response to questioning, Admiral Boyce mentioned some examples of decisions that were being held up by Blair's attempt to present one picture to the public (a desire to go down the UN route) while trying to prepare militarily. Specifically, he stated: 'I was not allowed to speak, for example, to the Chief of Defence Logistics – I was prevented from doing that by the Secretary of State for Defence, because of the concern about it becoming public knowledge'.[6]

The weakness in Blair's triangulation approach to communication threatened to destabilize his efforts. If the public were aware of what Blair was saying to the military and the extent of the military planning, even though it was not as much as the military wanted or needed, Blair's other message about the UN would have been undermined. Boyce was asked:

> Sir Roderic Lyne: Within these frank conversations, were there times when you had to express serious reservations or warnings to the Prime Minister about the course we were heading down?

LORD BOYCE: I would certainly, on a number of occasions, have expressed views about, for example, the holding up decisions to get reserves mobilised, the decision to go overt or to start allowing the preparations to be made, and whatever other problems as I saw them, as they came up, you know, which we would then go about solving.[7]

The defining illustration of inadequate or rushed preparations was probably the flawed distribution of body armour to front-line troops. The issue became politically explosive when it transpired that one of the first British soldiers killed after the commencement of the invasion, Sergeant Steven Roberts of the 2nd Royal Tank Regiment, had died after he had been ordered to hand over his body armour so that it could be reallocated to someone else deemed to be in greater need of protection. Before his death Roberts had communicated his concern about the lack of personal protection equipment in audio tapes that would later feature in the Inquest into his own death. He said, 'We've got nothing, it's disgraceful what we've got out here. It's pretty demoralising.' The recordings went further and criticized the upper echelons of the Army and the then Chief of the General Staff, General Sir Mike Jackson: 'General Jackson said "We're ready to go", and our vehicles are still in the boat ready to come into port. What a blatant lie ...'

From the moment it became public knowledge that Sergeant Roberts had been killed because his body armour had been taken from him Blair and his government were under pressure over their handling of preparations. It was a public relations disaster. The irony is that Blair's (and Campbell's) tactic of using individual cases of human tragedy as representative of more widespread evils – such as the terrified Iraqi woman he quoted in his eve-of-war speech – started to work against him. It did not matter how many thousands of soldiers had received the correct equipment, it was the failures that made the headlines, especially when those failures cost lives.

In his evidence to the Iraq Inquiry in January 2011 Admiral Boyce was asked whether, during a visit to Kuwait in March 2003 prior to the invasion, he had been made aware of shortages of equipment such as body armour. He replied that he had not. It is a military truism that s**t flows downhill: that is, from the upper ranks to the lower. The corollary to that timeless observation is that hot air floats upwards. When senior officers such as Admiral Boyce and others present their evidence to the Iraq Inquiry or compose their memoirs they can only refer to that which they have been told. What they cannot do is speak authoritatively about that which has been withheld from them.

Boyce himself was subject to the same pressure to send good news up the chain of command. In his 2009 evidence Admiral Boyce described how he would regularly brief Prime Minister Blair about the latest developments of difficulties he faced with military planning. Even he refers to being taken aside and asked to make his comments 'more of a half-full rather than a half-empty assessment'.[8] He was clearly not sending enough hot air up to the Prime Minister. Boyce also described his own view of the body armour fiasco in 2003: 'My understanding was everybody had body armour. Whether there was a sufficient number of enhanced body armour kits was something which didn't percolate out – and the need to redistribute such that appeared in theatre wasn't something which percolated up to the Chiefs of Staff'.[9]

Air Chief Marshall Sir Jock Stirrup was Deputy Chief of Defence Staff (Equipment Capability) from April 2002 until May 2003. He was asked about the difficulties of planning equipment procurement for the Iraq invasion with only four months' notice when the UK's most recent Strategic Defence Review had assumed a six-month lead in for an operation of that magnitude. Specifically, Stirrup was asked what difference the extra two months preparation time would have made. In response he said:

I think it would have made a significant difference. That's 50 per cent additional time and we were finding that, in a number of cases we were getting 100 per cent delivery about a month or two after the operation started. So I think that the six-month assumption wasn't a bad one.

I think the area where we could have done better is in terms of enhanced combat body armour. We didn't have enough of that in theatre at the time, and I think, in part, for both clothing and body armour, the issue was it was all being done so rapidly at the last minute no one was quite sure who had what. For example, just before the start of operation, the clear message that we were receiving in the Ministry of Defence was that all unit demands for enhanced combat body armour had been met, but quite clearly not everybody who needed it in theatre got it when they needed it, and had it been – had that been two months earlier, then those sorts of issues I think could have been untangled.[10]

Note the stark contrast in the language being used at the different levels of command. Sgt Roberts's comments from the front line: 'We've got nothing, it's disgraceful ... It's pretty demoralising ... What a blatant lie ...' ACM Stirrup felt that with an extra two months 'those sorts of issues I think could have been untangled'. While Admiral Boyce, Chief of Defence Staff noted: 'My understanding was everybody had body armour.' On weight of evidence – the evidence being the bullet that killed him, according to the Coroner, because he was not wearing enhanced body armour – Roberts's comments should be given greatest credence. The failure was not merely systemic and procedural: there was a moral failing by Blair's government towards Roberts when, because of the way the *ad bellum* justification was constructed, insufficient time was allocated to the fine-detailed preparations for war. Roberts and his family paid a high price and it enforced the increasingly-held view that the government was not properly supporting the troops. That view was played out in the national media over several years and it was played out on my own conversations with wounded and maimed personnel and with the next of kin of soldiers who were killed.

The other two high-profile shortages were of armoured patrol vehicles and battlefield helicopter provision. Although it is difficult to put an exact figure on the human cost of these shortages, it is likely that dozens of soldiers were killed, wounded or maimed by roadside improvised explosive devices (IEDs) because their thin-skinned Land Rovers could not withstand the blasts that they encountered. The restricted helicopter lift capability contributed to the difficulties of officers and soldiers on the ground because more patrols were forced to travel down booby-trapped roads rather than be moved by air.

These shortages had their origins in the Treasury, where the then Chancellor, Gordon Brown, was reluctant to invest the necessary level of funding to ensure that the best equipment – equipment that allies were already using – was available to British soldiers. From 2001 to 2007 Brown oversaw a huge expansion in public spending by the British government. The Defence budget grew minimally, even as two wars were being waged simultaneously, compared to the expansion of health, education and welfare budgets. Brown appeared before the inquiry into the Iraq War on 5 March 2010 and denied starving UK armed forces of equipment when he was Chancellor. He told the inquiry that the defence budget was 'rising in real terms every year' but House of Commons figures showed this was not the case.[11] In the financial years 2004/5 and 2006/7, at the height of the fighting in Iraq, funding for Defence fell in real terms. Brown subsequently informed the inquiry of his error.

As well as revealing the government's and the then Chancellor's priorities, the lack of investment in military equipment exposed the disjuncture between the sacrifices soldiers were making on the front line and the commitment of their political masters. It also exposed Blair's weakness that he was unwilling to confront an intransigent Chancellor over Defence funding. While the dysfunctional relationship between Blair and Brown went on to become the stuff of political legend, when viewed in terms of the deaths of soldiers that they sent into the field in inadequate vehicles, they were guilty of gross self-indulgence. They also breached the bond of trust between the military and the government, a trust that will not easily be regained.

Morality, legality and the will to fight

British soldiers, sailors and airmen are expected, in war, to conduct themselves in accordance with the law and to uphold high ethical standards. The corollary of this demand is that they expect to be sent to fight for good reasons. The military victories of which the British tend to be most proud are those that were achieved against an aggressor force and fought well, as far as wars can be fought well: for example, the Falklands Conflict, World War I and World War II. Both the Kosovo and Sierra Leone interventions are looked upon by many as positive examples of military force being used to save the lives of people in distant lands who would otherwise have been killed, wounded or displaced.

A common theme in most of my conversations with soldiers and airmen before the Iraq War began in 2003 was Blair's *ad bellum* justification of the intervention. The majority of people, as I was, were sceptical of Blair's arguments to a greater or lesser degree. Most of those who had participated in the 1991 Gulf War articulated a version of: 'It was clearcut the last time but this time it feels different.' There was a strong sense that in ejecting Saddam's forces from Kuwait in 1991 in response to an act of aggression, British and allied forces were not only enforcing the UN's will but acting in pursuit of a strong moral case as well. The case in 2002/3 was not so clear and not so convincing.

Even for those who had been expressing doubts, when the order was given to prepare and then to deploy a sense of duty and institutional loyalty took over. By the end of 2002 questions about how justified military action would be simply stopped, replaced by an intense focus on the task at hand. The doubts would not be raised with me again for several months until after the invasion began and I started working in a military hospital in support of those wounded or injured in and around the field of battle. The overwhelming majority of personnel involved in the 2003 invasion were willing to obey the orders given to them while many harboured doubts about the Prime Minister's arguments.

Once the decision was made to deploy, the focus shifted to reinforc-
ing the legal obligations that would be held by the combatants. There
are a large number of codes and conventions that govern the lives and
behaviour, especially in combat, of military personnel:

> Every officer is to make himself acquainted with, obey, and, so far
> as he is able, enforce, the Air Force Act, the Queen's Regulations for
> the RAF, and all other regulations, instructions and orders that may
> from time to time be issued. He is also to conform to the established
> customs and practices of the Service.[12]

This excerpt from Queen's Regulations illustrates the extent to which
the lives and conduct of military personnel are regulated in terms of
both military law and unwritten customs and practices. The former is
enforced by military police and judicial processes and, depending upon
the severity of the transgression, punished at either Orderly Room or
Courts Martial: both in peace-time and during war. The latter are enforced
through administrative action or the opprobrium of peers or superior
ranks. In times of war, every combatant is issued with guidance on the
law of armed conflict:

> All personnel must be aware of the basic rules of the law of armed
> conflict, including the practical application of the principles of mili-
> tary necessity, proportionality, distinction and humanity ... [And]
> Comply with the law of armed conflict and with Service law.[13]

These instructions provide explicit guidance on how combatants should
act in war: 'Comply with the law of armed conflict.'[14] Such law includes
the responsibilities of combatants under the Geneva Conventions, to
which the UK is a signatory. Consider two aspects of this instruction:
the means by which such compliance is achieved and the moral, in particular just war, discourses that this instruction draws upon. The Geneva
Conventions stipulate that combatants should be taught compliance
with the law of armed conflict as part of international humanitarian law.
Such compliance should be enforced through military instruction based
on military manuals 'in exactly the same way as the preparation for
combat'.[15] A number of supplementary instructional methods are specified: 'lectures, films, slides, audio-visual methods, war games including
questions and answers etc'.[16] The British armed forces – like many other
armed forces around the world – use such techniques to ensure that their

combatants are familiar with the law and know how to conform to it: conformity reinforced by disciplined repetition and training.

The aspects of law with which combatants must be concerned include 'the practical application of the principles of military necessity, proportionality, distinction and humanity'.[17] These principles are set out in a manner that suggests their use is unproblematic, yet even a brief look at the way the fighting in Iraq developed, in parallel with what was happening at the same time in Afghanistan, shows that this was not the case. If the 2003 invasion started off as a straightforward battle between Saddam's forces and those of the US/UK-led coalition, within months a different kind of war emerged. President Bush's bullish statement on 1 May 2003 on board USS *Abraham Lincoln* that major combat operations had ended could not have been more misplaced. The difficult fight was about to begin.

British and American soldiers were required, overnight, to move from an aggressive war-fighting posture to more of a peace-keeping role. With the Iraqi Army and the Iraqi Police Force disbanded and the coalition forces ill-equipped to replace them, any euphoria at the departure of Saddam's regime was short lived. An initial surge of criminal behaviour (looting, etc.) was followed by increasingly organized and aggressive sectarian violence between different Iraqi groups, most of whom had one common cause amidst their own internecine fighting: a desire to get rid of coalition forces from Iraqi soil. The insurgency began and it became clear as events unfolded in 2004 and beyond that the allied forces were ill equipped for the task and struggled to contain the rising tide of violence against them.

The individuals placed in greatest danger were those tasked with foot patrols in increasingly hostile and unpredictable areas. As soon as the British had taken control of Basra in 2003 the aggressive military posture was modified, berets replaced combat helmets as commanders on the ground sought to build relations with the local community. However, by the time the British withdrew from Basra Palace in September 2007 it was done under cover of darkness with combat air patrols circling overhead in case of attack by the now emboldened insurgent fighters. In the midst of the developing chaos on the ground, soldiers were being asked to fight with restraint against an enemy they could not see because they looked and dressed like all the other civilians around them. Furthermore, to combat the vast military advantages of coalition forces the insurgents adopted tactics that would make it difficult for those advantages to be brought to bear. Roadside IEDs became a daily hazard for those on patrol. Insurgent fighters from both Iraq and abroad were setting off bombs in public places to kill Iraqi civilians in an attempt to coerce the survivors into supporting anti-UK/US action.

British soldiers were placed in a very difficult situation where they were required, both legally and morally, to discriminate between enemy combatants and noncombatants, usually based solely on unpredictable actions at a moment's notice. There were no military uniforms to distinguish legitimate from illegitimate targets, with decisions on when to engage and when to open fire placing a great responsibility on young soldiers who had not, at least initially, expected such a war. When Blair's WMD case for intervention unravelled in rapid and spectacular style, for many soldiers a sense of moral and strategic purpose disappeared with it. Survival became an end in itself. The psychological pressures of war were magnified by the likelihood of killing women and children if artillery, mortars and the overwhelming firepower of strike aircraft were brought to bear in urban settings.

One battle-hardened non-commissioned officer (NCO) sat with me in 2007, ostensibly to talk about the difficulties he was facing in readjusting to family life after his third operational tour (Iraq and Afghanistan) in little over four years.[18] (In reality, his wife was threatening to leave if he didn't speak to someone.) I will call him 'Jim', though that was not his name. I asked Jim to tell me about his experiences on the front line first. After his first sentence he wept inconsolably and incoherently for 10–15 minutes, clenching his fists and his jaw by way of trying to regain control of his emotions. When that didn't work he gripped the arms of the chair and held on as though his life depended on it, slightly rocking backwards and forwards. Eventually he spoke.

Jim's first tour had been the most exhilarating time of his life. He had joined up to see action and by his own admittance didn't care much about the reasons for being in Iraq: there was a war on and he wanted to be part of it. He had tested himself in battle and come through. He described the euphoria with which he returned home at the end of the tour. Some mates had been badly hurt but he felt invincible. The only 'downer' was the speed with which his civilian friends and family lost interest in the most significant experiences of his life. After marrying his girlfriend his next tour was in Afghanistan against a different enemy but facing many similar tactics. By now he was an NCO and had some responsibilities for the newcomers who had never fought before. When one of them was killed by an IED he was responsible for picking up the smaller bits of his friend and putting them in a plastic bag to be sent back with the rest of his body. He stopped sleeping soon after that. The invincibility disappeared along with the sleep.

By the time Jim deployed again to Iraq he knew he was 'struggling' and almost obsessed with the thought that more friends might die. It became the focus of his thinking and decision making. He got increasingly 'f****d off' with fighting with one hand tied behind his back. I asked what he thought of the Geneva Conventions. 'We need to sort it [the Geneva Conventions] out and come down hard [on the enemy].' What did he think of things like the Abu Ghraib and other prisoner beatings and some of the allegations of atrocities against US Marines? 'Don't agree with it but that's easy to say sitting here.' He agreed to get further specialist help, though he did not know what good it would do. Jim received a medal on one of his tours but wanted to sell it and give the money to a military charity.

By the time I met him, Jim was utterly opposed to the UK's ongoing involvement in Iraq and Afghanistan. He was convinced we (the UK) were doing more harm than good and didn't see how dead Brits were helping solve anything on the ground. Despite being 'f****d up' and 'f****d off' Jim was prepared to deploy again if ordered to do so. He couldn't let the lads go without him. He saved his most shocking comment till last: 'You hate it and you love it. Being back is much harder.'

If Jim's is a tragic story of mental deterioration under the stress of combat, he is one of the luckier ones: he got help early on. In the US dozens of Iraq veterans have been imprisoned for murder, attempted murder or other violent crimes. Many more await trial. On both sides of the Atlantic a tsunami of Post Traumatic Stress will be throwing up 'Jims' for decades. He found it difficult to discuss ethical matters, despite having a clear sense of right and wrong. One source of anger was the different standards to which he and his colleagues were being held compared with the politicians that sent him. If he did something wrong the system would come down hard on him. Yet when politicians got it wrong (that is, by sending him there) nothing happened to them.

None of soldiers with whom I have discussed combat experiences in Afghanistan and Iraq limited their concerns to the *in bello* moral domain within just war. Most, if not all, were at least as concerned with the *ad bellum* justification of intervention – especially in Iraq. Their ethical thinking was not defined in terms of *ad bellum/in bello* distinctions. Despite an overwhelming sense in those I have met that Iraq and Afghanistan could not be 'won' in any traditional understanding of victory in war, soldiers continued to conduct themselves extraordinarily well in ambiguous circumstances. They risked their lives and health as soldiers have always done and do not limit their actions to the minimum required by the various legal codes that shape their conduct.

Men and women continue to go beyond the call of duty and the orders given to them, for the most part upholding high standards of personal conduct. Even when they either don't know what the overall mission aims are, don't care what the mission aims are, or think that the mission can't be achieved anyway.

The reasons for soldiers continuing to function effectively in morally ambiguous circumstances are as numerous as the individuals involved. For some it is about personal pride, for others, loyalty to their mates. A number truly identify with their regiments, squadrons and ships and the heritage of previous generations that they don't want to disappoint. A few regard their service as a form of divine calling on their lives (combatants that is, not just chaplains) while a small number will quietly refer to Queen and Country and carry granddad's/great granddad's World War II memorabilia or bible as a form of good luck charm. Perhaps a future book will focus entirely on what makes soldiers do what they do.

The people and war

In the UK, the Iraq War in particular has had an extraordinary impact upon the relationship between the government, the people and the armed forces. Since the low point of the prisoner beatings in 2003/4 when the British people (and most members of the military) were shocked by the conduct of a few soldiers, public support for those deployed on operations as gone up hugely. Donations to military charities have increased during a period of economic recession and Help for Heroes has achieved huge public visibility with the support of numerous celebrities and sports stars. At the same time as public support for military personnel has increased, the opposite is true of support for the politicians' insistence on maintaining operations in Iraq, and then Afghanistan.

While UK forces were withdrawn from Iraq in 2009 support for the operation in Afghanistan is becoming similarly unpopular to the extent that Prime Minister Cameron said in 2010 that combat operations will end by 2015. It is no coincidence that this planned date coincides with the expected run-up to the next General Election. There are no votes in lost limbs and expensive wars that cannot be won. The idea that fighting overseas is somehow reducing the terrorist threat in the UK and Europe is treated with increasing disdain by a sceptical public.

One expression of public support for the military and antipathy towards the government's use of the armed forces sprang up unbidden in the small market town of Wootton Bassett. What started as a private and local tribute to the fallen as flag-draped coffins were borne home through the town on the way from RAF Lyneham, took on a dynamic of its own. Where national remembrance has traditionally been an annual event controlled by the machinery of state and focused on the national memorial at the Cenotaph in Whitehall, London, grieving families and members of the public increasingly made Wootton Bassett the focus of their grief. Prime time news programmes regularly broadcast the parade of sorrow and emotion as flowers were strewn on the hearses, loved ones wept and the people of the town bowed in silent respect. In 2011, in recognition of the quiet, dignified and dedicated work of the people of Wootton Bassett the town was granted the prefix 'Royal' by the Queen.

Over the years however, unbidden by the people of Wootton Bassett, the occasions have begun to symbolize something greater than a simple acknowledgement of human loss. It became the People's remembrance, a symbol of unity and futility shared by many members of the public and the military. At the same time it has served as a rebuke to the politicians who have fractured the relationship with both groups: by ignoring the will of the people and, for years, neglecting the needs of the military until it became too politically costly to continue doing so. The lives of soldiers will continue to be lost and broken because of the political desire, in current and previous governments, to preserve political face both domestically and internationally. It happened in Iraq and it will happen in Afghanistan. When British and American forces are withdrawn from the latter, success will be proclaimed and responsibility handed over to Afghan political and military leaders. The polity that emerges is unlikely to match NATO's desire for democracy and stability.

More uncomfortably, there appeared at times to have been emotional, perhaps even spiritual, outpourings at Wootton Bassett that bore more than a passing resemblance to cultic religious practice. A highly developed ritual emerged, complete with objects of veneration (the draped coffins), sacrificial offerings (garlands and flowers) and the tears of the faithful: all led by the chief undertaker who walked the vehicles past the grieving devotees. Once participation in the remembrances moved beyond the townspeople and those whose fallen loved ones were returning home, something of a voyeuristic dimension developed that was never part of the original spontaneous reaction to loss on the battlefield.

The willingness of the British people to continue to provide even minimal support to the government's policy of keeping military personnel deployed in Afghanistan (and the same applied previously in Iraq) stands or falls on two issues: one operational and one ethical. Operationally, if Al-Qaeda or Taliban fighters were to be successful in shooting down a transport aircraft containing hundreds of soldiers it is unlikely that the country would be willing to continue operations with that level of loss. On the ethical side, if soldiers were found to have conducted some atrocity that shocked the conscience of humanity then it is unlikely that the British people would consent to ongoing representation by their armed forces abroad.

In 2004, when a number of British and American troops were found to have beaten, abused and even killed Iraqi prisoners and detainees in their charge, the impact went beyond the way they conducted themselves as ethical or unethical. The actions also impacted on the way that others around the world viewed the UK and US, and how citizens of the UK and US saw their values being represented or misrepresented through the actions of those soldiers. In other words, not only do soldiers represent the values of the societies they represent, when they commit war crimes they fundamentally alter the values of that society because they and its civilians are part of the same political community. In the eyes of the world, and most importantly the Arab world at that time, it was not British or American *soldiers* who beat, abused and killed prisoners: it was Britain and America. Blair dwelt on this point at length in his book, referring to how 'monstrously unfair' it had been that the good work carried out elsewhere in Iraq had been undermined by the actions of a few.[19]

The most high profile example, in recent decades, of gross misconduct in war impacting upon a nation's willingness to provide or withdraw its support is probably the My Lai massacre of 16 March 1968 in Vietnam. Professor William Eckhardt, Chief Prosecutor in the My Lai case at the height of the Vietnam War, has reflected on the events of that day when approximately 500 Vietnamese noncombatants were murdered by Charlie Company of the American Division led by Second Lieutenant William Calley. Charges for actions that included murder, rape and sexual assault were brought against 16 individuals, of whom five were tried and one – Lt Calley – was convicted.[20]

Eckhardt wrote of the My Lai killings: 'Revulsion from the extent and mindless brutality of the My Lai Incident caused a shift in public opinion toward opposition to involvement in Vietnam and in the Vietnam War.'[21] The events that took place at My Lai and public revulsion at what had been captured on camera and described in the press had a much broader impact. Eckhardt was not merely speculating when he referred to the shift in public opinion that resulted. Michal Belknap's book, *The Vietnam War on Trial*, covers the My Lai incident and the Court-Martial of Lt Calley and makes frequent use of opinion polls from that era. He noted that only two weeks after the guilty verdict was passed against Calley a major opinion poll showed that, for the first time, a majority of Americans were against continuing the war.[22]

There was undoubtedly a range of factors that influenced American thinking on continued support for the Vietnam War but the moral and legal outrages perpetrated in the name of the American people was a principle concern. If Vietnam was a war of ideology and anti-communist principle, any claimed moral high ground was surrendered among the violated corpses of My Lai. One of the most important breakdowns was the violation of trust between the American people and the Army whose first responsibility is to protect the Constitution and all that it entails. If the practices of a nation's armed forces reflect the dominant values in that society, and I believe they do, then the actions of those soldiers in My Lai violated not only their Vietnamese victims but the soul of the United States.

If any atrocity occurred in Iraq or Afghanistan, perpetrated by British personnel, which looked even vaguely like the events of My Lai, the British government's ability to sustain operations would, I submit, have evaporated almost instantly. One of the factors that made the events at My Lai both morally and legally abhorrent is that they were carried out against defenceless noncombatants. However, that was also the case with the prisoner abuse in Iraq. Although not of the same magnitude, the Iraq incidents were also against noncombatants. When a combatant is disarmed and taken prisoner he or she becomes a noncombatant for whom the capturing forces become both morally and legally responsible. The behaviour or tactics of the enemy, whether in Iraq, Afghanistan or Vietnam, is irrelevant when it comes to judging the legal and ethical conduct of our own troops. Enemy fighters, or even noncombatants in the enemy's country, are not part of the shared communal, political and moral collective that British soldiers represent. It is these shared values that must be upheld by the members of our armed forces when they are on operations, while these same shared values also demand that soldiers in the field are provided with the moral support of the country and the material support of the politicians under whose command they serve.

Summary

This book started with the voices of the wounded and since 2003 I have been particularly interested in how they view, or viewed, their relationship with the politicians who sent them to war. For many, especially among the lowest ranks, political leaders back in London were simply 'them': the ones who sent the soldiers but did not appreciate (or reward!) the dangers that were being faced. Perhaps in war it has always been thus. Further, among the Scottish and Lancastrian infantry soldiers with whom I have spent the most time there appears to be, for many, a deep seated understanding that their lives are expendable and there is very little expectation that 'the system' will put their needs first or value what they do. A significant proportion of infanteers in particular joined the Army as a way of escaping social deprivation or a lack of jobs and opportunities in the places they left behind. The cynicism, even humorous cynicism, of the PBI (Poor Bloody Infantry) is not something instilled during a couple of months of basic training. It was instilled by a lifetime of sub-standard housing, poor schooling and, in many cases, even worse parenting.

I have spoken to many combatants who have served in either the Iraq or Afghanistan wars – certainly numbering in the hundreds. The overwhelming majority view among soldiers and officers was that in Iraq (and also in Afghanistan) defining victory was almost impossible and achieving it harder still. In the latter stages of the UK's involvement in Iraq the chief aim of those deployed on operations was to get through their tours of duty and get home to loved ones, preferably with a full complement of testicles (for the men) and other body parts. No politician, senior military officer or other rank has been able to provide a one-line summary of the British missions in Iraq or Afghanistan. The communication principle goes back to Blair: if you can't put your message over in a straightforward way that people can understand then you will not convince them of its importance. With soldiers on the ground unable to buy into a sense of mission or higher purpose the default setting tends to be: protect your mates; protect yourself; go home.

Making the situation more difficult to understand is the reasonably high level of morale among those who have served in Iraq. For many, being tested in the heat of battle is a positive experience, at least until battle fatigue sets in or a major domestic difficulty presents itself back home (bereavement, illness of family members, partner leaves). On the ground, with the exception of the random and destructive effects of IEDs and the occasional mortar lobbed into the British-controlled bases, overwhelming allied firepower from both land and air ensured that almost every tactical encounter with enemy forces was won. That continues to be the case in Afghanistan where the future looks even more uncertain than it does in Iraq. In Vietnam, American forces won almost every tactical level encounter with the Viet Cong and North Vietnamese Army and yet lost the war. The same pattern is emerging in Afghanistan.

Into this mix is thrown the ethical conduct of British combatants, who typically seek to uphold the standards and values of the Navy, Army, Marines and Air Force and by extension society itself. While in an ideal world individuals would only be held morally accountable for their own actions and not the actions of others, this is not the case for the military. When someone in military uniform beats or tortures a prisoner, targets or accidentally kills a civilian – regardless of the person's actual, suspected or alleged actions – he or she violates the rights and body of the victim, the common life and values of the British society and the armed forces he or she represents. In addition, if a British Prime Minister sends soldiers into battle without a compelling and immediate moral case – as I have argued Blair did in Iraq – the values of society are also violated: a violation that cannot be papered over with a questionable letter of permission from an obliging Attorney General. Worse, Blair damaged the bonds of trust that necessarily exist between the government, the people and those who bear arms to protect them. The cancellation of the public launch of Blair's autobiography in London in 2010 was prompted by security fears about the threat posed to him, others and property by individuals still outraged by his actions towards Iraq. It is almost inconceivable that Blair will, in the short to medium term at least, be able to walk undisturbed and without security escort through the streets of the country he led for a decade.

9
Reflections

On 29 January 2010 Tony Blair appeared before the Iraq Inquiry to be questioned about his role in the justification and execution of the UK's military intervention in Iraq. Hundreds of protestors had gathered outside the Queen Elizabeth II Conference Centre near the Houses of Parliament in central London, determined to heckle him and highlight what they saw as his deception of the country as he took the UK to war against Iraq. The placards on display were adorned with phrases such as: 'Bliar', 'Blair lied, thousands died' and 'Judgement day for Blair'.[1] Unbeknown to the protesters, including relatives of soldiers who had died in Iraq, Blair had entered the building by the back door at 7.30 a.m. to avoid them. Though he was no longer Prime Minister, the intensity of the antipathy his Iraq policy had engendered in some members of the public was so great that police were concerned for his safety. By going to such lengths to avoid being confronted by parents mourning the deaths of their children in the war he advocated Blair enflamed the situation further, leading to strong condemnation and giving the impression, rightly or wrongly, that he had something to hide.

By the time he made this appearance, public opposition to the UK's involvement in Iraq had long been cemented. A YouGov poll at that time showed almost 60% of respondents thought Blair had misled Parliament, with a significant proportion holding the view that he had deliberately done so.[2] In previous chapters I advanced the view that he did not lie to Parliament but instead created a regime of truth about which he was personally, sincerely convinced. However, being personally convinced and being sincere about that conviction does not necessarily mean that his arguments and judgement were correct. In these final reflections I revisit some of the arguments made by Blair before the Iraq invasion and refer to some of the consequences of that intervention. In addition

I highlight how, after no WMD were found in Iraq, Blair's subsequent public discourse relied on his moral case for war to the exclusion of legal arguments, a disjuncture that also appeared during his questioning at the Iraq Inquiry.

The first section examines the ways that just war concepts were used in Blair's intervention discourse, pointing out the advantages and disadvantages of using historical arguments in the present. I also highlight how the philosophical underpinnings of commonly used just war arguments have radically changed over the centuries, to the point where even phrases like 'just cause' have conveyed very different meanings at different times. I go on to assess the impact of events in Iraq on the whole idea of humanitarian intervention. Specifically, I evaluate the extent to which Blair either reinforced or undermined the case for intervention he set out in his Doctrine of the International Community speech in 1999, taking both his moral and legal arguments into account. Has he helped to nudge the just war tradition in a pro-interventionist direction or did he prompt a more cautious reluctance to engage militarily across borders where there is a risk of encountering or engendering insurgency warfare? I tend towards the latter view while leaving open the possibility of small, low-level (in terms of cost and commitment) interventions. My concluding thoughts summarize some of the key arguments of the book and offer an overall assessment of Blair's military intervention in Iraq, highlighting why his moral case was, and remains, illusory.

Intervention revisited

A fundamental aspect of Blair's leadership style was to challenge the givens of the political landscape in which he operated, both domestically and internationally. He was not going to be deterred from military intervention on humanitarian grounds because customary law set out in the UN Charter prioritizes the rights of states to non-interference. When he set out his Doctrine of the International Community in Chicago in April 1999 Blair defined the conditions in which force should be used across borders for the protection of those were being killed, abused or displaced by their own political leaders. As I discuss in Chapter 1, his means of transcending or getting round the limits of international law was to appeal to moral arguments whose heritage not only preceded international law as we know it today but formed the basis of that very law.

The military historian Professor Lawrence Freedman provided Blair with a moral framework for military, or humanitarian, intervention that exhibits a number of clear links to the just war tradition. Here is a reminder of Blair's words in 1999:

> So how do we decide when and whether to intervene. I think we need to bear in mind five major considerations: First, are we sure of our case? ... Second, have we exhausted all diplomatic options? ... Third, on the basis of a practical assessment of the situation, are there military operations we can sensibly and prudently undertake? Fourth, are we prepared for the long term? ... And finally, do we have national interests involved?[3]

I previously made the case that these criteria set out by Blair correspond closely to key *ad bellum* criteria of the just war tradition: just cause, last resort, reasonable chance of success, proportionality and right intention. The main advantage of using these moral considerations is that they have been embedded in Western thought for millennia: even those unfamiliar with the finer points of international relations would recognize the arguments from problems that arise in routine personal interactions.

At the time when Blair made these arguments NATO aircraft were already bombing targets in Bosnia as a means of coercing President Slobodan Milosevic into stopping his ethnic cleansing of Kosovo Albanians. On one level Blair was simply making public a moral case that had already proven successful when he earlier attained support from other major nations for this military intervention. More importantly for Blair and like-minded interventionists in the short to medium term, given that the UN Security Council had refused to sanction military action against Milosevic, he provided a moral basis for avoiding the constraints of international law. Few have argued since that the Kosovo intervention should not have taken place. Similarly, the intervention in Sierra Leone in 2000 is widely accepted to have been a timely and worthwhile act, made all the more urgent by the ongoing atrocities at that time. While basking in the glory of what were widely considered to be just interventions, Blair did not carry forward one crucial lesson from both of those campaigns into the Iraq situation: the imminence of danger to civilians. The abuses in Kosovo and Sierra Leone were taking place live on 24-hour news television, while the worst of the Iraq atrocities – the ones which Blair featured in his speeches so regularly – took place a decade and more earlier.

Both before and after the later invasion of Iraq Blair has appeared bemused, defensive and occasionally hostile when his case for action has been called into question. However, the one thing he should not have been was surprised. Within weeks of the coalition's initial swift victory against Saddam Hussein's forces it became clear that the WMD-centred basis of the legal case for invasion was evaporating faster than water in the desert sun. He recalls:

> By the time of my visit to Basra at the end of May, Donald Rumsfeld had somewhat unhelpfully suggested that we may never find WMD, a prediction that turned out to be true but needed to be handled with some care. It was, after all, the *casus belli*.[4]

I have already discussed the place of communications and 'spin' at the heart of Blair's political strategy, masterminded by Alastair Campbell. When Rumsfeld produced an honest evaluation of the situation on the ground in Iraq concerning the lack of WMD, it was not seen by Blair as a self-evident truth that had to be faced but as something 'to be handled with some care'.[5] Large swathes of the British public were already convinced that Blair had misled the country in the push to war. Blair's view that the truth was something to be 'handled' rather than simply stated or even apologized for merely reinforces the view that Blair's communications department was spinning against the British people almost as much as it was providing propaganda against Saddam Hussein.

The impression that emerged, reinforced by Blair's appearances before the Iraq Inquiry and the publishing of his memoirs, was of a Prime Minister and government more concerned to protect their own reputations than confront the paucity of their carefully constructed but crumbling cause for war. The desire to constantly control, or at least influence, the flow of information to the public gave the impression that Blair and his team had something to hide. MPs, members of the public and especially relatives of dead British soldiers who, at the time of the war and subsequently, wanted greater detail than was being provided were often left feeling that they would not and should not be trusted with the bald facts. The ability of the public to ascertain the truth of the events surrounding the Iraq invasion is limited by the capacity and willingness of Blair's and subsequent governments to restrict the flow of information.

The Hutton Inquiry, the Butler Review and the Iraq Inquiry share a number of common characteristics. Each was presented by the Prime Minister of the day who ordered them as a means of establishing the truth about particular events: be it the death of the weapons inspector David Kelly, the use of intelligence on weapons of mass destruction, or lessons to be learned about the war as a whole. The personnel charged with undertaking the inquiries were appointed by the government whose actions were being investigated, leading to accusations that political placemen and women were being used as a means of limiting the degree to which inquiries would be pursued. The terms of reference for each of the inquiries were set by the government, thus constraining the scope of explorations. Lastly and most significantly, the inquiries, while intended to give the impression of robustness and credibility through the employment of individuals of some repute, carried no independent judicial powers. They could not summon witness, take evidence under oath or subpoena evidence that the government, key ministers or Blair himself decided should be kept hidden from public scrutiny. Blair simply refused to make public letters he wrote to President Bush in the build-up to the 2003 war and the Chair of the Iraq Inquiry, Sir John Chilcot, was utterly powerless to compel him to do otherwise.

None of this automatically means that Blair, his ministers or the later government of Gordon Brown were deliberately colluding to mislead the British people about events surrounding the Iraq War. It does mean that Blair cannot claim that he has been fully open and transparent about his motivations and the way he took the UK to war. A full judicial inquiry with scrutiny conducted by qualified legal experts backed by the full might of the law might have produced some different findings.

Just war: tradition or collection

This discussion of Blair's moral case for intervening in Iraq has highlighted a number of benefits, and problems, when drawing upon culturally embedded historical just war ideas to justify military action in the present. Specifically, it highlights the extent to which just war is more of a collection of ideas loosely related through a common theme and overlapping vocabulary than a unitary, evolving school of thought. Rather than being a tradition that has exhibited a smooth or even logical progression over the centuries, just war is more accurately characterized as a number of situated arguments with distinct philosophical foundations, separated by conceptual breaks. To further reinforce this line of reasoning I will compare the most important single, underlying principle of the just war tradition – that we should only go to war to achieve a better state of peace afterwards – with a segment of Blair's eve-of-war statement to Parliament on 18 March 2003.

Blair said to MPs in the House of Commons and a much wider audience following the debate on television: 'And now the world has to learn the lesson all over again that weakness in the face of a threat from a tyrant, is the surest way not to peace but to war.'[6] At first glance these words almost invite a satirical reading along the lines of Joseph Heller's

Catch-22: if we pursue peace we will go to war; if we go to war we go to war. The solution is therefore to go to war. However, Blair's words show strong similarities to much older moral arguments for going to war. Compare his words with the words of Augustine written in the fifth century: 'Peace is not sought in order to provoke war, but war is waged in order to attain peace.'[7]

Superficially at least, Blair's argument for going to war against a tyrant to achieve peace is consonant with Augustine's fifth-century just war thinking. However, if the words of Augustine are located more fully in their original context, another aspect of his discourse reveals itself:

> The will should be concerned with peace and necessity with war, so that God might liberate us from necessity and preserve us in peace. Peace is not sought in order to provoke war, but war is waged in order to attain peace. Be a peacemaker, then ... 'Blessed are the peacemakers,' says the Lord, 'for they will be called children of God' (Matthew 5:9).[8]

Augustine was not concerned with peace in the international system *per se*. At that time there was no international system as we might recognize it today. Augustine was concerned, first of all, with maintaining divine order – God's peace on earth – and, secondly, with the Roman Empire and those who might attack it or be attacked by it. In addition, the enforcement of divine order through the pursuit of peace was a response to God's direct command to his people to be peace-makers, a command set out in Matthew's gospel.

When we contrast Augustine's words with those of Blair we soon see the areas in which there is continuity of thought and the areas where Blair has excluded the earlier ideas from his war discourse. Blair was happy to put before Parliament the idea that facing up to the threat from Saddam the tyrant would lead to peace. This line of argument shows Blair to have been consistent with the historical moral discourse of Augustine. However, Blair did not include in his speech any mention of God, divine order or the biblical command to be a peace-maker – these aspects of Augustine's just war were left firmly in the past. As a Christian, perhaps even a devout Christian, Blair may personally have believed in the authority of the bible and set great store by the commands set out in Matthew's gospel. It did not, however, feature in the justification of the Iraq invasion he set before MPs.

Similarly, if we revisit Grotius's seventeenth-century just war writings, we see how Blair emerges as ethical in relation to those historical arguments. Grotius wrote:

> But if the injustice [of a ruler against that ruler's subjects] be visible ... such tyrannies over subjects as no good man living can approve of, the right of human society shall not therefore be excluded ... And indeed tho' it were granted that subjects ought not, even in the most pressing necessity, to take up arms against their Prince ... we should not yet be able to conclude from thence, that others might not do it for them.[9]

Grotius was writing as the concept of state sovereignty and a precursor to the modern international system began to emerge in Europe. The crucial difference between Grotius's idea of inter-state relations and current international relations is found in the relationship between individuals and states. For Grotius, states were entities that existed within the greater 'human society'.[10] Consequently for him, protecting citizens in a neighbouring state from the abuse of their tyrannical leader was possible because wider humanity was prioritized over individual statehood. Conversely, the international system today gives priority to the state, with states' rights being protected by international law. Human society today is divided into multiple human societies that exist within the geographical boundaries of sovereign states. When the state is prioritized in this way the rights of individual citizens are not automatically protected in the same way by the UN Charter as the rights of states.

The interventionist doctrine that Blair proposed in 1999 was entirely consistent with Grotius's regard for the protection of the vulnerable from the tyrant. If the present international system prioritized human society over the society of states,[11] Blair would not have had to work so hard to create a humanitarian justification for crossing state borders to aid the victims of tyranny. That said, even under Grotius's just war principles it would be necessary to demonstrate serious and widespread, imminent or ongoing threat to the lives and bodies of the persecuted: something that Blair was unable to do in the case of Iraq.

Iraq and its consequences

The repercussions of the 2003 Iraq invasion and its aftermath are only beginning to be felt and, if the history of statecraft and war is any guide, its implications will not be reasonably assessed until the twenty-second century. The few Iraqis I have been able to question have all been reasonably optimistic that some form of democracy will be sustained in Iraq: 'Under a strong leader! It is the Iraqi way.' Beyond Iraq, I have selected a number of areas for comment in the short term: Blair's personal standing; the UK and war; and the impact of Iraq on humanitarian intervention as an international doctrine.

Blair's personal standing as a man and as a politician in the wake of the Iraq war might best be described as varied, depending on where the question is asked. In the US he is still held in high regard by many because of the immediate pledge of support he gave to the American people in the wake of the 9/11 attacks. That high regard is regularly repaid in dollars and cents when Blair is well rewarded for lectures and speeches. It is difficult to gauge how he is received by leaders in the Middle East, a part of the world that prides itself on its hospitable and respectful treatment of guests. Is his acceptance a reflection of his standing as a statesman and former politician or is he tolerated because he was appointed as a special envoy by the United States? I suspect it is the latter but I leave open the possibility that he is, and has been, genuinely welcomed by leaders who are grateful for his advice and counsel on how to bring peace to the Gulf region. Colonel Gaddafi certainly seems to have been grateful for Blair's interventions on his behalf.

Privately, any comments made to me by Iraqis, Israelis, Jordanians and Iranians about Blair's appointment by the US as a peace envoy to the Middle East with particular interest in Israel/Palestine have been highly critical. The common, politely expressed view is that Blair's involvement is well intentioned but highly inappropriate. A more colourful description by a Palestinian living and teaching in London is that it is like Joseph Mengele being asked to develop child protection policy, a symbol of high-handedness and insensitivity from key Western powers.

The protests at his appearances before the Iraq Inquiry, the protests at his book launch in Dublin in 2010 and the cancellation of his book launch in London shortly afterwards point to a man who is now, in the eyes of many, an embarrassing guest in his own country. I have set down at length some of the reasons for this antipathy but they always point back to the way he took the UK to war in Iraq and the perception that he was being less than fully honest. The UK's history is highly militaristic and some of the events remembered with greatest pride by the British people are victories in war: Waterloo, the two World Wars and so on. Accordingly, the political and military leaders who oversaw these victories have been decorated in life and commemorated in death. These wars, and others, were fought for clear strategic reasons that were supported, to a large degree, by the British people. Blair's inability to provide one overriding, clear, convincing reason for taking action against Iraq in 2003 was his problem at the time and continues to dog his *post bellum* justifications. A 2009 television interview with Fern Britton illustrates this point:

> BRITTON: If you had known then that there were no WMDs, would you still have gone on?
>
> BLAIR: I would still have thought it right to remove him. I mean, obviously, you would have to use ... errm ... deploy different arguments about the nature of the threat. But I find it quite hard because I spend so much of my time out there now and, you know, they're about to have an election which will be probably the single most significant thing that's happened in that region for many years. Because they've managed, at long last, to break out of – actually – the religious divide. So you've got groupings for the first time standing there for election who are going to be broad based. We hope it works ... I can't really think we'd be better with him and his two sons still in charge ... for me, in the end, I had to take the decision.[12]

With these words Blair damned all his other claims to be primarily motivated by a need to rid the region of WMD to make world a safer place. He reinforced the arguments I made in Chapter 5 that his primary aim was regime change and that all of his other moral arguments were a means of achieving that end. Other reasons for going to war, such as WMD, remained secondary considerations. It is inconceivable that one of the great political communicators simply had a momentary lapse when he stated that he 'would still have thought it right to remove' Saddam.[13] Yet when challenged about the comment at the Iraq Inquiry Blair was able to claim without blushing 'even with all my experience in dealing with interviews, it still indicates that I have got something to learn about it'.[14]

Blair went on to say: 'The point that I'm making is very simply this: I did not use the words "regime change" in that interview, and I did not in any sense mean to change the basis [of his position].'[15] Incredibly, Blair's defence of his statement to Fern Britton was centred around the fact that he had not used the phrase 'regime change'. I leave you, the reader, to consider whether it would have been in any way possible to remove Saddam without also having regime change in Iraq. If Blair had simply made the comment about removing Saddam in isolation then his slip-of-the-tongue defence may have been more credible. However, he expanded upon his point by explaining to Fern Britton how he would have had to 'deploy different arguments about the nature of the threat'.[16] Given that Blair deployed every conceivable argument in his desperate attempt to make a case for military action against Saddam and Iraq, it is difficult to see what he could possibly have done differently. On 8 July 2003 he gave evidence to the House of Commons Liaison Committee and stated: 'I accept entirely the legal basis for action was through weapons of mass destruction.'[17] Six years later, on British television, Blair stated that even without WMD – his legal basis for war – he would still have thought it right to remove Saddam and that he would have had to deploy different arguments to do so. With Blair prepared to discount his legal basis for war the only justifications that would be left to him would have been the moral arguments, which he had already deployed at length.

Looking beyond Blair and his Iraq discourse to the legacy he left for subsequent Prime Ministers it is clear that the degree of distrust engendered in the British people by his justification of the 2003 invasion will take a long time to dissipate. In March 2011 the UK embarked upon another military intervention, this time in Libya. Prime Minister Cameron, when appearing before the House of Commons to seek a vote in support of military action, went to great lengths to reassure MPs that the intervention had been approved by the UN Security Council in Resolution 1973: a resolution that called upon states to use all means necessary to protect Libyan civilians. By mid-April 2011 cautious MPs, journalists and members of the public were voicing concern when Cameron, in conjunction with President Sarkozy and President Obama, began to talk of regime change, something not authorized by the UN.

It is impossible to tell with any accuracy the extent to which Blair's legacy from Iraq is behind the prompt criticism of any action that goes beyond the Security Council remit. However, the whole 'regime change' controversy that surrounded Blair, Iraq and Saddam Hussein seems to have raised a public awareness of this particular means of violating international law. As talk of 'mission creep' in Libya grows louder it would seem that only a timely and effective conclusion to that particular intervention will restore faith in the principle of helping others across borders using military force. The fact that Cameron felt the need to secure a level of UN Security Council approval that Blair did not achieve in the case of Iraq suggests that the bar of legitimacy has already been set higher in the minds of British politicians and the British people.

One final cautionary note on humanitarian intervention should be mentioned and it has been voiced most clearly and passionately by Alan Kuperman. He argues that the West's willingness to undertake humanitarian intervention creates a 'moral hazard' whereby that very willingness may be prompting the atrocities that in turn create the need for intervention.[18] He writes:

> The emerging norm, by raising expectations of diplomatic and military intervention to protect these groups, unintentionally fosters rebellion by lowering its expected cost and increasing its likelihood of success. In practice, intervention does sometimes help rebels attain their political goals, but usually it is too late or inadequate to avert retaliation against civilians.[19]

Kuperman's thesis is that groups who wish to rebel against their governing authorities have a vested interest in making sure that it commits or provokes the crossing of a threshold of violence towards civilians to draw into the conflict the military resources of the West. In other words, without the West's willingness to conduct humanitarian intervention, vulnerable or rebel groups would be less likely to engage in violent protest or uprising if they knew they faced defeat and possible eradication. Kuperman, in discussing the Bosnian conflict of the early 1990s, quotes Bosnia's subsequent Prime Minister Edhem Bicakcic who said: 'We absolutely believed that UN recognition would guarantee military protection.'[20] The warning from Kuperman is that the whole doctrine of humanitarian intervention may well have the unintended moral consequence of provoking the very violence it aims to stop. There is not the scope here for a full engagement with Kuperman's ideas. However, regardless of the degree to which his ideas are accepted or rejected it is important to engage with them and ensure that intervention is only undertaken with a clear strategy in mind, using a proportionate degree of force to ensure that protection of one group of people does not escalate into the oppression of a rival group.

Ironically, given the criticism I have levelled at his justification of the Iraq intervention, the interventionist doctrine Blair set out in 1999 remains highly relevant as I write in 2011. It set out a number of conditions which, if taken and applied seriously, would to a reasonable degree guard against abuses by those who would use the doctrine of humanitarian intervention to their own political advantage. In the long term this doctrine may turn out to be Blair's legacy to the world and to vulnerable individuals abused at the hands of tyrants and despots: a logical and coherent moral framework for assessing when and how to intervene with military force. If he had gone to greater lengths to conform to his own, just war-based doctrine more assiduously he may well have avoided much of the anguish he brought upon others and himself. Inconveniently, however, it is unlikely that he would have been able to engage in the war that he was so determined to undertake alongside President Bush – at least not at that time.

Conclusion

In a speech to the Labour Party conference shortly after 9/11 Blair set out his vision for the future: 'The kaleidoscope has been shaken, the pieces are in flux. Soon they will settle again. Before they do let us reorder this world around us.'[21] His subsequent actions show that this was not mere rhetoric, Blair truly wanted to reshape the world and the way international politics was conducted, especially to help the oppressed. As this book has set out, beginning with his Chicago Speech of April 1999, Blair was quite consistent over his years in office about the types of moral arguments he made to justify his interventions: protecting the weak and vulnerable, opposing the tyrant, confronting evil. Any attempt to limit his morally-inspired interventions through the UN or international law were viewed by him as an inconvenience to be circumvented or ignored – at least in the cases of Kosovo and Sierra Leone. His greatest difficulty arose in relation to Iraq when many in his own political party, in Parliament and in the public at large were not convinced by his legal case, his moral arguments or a combination of both. As a result they would not allow him simply to bypass the constraints and inconveniences of the United Nations and the Security Council.

One of the reasons that Blair's honesty has been loudly called into question so frequently over the years in public protests and in the British media in particular is the perception that he was always trying to square the circle between a commitment to Bush and the US on the one hand and the reality of the constraints imposed by his domestic political situation on the other. When questioned on the matter, either at the Iraq Inquiry or elsewhere, Blair's frustration is palpable on the issue of his case for the 2003 Iraq invasion. He does not seem able to understand why anyone would take a different view to his, especially when presented by the moral arguments on which his views were – and remain – based. Despite all the evidence to the contrary he gives the impression that if he only repeats himself loudly enough and often enough then people will eventually see what he saw.

I share the same hope for Iraq that Blair set out several years ago: that it will be a beacon of political stability, democratic freedom and economic prosperity. However, I do not share Blair's optimism that democracy – or at least a Western conception of democracy – can be imposed or even 'encouraged' by the use of military force. I would go even further. No country deserves to have democracy if they have not fought and died for it on their own terms and in their own time. History shows, though I will be happy to be proved wrong in Iraq and Afghanistan, democracy cannot be given as a gift. It has historically been bought and paid for with blood. Democracy is valued and defended by those who have gained it for themselves precisely because of the terrible price that it demands.

Why then, several years after the fact, do so many people remain fascinated, or appalled, by Blair's justification of the Iraq War? This book has explored a number of facets of this question but perhaps the lingering reason is this: war is a special category of political activity with an inherent moral dimension that can never be overlooked or distorted. Domestic policy decisions both reflect and shape how the British people live in a political community; foreign policy decisions reflect and shape the way that the UK relates to other political entities in the international arena, to both states and sub-state actors. The way that war is justified and the subsequent way that it is fought goes to the heart of who the British (or any other) people are and the values through which their shared existence is defined and contested. Blair did not subvert a political system; he subverted the values that underpin a political system. In particular he undermined the bond of trust between a government and its people: those who expect that their children, partners, parents or friends in the armed forces will be put in harm's way – or asked to take the lives of others – for only the most just and justifiable of reasons. Detailed analysis of Blair's Iraq justification has exposed the illusion of morality he created. Like all illusions, once it has been exposed it ceases to work its magic: except, it seems, on Blair himself.

Notes

Introduction

1. Sir John Chilcot, 30 July 2009, Iraq Inquiry's Terms of Reference, from http://www.iraqinquiry.org.uk, accessed 27 January 2010.
2. In this book the word 'moral' is understood as relating to codes, written and unwritten, that govern our behaviour. The word 'ethical' relates to the individual choices that individuals make in shaping their own behaviour by either conforming to the codes (including law) or not. These conceptions of morality and ethics are based on ideas articulated by the French philosopher and cultural historian Michel Foucault. See Foucault, M., *The Use of Pleasure*, Trans. R. Hurley (London: Penguin Books, 1984).
3. Just war principles can be found in every part of the world and have been shaped by the political, military, moral and religious histories of the peoples concerned. As a result 'just war' does not have one universal meaning. This book, however, refers to a distinct Western understanding and history of just war.
4. These ideas are drawn from the later works of Michel Foucault, where he sought to understand the constitution and creative self-constitution of the ethical, desiring subject as a means of comprehending broader questions about how individuals form themselves as subjects: drawing on both contemporary and historical discourses.
5. For further details see The Ministry of Information, in The National Archives, located at http://www.nationalarchives.gov.uk/theartofwar/inf3.htm, accessed 4 February 2011.
6. These questions are adapted from ideas found in Foucault, M., 'On the Genealogy of Ethics', in Foucault, M. and Rabinow, P. (Eds.) *The Essential Works of Michel Foucault 1954–1984 Volume 1: Ethics – Subjectivity and Truth* (New York: The New Press, 1997) pp. 263–5.
7. Perhaps a stronger word than 'enforcing' would be 'constitutive': where political actions and argument *create* as well as enforce related moral positions.
8. Rumsfeld, Donald, speech to the United States Senate Armed Forces Committee, 9 July 2003, located at http://news.bbc.co.uk/, accessed 10 July 2003.
9. *Ibid.*
10. Blair, 24 September 2002, Iraq Statement to Parliament. Details of Blair's Prime Ministerial Speeches, Parliamentary Statements and press conferences quoted or referred to in the text can be found on p. 201. All transcripts located at http://www.pm.gov.uk, accessed 19 June 2006. Subsequent speech citations will take the form Blair, 24 September 2002.
11. Drake, S., *Galileo At Work* (Chicago: University of Chicago Press, 1978) p. 367.
12. The concept of a regime of truth is used in this book in the Foucauldian sense. That is, truth does not have an independent existence of its own but is produced and reinforced within societies using political, educational, religious and other mechanisms for deciding what counts as true and what counts as

false. Those who wield political and institutional power have a greater means of shaping what counts as truth than those who would oppose them. For further reading see Foucault, M., 'Truth and Power', in Foucault, M. and Faubion, J.D. (Eds) *The Essential Works of Michel Foucault 1954–1984 Volume 3: Power* (London: Allen Lane, 2001) pp. 111–33.

13. I mention Afghanistan sparingly because military action against the Taliban regime was prompted primarily not by humanitarian catastrophe but in response to 9/11 and the Al-Qaeda leaders and activists who operated out of Afghanistan.

1   Blair and just intervention

1. Blair, Tony, *A Journey* (London: Hutchinson, 2010) p. 228.
2. *Ibid.*, p. 229.
3. *Ibid.*, p. 271.
4. *Ibid.*
5. Blair, 24 April 1999.
6. 'All Members shall refrain in their international relations from the threat or use of force against the territorial integrity or political independence of any state, or in any other manner inconsistent with the Purposes of the United Nations.' Charter of the United Nations, Art. 2, Para. 4. This and all subsequent references to the UN Charter located at http://www.un.org, 4 December 2008.
7. Blair, 24 April 1999.
8. *Ibid.*
9. Just war is commonly seen today to consist of three separate moral domains: *jus ad bellum*, *jus in bello* and *jus post bellum*. These refer to the moral justification of going to war in the first place, the morality of the way in which the war is fought, and the justice of post-war events as peace is restored and civic life resumed. *Jus post bellum* is the most recent of the three to be the focus of philosophical inquiry and practical application, interest in the field accelerated by events in Iraq and Afghanistan in the first decade of the twenty-first century.
10. For extended descriptions of just war criteria see Norman, R., *Ethics, Killing and War* (Cambridge: Cambridge University Press, 1995) p. 118. For similar summaries see Bellamy, A.J., *Just Wars: From Cicero to Iraq* (Cambridge: Polity Press, 2006) pp. 121–3; McMahan, J., 'Just Cause for War', *Ethics & International Affairs*, Volume 19, No. 3 (Fall 2005) p. 5; or Rengger, N., 'The Ethics of War: The Just War Tradition', in Bell, D., (Ed.) *Ethics and World Politics* (Oxford: Oxford University Press, 2010) pp. 296–8.
11. There are numerous ethical approaches to war, both in Europe and every other region of the world. While some, even many, aspects of these different ethical approaches appear to overlap – such as the need for a just cause for war – they also reflect localized, shared political, cultural and religious histories. For further reading see Sorabji, R. and Rodin, D. (Eds) *The Ethics of War: Shared Problems in Different Traditions* (Aldershot: Ashgate Publishing, 2006).
12. These events were confirmed by Professor Freedman in a letter to the Iraq Inquiry Chairman, Sir John Chilcot, dated 18 January 2010, six months after

the Inquiry was launched. This and subsequent references to evidence to the Iraq Inquiry located at http://www.iraqinquiry.org.uk, Crown Copyright, accessed 20 February 2011.

13. Freedman, Lawrence, 16 April 1999, Memo to Blair's Chief of Staff, Evidence to the Iraq Inquiry.
14. *Ibid.*
15. Brown, Gordon, 15 June 2009, Statement to the House of Commons, http://www.publications.parliament.uk, accessed 8 February 2011.
16. Blair, 2010, p. 228.
17. Blair, 24 April 1999.
18. *Ibid.*
19. *Ibid.*
20. *Ibid.*
21. Exodus 20:13, 15. This and subsequent biblical quotations are from the *New International Version.*
22. Charter of the United Nations, Art. 51: 'Nothing in the present Charter shall impair the inherent right of individual or collective self defence if an armed attack occurs against a member of the United Nations, until the Security Council has taken measures necessary to maintain international peace and security.'
23. Charter of the United Nations, Art. 39: 'The Security Council shall determine the existence of any threat to the peace, breach of the peace, or act of aggression and shall make recommendations, or decide what measures shall be taken in accordance with Articles 41 and 42, to maintain or restore international peace and security'.
24. Blair, 24 April 1999.
25. United Nations Security Council Resolution 1244 adopted on 10 June 1999, found at http://www.nato.int/kosovo/docu/u990610a.htm, accessed 16 September 2010.
26. UN International Criminal Tribunal for the former Yugoslavia, proceeding located at http://www.icty.org/, accessed 10 February 2011.
27. For a more extensive appraisal of the Rambouillet Conference and its consequences see Weller, Marc, The Rambouillet Conference on Kosovo, *International Affairs*, Vol. 75, No. 2 (Apr 1999) pp. 211–51.
28. Kissinger, Henry, *Daily Telegraph*, 28 June 1999.
29. Bull, H., *The Anarchical Society: A Study of Order in World Politics*, 3rd edn. (Basingstoke and New York: Palgrave, 2002).
30. Blair, 24 April 1999.
31. Blair, 2010, p. 229.
32. Charter of the United Nations, Art. 2.
33. The Universal Declaration of Human Rights, 10 December 1948, Preamble, located at http://www.un.org, accessed 26 August 2010.
34. *Ibid.*, Articles 3 and 5.
35. Blair, 2010, p. 248 (Italics added for emphasis).
36. *Ibid.*, p. 246.
37. Blair, 13 November 2000, Mansion House Speech.
38. Blair, 7 April 2002, Speech at the George Bush Senior Presidential Library.
39. Blair, 2010, p. 433.
40. *Ibid.*, p. 246.

41. *Ibid.*, p. 249.
42. Blair, 24 April 1999.

2   Are we sure of our case?

1. Blair, 24 April 1999.
2. Blair, 18 March 2003.
3. Blair, 2010, p. 432.
4. Campbell, Alastair, 'It's time to bury spin', *British Journalism Review*, Vol. 13, No. 4, 2002, p.18.
5. Foucault, M., *Power/knowledge: Selected Interviews and Other Writings by Michel Foucault, 1972–1977* (New York: Pantheon Books, 1980) p. 131.
6. Turnbull, Lord, 25 January 2011, Evidence to the Iraq Inquiry.
7. O'Donnell, Sir Gus, Evidence to the Iraq Inquiry, 28 January 2011.
8. *Ibid.*
9. Blair, 2010, p. 405 (My italics). Blair was describing his approach to the Iraq question back in July 2002.
10. *Ibid.*, p. 407.
11. Manningham-Buller, Elizabeth L., 20 July 2010, Evidence to the Iraq Inquiry.
12. Manningham-Buller, Elizabeth L., 22 March 2002, Letter to John Gieve, Home Office, Evidence to the Iraq Inquiry.
13. Blair, 7 April 2002.
14. Blair, 2010, pp. 451–2 (Original italics).
15. Blair, 25 February 2003.
16. Blair, 18 March 2003.
17. Blair, 8 July 2003, Evidence to the Liaison Committee, Select Committee on Liaison Minutes of Evidence http://www.publications.parliament.uk, accessed 3 July 2006.
18. For a more thorough examination of the history of weapons inspections in Iraq see the CRS Report for Congress No. RL31671, 7 October 2003, 'Iraq: U.N. Inspections for Weapons of Mass Destruction', located at http://www.fas.org, accessed 3 September 2010, p. 4ff. See also the Amorim Report to the UN Security Council, S/1999/356, 30 March 1999, 'Concerning disarmament and current and future ongoing monitoring and verification issues'.
19. Rumsfeld, Donald, 9 July 2003, Comments on Report to the US Senate Armed Services Committee, located at http://news.bbc.co.uk/1/hi/world/americas/3054423.stm, accessed 10 September 2006.
20. Blair, 2010, p. 399.
21. House Joint Resolution 114: To authorize the use of United States Armed Forces Against Iraq, 2 October 2002, located at http://usgovinfo.about.com, accessed 14 September 2010.
22. Rockefeller, J.D., 5 June 2008, Comments on the Press Release of the Intelligence Committee – Two Bipartisan Reports Detail Administration Misstatements on Prewar Iraq Intelligence, and Inappropriate Intelligence Activities by Pentagon Policy Office, located at http://intelligence.senate.gov, accessed 14 September 2010.
23. Blair, 10 April 2002.
24. Blair, 7 April 2002.

25. *Ibid.*
26. Blair, 10 April 2002.
27. Blair, 10 September 2002.
28. *Ibid.*
29. Blair, 11 November 2002.
30. Blair, 7 January 2003. In addition to these references further examples can be found in Blair's speeches of 3 and 25 February; 16, 17 and 18 March 2003.
31. Blair, 10 September 2010.
32. Manningham-Buller, Elizabeth L., 20 July 2010, Evidence to the Iraq Inquiry.
33. *Ibid.*
34. Roland Barthes, French philosopher and linguist, explored this phenomenon at great length. He referred to writerly text where the reader, or listener, plays an active role in the creation of meaning. Blair's Iraq discourse provides repeated examples of where the reader or listener was invited to take a number of ingredients such as threat, Iraq, WMD and terrorism and create their own meaning from them. Blair did not simply persuade people, he gave them the ideas with which to persuade themselves. Of course, it did not work for everyone. For further reading see Barthes, R., *The Pleasure of the Text*, Trans. Richard Miller (New York, Hill and Wang, 1975).
35. Goldsmith, Lord Peter, 27 January 2010, Evidence to the Iraq Inquiry.
36. Blair, 24 September 2002.
37. Dearlove, Richard, 15 September 2003, Evidence to the Hutton Inquiry.
38. Blair, 24 September 2002, *Iraq's Weapons of Mass Destruction: The Assessment of the British Government*, Foreword, p. 4, Crown Copyright, located at www.pm.gov.uk accessed 28 February 2008.
39. Scarlett, J., 20 September 2002, Memo – Iraqi WMD: Public Presentation of Intelligence Material, Crown Copyright, located at http://news.bbc.co.uk, accessed 18 February 2008.
40. September Dossier Conclusion (left out of final draft), Crown Copyright, located at http://news.bbc.co.uk, accessed 18 February 2008.
41. Intelligence and Security Committee Report on Iraqi Weapons of Mass Destruction, 11 September 2003, presented to Parliament by Prime Minister Tony Blair, p. 31, para. 111, Crown Copyright, located at http://www.cabinetoffice.gov.uk/, accessed 20 February 2011.
42. *Ibid.*, para. 112.
43. Government Response to the Intelligence and Security Committee Report on Iraqi Weapons of Mass Destruction – Intelligence and Assessments 11 September 2003, February 2004, para. 14, Crown Copyright located at http://www.cabinetoffice.gov.uk, accessed 20 February 2011.
44. Blair, 2010, pp. 451–2.
45. Blair, Minute to Jonathan Powell, 17 March 2002, Evidence to the Iraq Inquiry.
46. *The Sun*, 25 September 2002.
47. *Daily Star*, 25 September 2002.
48. Blair, 2010, p. 406.
49. Blair, 29 January 2010, Evidence to the Iraq Inquiry.
50. Blair, 18 March 2003.
51. *Ibid.*
52. *Ibid.* (Italics added for emphasis)

53. *Ibid.*
54. CRS Report for Congress – Iraq: U.N. Inspections for Weapons of Mass Destruction, 7 October 2003, Copyright House of Congress, located at http://www.fas.org/man/crs/RL31671.pdf, accessed 9 September 2010, p. 10.
55. *Ibid.*, pp. 10–11, 17 (Italics added for emphasis).
56. *Ibid.*, p. 11, Note 35.

3   Views from the academy

1. Walzer, M., *Arguing About War* (New Haven and London: Yale University Press, 2004) p. 6ff.
2. Walzer, M., *Just and Unjust Wars*, 3rd Edition (New York: Basic Books, 2000) p. xxii.
3. *Ibid.*, p. 44.
4. Walzer, M., *Interpretation and Social Criticism* (Cambridge and London: Harvard University Press, 1987) p. 19.
5. Walzer, 2000, p. xx.
6. *Ibid.*, p. 54.
7. Walzer, M., 'The Communitarian Critique of Liberalism', *Political Theory*, Vol. 18, No. 1 (Feb 1990) p. 21.
8. Walzer, M., 'The Moral Standing of States: A Response to Four Critics', *Philosophy and Public Affairs*, Vol. 9, No. 3 (Spring 1980) p. 210.
9. *Ibid.*, p. 226.
10. Walzer, M., *Thick and Thin* (Notre Dame: University of Notre Dame Press, 1994) p. 81.
11. Walzer, 2000, pp. 86–108.
12. *Ibid.*, p. xi.
13. Walzer, 2004, p. xv.
14. *Ibid.*
15. *Ibid.*, pp. xii/xiii.
16. Walzer, 2000, p. xi.
17. Walzer, M., *Just and Unjust Wars*, 4th Edition (New York: Basic Books, 2006) p. ix.
18. *Ibid.*, p. xiii.
19. *Ibid.*, p. xvii.
20. *Ibid.*
21. Walzer, M., *Spheres of Justice: A Defense of Pluralism and Equality* (United States of America: Basic Books, 1983) p. 313.
22. *Ibid.*
23. Jeff McMahon is critical of Walzer's view of the moral equality of soldiers. A good example of his critique can be found in McMahan, J., 'Collectivist Defenses of the Moral Equality of Combatants', *Journal of Military Ethics*, Vol. 6, No. 1 (2007) pp. 50–9.
24. Walzer, 2000, p. 146.
25. *Ibid.*, p. 141.
26. *Ibid.*, p. 36.
27. *Ibid.*
28. *Ibid.*, p. 188ff.

29. Elshtain, J.B., 'Just War and Humanitarian Intervention', *Ideas*, Vol. 8, No. 2 (2001) p. 2.
30. Elshtain, J.B., *Just War Against Terror* (New York: Basic Books, 2004) p. 56 (Original italics).
31. Elshtain, J.B. (Ed.) *Just War Theory* (New York and London: New York University Press, 1992) p. 323.
32. Walzer, 2000, p. 61.
33. Elshtain, J.B., *Sovereignty: God, State, and Self* (New York: Basic Books, 2008) p. 159.
34. Elshtain, 2004, p. 214.
35. *Charter of the United Nations*, Art. 39.
36. Elshtain, J.B., *Augustine and the Limits of Politics* (Notre Dame: University of Notre Dame Press, 1995) p. 114.
37. *Ibid.*
38. Elshtain, 2008, p. 10.
39. *Ibid.*, p. 228.
40. *Ibid.*
41. Elshtain, J.B., 'The Third Annual Grotius Lecture: Just War and Humanitarian Intervention', *American University International Law Review*, Vol. 17, No. 1 (2001a) p. 2.
42. *Ibid.*
43. *Ibid.*
44. Elshtain, 2004, p. 168.
45. *Ibid.*
46. *Ibid.*, p. 170.
47. *Ibid.*, p. 241.
48. *Ibid.*, p. 185.
49. *Charter of the United Nations*, Art. 2.
50. *Ibid.*, Art. 51.
51. Walzer, M. 'On Fighting Terrorism Justly', *International Relations*, Vol. 21, No. 4 (2007) p. 480.
52. Elshtain, J.B., 'A Response', *International Relations*, Vol. 21, No. 4 (2007) p. 502.
53. *Ibid.*, p. 503.
54. *Ibid.*, p. 505.
55. *Ibid.*

4   Authority, legitimacy and war

1. Aquinas, Thomas, *Summa Theologica*, Trans. Fathers of the English Dominican Province, Rev. Edn, Benzinger Brothers, 1948 (Reprinted Westminster, MD: Christian Classics, 1981), Second Part of the Second Part, Question 40, Article 1, p. 1813/4. Henceforth cited in the format: *Summa*, II-II, Q. 40, A. 1, pp. 1813–4.
2. UNSCR 660, 2 August 1990, text located at http://www.un.org/Docs/sc/unsc_resolutions11.htm, as are all subsequent UNSCR references.
3. UNSCR 678, 29 November 1990, *Ibid.*
4. UNSCR 687, 3 April 1991, *Ibid.*

5. Bush, G.W. and Blair, A., 23 February 2001, Joint Press Conference at Camp David. Transcript located at http://www.fas.org/news/usa/2001/usa-010223zwb.htm, accessed 16 September 2010.
6. Blair, 2010, p. 342.
7. Blair, Statement in response to terrorist attacks in the United States, 11 September 2001.
8. Press Conference: Prime Minister Tony Blair and President George Bush, 6 April 2002.
9. *Ibid.*
10. Goldsmith, Lord Peter, 27 January 2010, Evidence to the Iraq Inquiry.
11. *Ibid.*
12. *Ibid.*
13. *Ibid.*
14. Prescott, John, 30 July 2010, Evidence to the Iraq Inquiry.
15. Blair, 14 January 2001, Statement to the Iraq Inquiry.
16. UNSCR 678, 29 November 1990.
17. Goldsmith, Lord, 4 January 2011, Statement to the Iraq Inquiry, para 2.15.
18. Blair, Tony, 21 January 2011, Evidence to the Iraq Inquiry.
19. Wilson, Lord, 25 January 2011, Evidence to the Iraq Inquiry.
20. Short, Clare, 2 February 2010, Evidence to the Iraq Inquiry.
21. Wilson, Lord, 25 January 2011, Evidence to the Iraq Inquiry.
22. Goldsmith, Lord, 4 January 2011, Statement to the Iraq Inquiry, para. 1.16.
23. *Ibid.*, para. 1.3.
24. *Ibid.*
25. Wood, Sir Michael, 26 January 2010, Evidence to the Iraq Inquiry.
26. *Ibid.*
27. UNSCR 1441, 8 November 2002.
28. Straw, Jack, 2 February 2011, Evidence to the Iraq Inquiry.
29. Pattison, Stephen, 31 January 2011, Evidence to the Iraq Inquiry.
30. Wood, Sir Michael, 23 January 2003, cited in Evidence to the Iraq Inquiry, 26 January 2010.
31. UNSCR 84, 7 July 1950 (Italics added).
32. UNSCR 770, 13 August 1992 (Italics added).
33. UNSCR 1973, 17 March 2011.
34. Turnbull, Lord, 25 January 2011, Evidence to the Iraq Inquiry.
35. Blair, 20 December 2002, Interview with British Forces Broadcasting Service.
36. Blair, 21 January 2003, Select Committee on Liaison Minutes of Evidence, http://www.publications.parliament.uk, accessed 3 July 2006.
37. *Ibid.*
38. *Ibid.*
39. Blair, 18 February 2002, Press Conference.
40. *Ibid.*
41. Blair, 11 March 2003, Press Conference.
42. Goldsmith, Lord, 4 January 2011, Statement to the Iraq Inquiry, para. 4.1 ff.
43. Blair, 21 January 2011, Evidence to the Iraq Inquiry.
44. *Ibid.*
45. *Ibid.*
46. Blair, 2010, p. 424.
47. Blair, 18 March 2003.

48. Jack Straw memo to No 10, Conversation between himself and the French Foreign Secretary, 13 March, 2010, Evidence to the Iraq Inquiry.
49. *Ibid.*
50. Blair, 2010, p. 432.
51. *Ibid.*
52. *Ibid.*, p. 436.
53. Wood, Sir Michael, 26 January 2010, Evidence to the Iraq Inquiry.
54. Wood, Sir Michael, 15 January 2010, Statement to the Iraq Inquiry, para. 36.
55. Wilmshurst, Elizabeth, 26 January 2010, Evidence to the Iraq Inquiry.
56. Blair, 2010, p. 432.
57. *Ibid.*, p. 433 (My italics).
58. *Ibid.*

5   Regime change

1. Aquinas, Thomas, '*Summa Theologiae*, IIaIIae 64.7' in Dyson, R.W. (Ed.) *Aquinas: Political Writings*, Trans. R.W. Dyson (Cambridge: Cambridge University Press, 2002) pp. 263–4.
2. Blair, 7 April 2002.
3. *Ibid.*
4. *Ibid.*
5. *Ibid.*
6. Blair, 17 March, Minute to Jonathan Powell, Evidence to the Iraq Inquiry.
7. Blair, Evidence to the Iraq Inquiry, 21 January 2011.
8. Goldsmith, Lord, 27 January 2010, Evidence to the Iraq Inquiry.
9. Charter of the United Nations, Art. 2.
10. Blair, Minute to Jonathan Powell, 17 March 2002.
11. Blair, Evidence to the Iraq Inquiry, 21 January 2011.
12. Blair, 2010, p. 248.
13. Blair, Evidence to the Iraq Inquiry, 21 January 2011.
14. Blair, *On The Record*, BBC1, 16 November 1997, cited at http://news.bbc.co.uk/1/hi/uk/31780.stm, accessed 11 March 2011.
15. Cook, Robin, 18 March 2003, Resignation Speech to the House of Commons, transcript located at http://www.globalpolicy.org, accessed 17 April 2006.
16. Blair, 2010, p. 400.
17. Campbell, Alastair, 23 March 2011, Interview, *5 Live Breakfast*, BBC Radio 5 Live.
18. Press Conference, 6 April 2002, Prime Minister Tony Blair and President George W. Bush.
19. *Ibid.*
20. Blair, 2010, p. 400.
21. *Ibid.*
22. Blair, 20 June 2002.
23. Blair, Evidence to the Iraq Inquiry, 21 January 2011.
24. Powell, Jonathan, 19 July 2002, Minute to Prime Minister, Evidence to the Iraq Inquiry.
25. Straw, Jack, 8 July 2002, 'Iraq: Contingency Planning', Evidence to the Iraq Inquiry.

26. Wilson, Lord, 25 January 2011, Evidence to the Iraq Inquiry.
27. Blair, 3 September 2002.
28. *Ibid.*
29. Lord Goldsmith, 27 January 2010, Evidence to the Iraq Inquiry.
30. Bush, President G.W., 21 October 2002, Transcript of Remarks Following Discussions with Secretary General Lord Robertson of the North Atlantic Treaty Organization and an Exchange with Reporters, located at http://www. presidency.ucsb.ede, accessed 16 November 2008.
31. Blair, 2010, p. 412.
32. Hans Blix's official title was Executive Chairman of the United Nations Monitoring, Verification and Inspection Commission (UNMOVIC).
33. Cook, 18 March 2003.
34. Blair, 18 February 2003, Press Conference (Italics added).
35. Blair, 20 March 2003.
36. *Ibid.*
37. Blair, 2010, p. 424.
38. Blair, 24 March 2003, Statement to the House of Commons.
39. Blair, 2010, p. 446.
40. *Ibid.*
41. Blair, 14 January 2011, Statement to the Iraq Inquiry.
42. Walzer, 2006, p. xiii.
43. Blair, 2010, p. 479.

6   Confronting tyranny

1. Blair, Tony, 18 March 2002.
2. *Ibid.*
3. Augustine, *Against Faustus the Manichean*, Ch. XXII.74, in Fortin, E.L. and Kries, D. (Eds) *Augustine: Political Writings*, Trans. Tkacz, M.W. and Kries, D. (Indianapolis: Hackett, 1994) pp. 221–2.
4. Elshtain, 2004, p. 186.
5. *Ibid.*
6. Elshtain subsequently provided further clarification of this disjuncture. In *Sovereignty: God, State, and Self* (New York: Basic Books, 2008) she charts the different conceptions of sovereignty in the book title, seeking to understand how the constitution of each draws upon its predecessor(s). In a 'history of ideas' (p. xvi) approach she points out that Augustine's 'moral conception of sovereignty was *not* attached to a notion of territory but assigned as one of God's powers, the heart of God's authority over all creation' (2008, p. 2). Her thesis is that the trajectory of Western notions and prioritizations of sovereignty moved from the divine to the sovereign state and then to the self.
7. Aquinas, Thomas, *Scripta super libros sententiarum*, Bk. II, D. 44, Q. 2, A. 2, from Dyson, 2002, pp. 72–3.
8. *Ibid.*
9. Cicero, Marcus Tullius, *On Duties*, Bk. III, Sect. 29–32, from Reichberg, G.M., Syse, H. and Begby, E. (Eds) *The Ethics of War* (Oxford: Blackwell Publishing, 2006) p. 59.

10. Grotius, H., *The Rights of War and Peace*, Edited by Richard Tuck from the Jean Barbeyrac Edn, Trans. 1738 by John Morrice (Indianapolis: Liberty Fund, Inc., 2005) II.I.II.II, p. 395.
11. Aquinas, *Summa*, II-II, Q. 40, A. 1, p. 1814.
12. *Ibid.*
13. Grotius, *The Rights of War and Peace*, II.I.III, p. 397.
14. Vattel, E. de, *Essay on the Foundation of Natural Law and on the First Principle of the Obligation Men Find Themselves Under to Observe Laws*, Trans. T.J. Hochstrasser , in Vattel, E. de, *The Law of Nations, or, Principles of the Law of Nature, Applied to the Conduct and Affairs of Nations and Sovereigns* (1797 Edn.) Trans. Nugent, T. (Indianapolis: Liberty Fund Inc., 2008) XX, p. 753.
15. Bush, President George W., 1 June 2002, Speech at US Military Academy Graduation, transcript located at http://www.globalsecurity.org, accessed 20 March 2011.
16. *Ibid.*
17. Vattel, *Law of Nations*, II.IV.56, pp. 290–1.
18. *Ibid.*
19. Elshtain, 2004, p. 186.
20. Vattel, *Law of Nations*, II.IV.56, pp. 290–1.
21. *Ibid.*
22. *Ibid.*
23. Elshtain, 2004, p. 189.
24. *Ibid.*
25. Grotius, *The Rights of War and Peace*, II.I.III, p. 397.
26. Vattel, *Law of Nations*, II.IV.56, pp. 290–1.
27. Walzer, 2000, p. 107.
28. *Ibid.*, p. 101.
29. Walzer, 2004, p. 81 (Original italics).
30. *Ibid.*
31. Blair, 29 January 2010, Evidence to the Iraq Inquiry.
32. Bush, 31 January 2003, Press Conference with Prime Minister Tony Blair and President Bush at the White House. Transcript located at http://www.pm.gov.uk/output/Page5087.asp. Accessed 19 Jun 2006.
33. Blair, 11 November 2002, Speech at the Lord Mayor's Banquet (Italics added for emphasis).
34. For example, see Blair, 18 March 2003.
35. Blair, 2010, p. 248.
36. Blair, 18 March 2003.
37. Blair, 2010, p. 439.
38. UNSCR 612, 9 May 1988.
39. Chemical Ali would eventually receive five death sentences for his various crimes against humanity and against the Iraqi people.
40. Blair, 2010, p. 436.
41. Blair, 29 March 2001.
42. Blair, Interview with Fern Britton, Broadcast Sunday 13 December 2009, BBC 1 TV.
43. Blair, 17 December 1998.
44. Blair, 24 April 1999.
45. Blair, 28 January 2001.

46. Blair, 11 September 2001.
47. Matthew 12: 30.
48. Bush, 8 November 2001, Press Conference: Prime Minister Tony Blair and President George Bush.
49. Blair, 18 July 2003.
50. Ephesians 6: 12, 13, 16.
51. Vattel, *Law of Nations*, II. IV.49, p. 288.
52. *Ibid.*, Para. 50, pp. 288–9.
53. *Ibid.*, Para. 51, p. 289.
54. *Ibid.*

7   Protecting the weak

1. See Blair, 2010, p. 629.
2. Augustine, *The City of God Against the Pagans,* Ed. and Trans. R.W. Dyson (Cambridge: Cambridge University Press, 1998) XIX.7, p. 929.
3. Augustine, *On Free Choice of the Will*, Bk 1, Ch. 5, in Reichberg *et al.*, 2006, p. 75.
4. *Ibid.*, p. 76.
5. Exodus 20: 13.
6. Luke 6: 29.
7. Grotius, *The Rights of War and Peace*, II.XXV.VIII, pp. 1161–2.
8. *Ibid.*
9. Augustine, *City of God Against the Pagans*, XIX.7, p. 929.
10. Blair, 18 March 2003.
11. *Ibid.*
12. Blair, 10 April 2002.
13. Blair, 10 September 2002.
14. Blair, 24 September 2002.
15. Blair, 18 March 2003.
16. Alastair Campbell, 16 September 2010, http://www.alastaircampbell.org, accessed 21 September 2010.
17. Confirmation at the Order for Celebration of Holy Communion, http://www.cofe.anglican.org, accessed 25 September 2010.
18. Blair, 2010, p. 79.
19. Blair, 2010, p. 629.
20. Burton, John and McCabe, Eileen, *We Don't Do God*: *Blair's Religious Belief and its Consequences* (London: Continuum, 2009) pp. 225–6.
21. Blair, 3 September 2002.
22. Blair, Interview with Michael Parkinson, 4 March 2006, transcript located at http://news.bbc.co.uk/1/hi/uk_politics/4773874.stm, accessed 22 September 2010.
23. Burton and McCabe (2009, pp. 214–5) point out some of the key Christian liberal priests and theologians that have influenced Blair over many years.
24. Blair, 5 February 2009, Speech to the National Prayer Breakfast, Washington DC, from http://www.tonyblairoffice.org, accessed 30 March 2011.
25. *Ibid.*
26. Blair, 2010, p. 228.
27. Burton and McCabe, 2009, p. 133.

28. Blair, 24 April 1999.
29. Blair, 7 April 2002.
30. Blair, 17 December 2001.
31. Blair, 21 December 2001.
32. Blair, 7 April 2002.
33. Blair, 25 March 2003.
34. *Ibid.*
35. Blair, 27 March 2003.
36. Blair, 8 April 2003.
37. Luke 4: 18.
38. Blair, 18 March 2003.
39. Cameron, D., 24 August 2005, Speech to the Foreign Policy Centre, located at http://fpc.org.uk/fsblob/560.pdf, accessed 5 October 2010.
40. Blair, 2010, p. 439.

8 Fighting the fight

1. This abridged version of the Military Covenant is located at the Army Recruitment website, http://www.armyjobs.mod.uk, accessed 3 April 2011, Crown Copyright. An expanded and revised version can be located in Army Doctrine Publication (ADP) Operations, 2010, at http://www.mod.uk.
2. Augustine, *The City of God Against the Pagans*, I.26, p.39.
3. *Ibid.*, p. 82.
4. Boyce, Admiral Lord Michael, 3 December 2009, Chief of the Defence Staff, 2001–3, Evidence to the Iraq Inquiry.
5. *Ibid.*
6. *Ibid.*
7. *Ibid.*
8. *Ibid.*
9. Boyce, Admiral Lord Michael, 27 January 2011, Evidence to the Iraq Inquiry.
10. Sir Jock Stirrup, 1 February 2010, Evidence to the Iraq Inquiry.
11. Brown, Gordon, 5 March 2010, http://news.bbc.co.uk/1/hi/uk_politics/8572372.stm.
12. The Queen's Regulations for the Royal Air Force, Para. 989, Parts 1 and 4, pp. 15–1, Crown Copyright.
13. Aide Memoire on the Law of Armed Conflict, JSP 381, Para. 4, Revised February 2005, Ministry of Defence, Crown Copyright, located at http://www.mod.uk/, accessed 10 January 2009.
14. *Ibid.*
15. Programmes of military instruction, Protocol Additional to the Geneva Conventions of 12 August 1949, and relating to the Protection of Victims of International Armed Conflicts (Protocol I), 8 June 1977. Part 5, Section 1, Article 83, Para. 3376, located at http://cicr.org, accessed 15 January 2010.
16. *Ibid.*
17. Aide Memoire, *op. cit.*
18. 'Jim' was happy for his story to be told as long as identifying details were omitted.

19. Blair, 2010, p. 467.
20. Eckhardt, William George, Essay – 'My Lai: An American Tragedy', 2000, located at http://www.law.umkc.edu/faculty/projects/ftrials/mylai/ecktragedy. html, accessed 16 November 2010, p. 12.
21. *Ibid.*, pp. 37–8.
22. Belknap, Michal, *The Vietnam War on Trial* (Kansas, University Press of Kansas, 2002) p. 212.

9   Reflections

1. Photographs of the protest and the protestors' banners can be seen at http:// www.dailymail.co.uk/news/article-1246958/Tony-Blair-Iraq-inquiry-Former-PM-refuses-face-public-sneaks-early.html, accessed 14 April 2011.
2. Full details available at http://www.yougov.co.uk/extranets/ygarchives/ content/pdf/trackerIraqTrends_060403.pdf, accessed 14 April 2011.
3. Blair, 24 April 1999.
4. Blair, 2010, pp. 451–2 (Original italics).
5. *Ibid.*
6. Blair, 18 March 2003.
7. Fortin and Kries, 1994, p. 220.
8. *Ibid.*
9. Grotius, *The Rights of War and Peace*, II.XXV.VIII, pp. 1161–2.
10. *Ibid.*
11. The expression 'society of states' is most commonly associated in International Relations with the work of Hedley Bull.
12. Blair, 13 December 2009, Interview with Fern Britton, BBC1 TV.
13. *Ibid.*
14. Blair, 29 January 2010, Evidence to the Iraq Inquiry.
15. *Ibid.*
16. Blair, 13 December 2009, Interview with Fern Britton, BBC1 TV.
17. Blair, 8 July 2003, Select Committee on Liaison Minutes of Evidence, http:// www.publications.parliament.uk/, accessed 3 July 2006.
18. Kuperman, Alan J., 'The Moral Hazard of Humanitarian Intervention: Lessons from the Balkans' in *International Studies Quarterly* (2008) No. 52, pp. 49–80.
19. *Ibid.*, p. 49.
20. *Ibid.*, p. 61.
21. Blair, 2 October 2001, Speech to the Labour Party Conference. Transcript located at http://www.guardian.co.uk/politics/2001/oct/02/labourconference. labour7, accessed 17 September 2010.

Speeches by Prime Minister Tony Blair

17 December 1998, Statement to Parliament concerning Iraq.
24 April 1999, Doctrine of the International Community speech at the Economic Club, Chicago.
13 November 2000, Mansion House Speech.
28 January 2001, Speech on the Holocaust.
29 March 2001, Speech to the Christian Socialist Movement at Westminster Central Hall.
11 September 2001, Statement in response to terrorist attacks in the United States.
8 November 2001, Press Conference: Prime Minister Tony Blair and President George Bush.
2 October 2001, Speech to the Labour Party Conference.
17 December 2001, Statement to Parliament.
21 December 2001, Interview with the BBC World Service.
18 February 2002, Press Conference.
6 April 2002, Press Conference: Prime Minister Tony Blair and President George Bush.
7 April 2002, Speech at the George Bush Senior Presidential Library.
10 April 2002, Statement to Parliament on the situation in the Middle East.
20 June 2002, Press Conference.
3 September 2002, Press Conference.
10 September 2002, Speech to the TUC Conference in Blackpool.
24 September 2002, Iraq Statement to Parliament.
11 November 2002, Speech at the Lord Mayor's Banquet.
20 December 2002, Interview with British Forces Broadcasting Service.
7 January 2003, Speech at the Foreign Office Conference.
31 January 2003, Prime Minister Tony Blair and President Bush at the White House.
3 February 2003, Statement to Parliament.
25 February 2003, Statement to Parliament.
11 March 2003, Press Conference.
16 March 2003, Statement following the Azores Summit.
17 March 2003, A Vision for Iraq and the Iraqi People.
18 March 2003, Statement Opening the Iraq Debate.
20 March 2003, Address to the Nation.
24 March 2003, Statement to the House of Commons.
25 March 2003, Press Conference.
27 March 2003, Joint Press Conference with President Bush at Camp David.
8 April 2003, Joint Press Conference with President Bush.
18 July 2003, Speech to the US Congress.

Index